JESUS IN
THE FIRST THREE
GOSPELS

Millar Burrows

JESUS IN THE FIRST THREE GOSPELS

Abingdon / Nashville

JESUS IN THE FIRST THREE GOSPELS

Library of Congress Cataloging in Publication Data

BURROWS, MILLAR, 1889-
  Jesus in the first three Gospels.
  Includes index.
  1. Jesus Christ—History of doctrines—Early church, ca. 30-600. 2. Bible. N.T.
Gospels—Criticism, interpretation, etc. I. Title.
BT198.B86   232.9′01   77-3568

ISBN 0-687-20089-X

MANUFACTURED BY THE PARTHENON PRESS AT
NASHVILLE, TENNESSEE, UNITED STATES OF AMERICA

DEDICATION

To the Memory
of my
Brave, Loyal Wife,
of whom the world was not worthy

PREFACE

For economic reasons the text of this book has been severely compressed and abridged, and the apparatus of scholarship has been almost entirely jettisoned. It would be pleasant, therefore, to name here some of the scholars to whom I am indebted, but there are too many of them. Not to mention my own teachers, time would fail me to tell of the host—from Dibelius and Bultmann to, say, Via and Crossan—by whose work I have profited even when I could not agree with them.

I do want to express my appreciation of the competent secretarial assistance and encouraging interest of Deborah L. Wettstein and Ellen W. Emerson. For making their services available and providing facilities, I am grateful to Dr. A. Arnold Wettstein of Rollins College.

This is the first time I have been unable to thank my wife for help with a book; yet the thought of her has been a constant support and stimulus. Dedicating my work to her memory is the least and perhaps the most I can do.

In a way I have been writing this book all my life, and from childhood that life has been consecrated to him of whom I write. If what I have written is disturbing to some readers, I hope it will help others to reach a truer understanding of Jesus and a deeper devotion to him.

MILLAR BURROWS

PALESTINE IN THE TIME OF JESUS

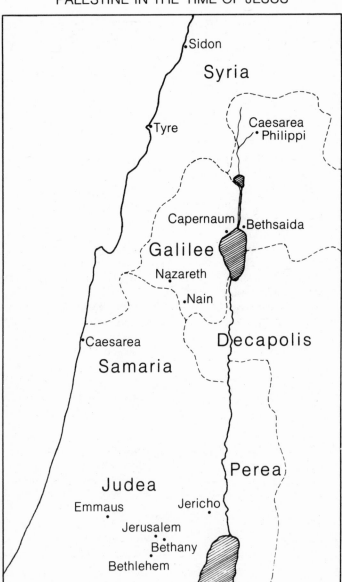

ABBREVIATIONS

CD   Damascus Document
1, 2 Chron   1, 2 Chronicles
Col   Colossians
1, 2 Cor   1, 2 Corinthians
Deut   Deuteronomy
Eph   Ephesians
Ex   Exodus
Ezek   Ezekiel
Gal   Galatians
Gen   Genesis
Hab   Habakkuk
Hag   Haggai
Heb   Hebrews
Hos   Hosea
Is   Isaiah
JB   Jerusalem Bible
Jer   Jeremiah
Jn   John
1, 2, 3 Jn   1, 2, 3 John
Judg   Judges
KJV   King James Version
Lev   Leviticus
Lk   Luke
1, 2 Macc   1, 2 Maccabees
Mal   Malachi
Mic   Micah
Mk   Mark
Mt   Matthew
NAB   New American Bible
NEB   New English Bible
NJV   New Jewish Version

Num   Numbers
1, 2 Pet   1, 2 Peter
Phil   Philippians
Philem   Philemon
Prov   Proverbs
Ps   Psalm, Psalms
1QH   Hodayot (Thanksgiving Psalms)
1QpHab   Habakkuk Commentary
1QS   Manual of Discipline
Rom   Romans
RSV   Revised Standard Version
Rev   Revelation
1, 2 Sam   1, 2, Samuel
Sir   Sirach (ben Sira)
TEV   Today's English Version
Test Dan   Testament of Dan
Test Iss   Testament of Issachar
Test Levi   Testament of Levi
1, 2 Thess   1, 2 Thessalonians
1, 2 Tim   1, 2 Timothy
v, vv   verse, verses
Wis   Wisdom of Solomon
Zech   Zechariah
Zeph   Zephaniah

CONTENTS

throughout Galilee. (Mt 4:12-25; Mk 1:14-39; Lk 4:14-44; 5:1-11)

IV. THE SERMON ON THE MOUNT
AND THE SERMON ON THE PLAIN 57

Beatitudes and woes. Salt and light. Fulfillment of prophecy and the law; exceeding the righteousness of the scribes and Pharisees. Murder, adultery, the offending eye or hand, divorce, oaths. Nonresistance. Love of neighbor and enemy, being sons of God, perfection. Ostentatious piety: charity, prayers. The Lord's Prayer. Fasting. Treasure in heaven. Light within. God versus Mammon. Anxiety. Seeking God's kingdom and righteousness. Judging others. Respect for what is holy. Confident prayer. The Golden Rule. The narrow gate. False prophets. Profession versus performance; the two builders. (Mt 5:1-48; 6:1-34; 7:1-29; Lk 6:20-49)

V. THE SECOND PART OF THE GALILEAN
MINISTRY 87

A leper healed. The centurion's slave. Foxes and birds and the homeless Son of man. Leaving the dead to bury their dead. A paralytic healed; opposition begins. Matthew (Levi) called; more opposition. A discussion of fasting. New patches and new wine. The mission of the twelve and their instructions. (Mt 8:1-22; 9:1-17, 35-38; 10:1-42; 11:1; Mk 1:40-45; 2:1-22; 6:6-13; Lk 5:12-39; 7:1-10; 9:1-6)

VI. THE THIRD PART OF THE GALILEAN
MINISTRY 101

John's question and Jesus' tribute to John. Woes on Galilean cities. Thanksgiving for revelation to babes. Jesus' easy yoke. Plucking grain on the Sabbath. The man with a withered hand. Multitudes healed. Appointment of the twelve. The widow's son at Nain. The women who provided for Jesus and the disciples. Jesus' friends try to restrain him. The Beelzebul controversy; blasphemy against the Holy Spirit. The sign of Jonah. The demon's return. Jesus' relatives. (Mt 11:2-30; 12:1-50; Mk 2:23-28; 3:1-35; Lk 6:1-19; 7:11-50; 8:1-3, 19-21)

VII. TEACHING BY PARABLES 118

Parables and interpretations: the sower, seed growing of itself, weeds, mustard seed and leaven, treasure and pearl,

Mary. Jesus refuses to adjudicate a dispute. The rich fool. Three metaphors for God. Jesus must cast fire on the earth and undergo a baptism. Galileans massacred; the tower in Siloam. A crippled woman healed. (Mt 19:1-12; Mk 10:1-12; Lk 9:51-62; 10:1-42; 11:1-54; 12:1-59; 13:1-30)

XI. LUKE'S SPECIAL SECTION CONTINUED

Jesus warned that Herod wants to kill him. His lament over Jerusalem. A Sabbath dinner at a Pharisee's house; a man with dropsy healed. Humility recommended. The great banquet. Counting the cost of discipleship. The lost sheep and coin and the prodigal son. The dishonest steward. Pharisees condemned as men-pleasers. The rich man and Lazarus. The unprofitable servant. Ten lepers healed. The kingdom in the midst (or within). The days of the Son of man. The corrupt judge. The Pharisee and the tax collector. (Mt 22:1-14; Lk 13:31-35; chapters 14–17; 18:1-14)

XII. THE CONCLUSION OF THE JOURNEY TO JERUSALEM

Jesus blesses children. The unsatisfied rich man. The disciples reassured. Thrones promised to the twelve in the Son of man's kingdom. Renunciation and following. The laborers hired at different hours. Jesus' third prediction of his death and resurrection. The ambitious sons of Zebedee. The disciples' lack of understanding. The Son of man's death a ransom. Jesus reaches Jericho. Blind Bartimaeus healed. The conversion of Zacchaeus. The pounds (or talents). (Mt 19:13-30; 20:1-34; Mk 10:13-52; Lk 18:15-43; 19:1-27)

XIII. THE FIRST DAYS AT JERUSALEM

Jesus reaches Jerusalem; his approach to the city; he predicts its destruction. He enters and goes to the temple; blind and lame people healed. Children acclaim Jesus, and he defends them. A fig tree, cursed by Jesus, withers. The cleansing of the temple. Controversies: first, Jesus' authority challenged. The two sons. The rebellious tenants. Second controversy: paying taxes to Rome. Third, the resurrection of the dead; fourth, the greatest commandment; fifth, David's son. (Mt

INTRODUCTION

SUBJECT, PROBLEMS, AND APPROACH

Many dedicated Christians, who love Jesus sincerely and feel that they know him as their dearest personal friend, have very vague ideas about him. Personal experience and heartfelt devotion are of course more important than their intellectual expression. The danger is that there will be nothing distinctively Christian in them. They must be brought into focus by the Word made flesh (Jn 1:14).

One of the first heresies rejected by the early church was the denial of Jesus' real and full humanity. "Beloved, do not believe every spirit. . . . By this you know the Spirit of God: every spirit which confesses that Jesus Christ has come in the flesh is of God" (1 Jn 4:1-2; cf. 2 Jn v 7). When faith loses touch with the flesh-and-blood person whom his disciples lived with and knew, it ceases to be truly Christian.

An honest, realistic attempt to know Jesus as a real man, however, is fraught with difficulties. First of all, do we really know that he ever lived? Outside of the New Testament there is little if any contemporary evidence of his existence. That is not surprising. He wrote no books, left no coins or inscriptions. There was no reason, so far as anyone could have seen at the time, that historians should have considered him important, if they ever heard of him. The Gospels themselves, however, are sufficient evidence that Jesus lived.

How well then can we know what he taught and what he was? The Gospels do not afford the kind of evidence needed to trace the course of his life or to explore his mind and personality. They were not written for that purpose. Their authors selected, arranged, and presented the material available to them with a view to the practical religious ends of evangelism, edification, and guidance. The Gospels, however, are the only records we have of Jesus' life on earth.

Many questions confront a serious student of the Gospels. Why, for instance, do we have not one Gospel but four in the New

17

Testament? They cover in general the same ground, though each has also something not contained in the others. The main problem, however, is that there are perplexing differences among them. How can this be if they are all the inspired word of God? Several observations are in order here.

A valid understanding of the inspiration of the Bible, including the Gospels, must be consistent with manifest and undeniable facts. The differences among the Gospels are facts that anyone can observe for himself. What the Gospels have in common is usually more important than the points on which they differ, but not always. There are often two or three reports of the same event or saying that cannot be equally correct. We shall encounter many instances of this.

If it is assumed that every item in the sacred text must be factually accurate, these differences constitute a formidable difficulty. But if the inspiration of Scripture is to be found not in exact wording or factual details, but in profound spiritual insights concerning the source and meaning of existence and the true ends of life, then the differences between one account and another present an interesting problem for investigation but no difficulty for faith.

So regarded, the Gospels supplement one another, each making a unique contribution to a rounded view of their common subject. Attempts have often been made to harmonize them and combine them into a single Gospel. We may be thankful that such efforts have never been successful. The difficulties and differences in the records can at least preserve us from slavery to the letter and compel us to seek the true spirit of the gospel.

What then are these perplexing differences? First of all, even a superficial comparison of the Gospels encounters at once a sharp contrast between the first three and the fourth. Matthew, Mark, and Luke have the same general point of view, share much of the same material, and present it in much the same way. For that reason they are called the Synoptic Gospels. There are differences among them also, but the Fourth Gospel differs from all three much more than they differ among themselves.

To be more specific, the Synoptic Gospels represent Jesus'

ministry as exercised chiefly in Galilee until about the last week of his life; John has much to say of a ministry in Judea before Jesus began his work in Galilee. The Synoptic Gospels tell of only one visit to Jerusalem after the beginning of the public ministry; in John there are several. The cleansing of the temple comes near the beginning of Jesus' ministry in the Fourth Gospel, near the end in the others. Instead of the characteristic parables and pithy sayings about the kingdom of God in the Synoptic Gospels, John gives a series of long discourses concerned mainly with the exalted nature of Jesus himself. Instead of miracles performed in compassionate response to human needs, John has a series of selected "signs" by which he "manifested his glory" (Jn 2:11). The Synoptics abound in stories of casting out demons; the Fourth Gospel has none. Most important of all, the picture of Jesus in the Fourth Gospel is quite different from that in the other three. The Synoptic Jesus is divine; the Johannine Jesus seems more conscious of his divinity. The Johannine Jesus is human, but the Synoptic Jesus is much more so.

The historical value of the Fourth Gospel is still a matter of debate and uncertainty, but as a historical document John is clearly less reliable than the others. It is a magnificent expression of early Christian faith, with great literary and devotional value. Scholars at present seem inclined to recognize more history in it than their predecessors did a generation or two ago. Matthew, Mark, and Luke, however, certainly give more and better information about the real Jesus of Nazareth.

So great is the contrast between the first three Gospels and the Fourth that any attempt to follow the course of Jesus' life and the content of his teaching in all four of them together is doomed to failure. The only fruitful procedure is to study the Synoptics and John separately before attempting any synthesis. In this study I shall depend almost entirely on the Synoptic Gospels, referring to John only when there is some special reason to do so.

Among themselves the Synoptic Gospels differ less widely, but the differences are significant and sometimes formidable. A conspicuous example appears at the very beginning of the Gospel story. The first chapter of Matthew, which is also the first chapter

19

of the New Testament, contains a genealogy of Jesus (Mt 1:1-17). Luke also has a genealogy, not at the beginning of the Gospel but after Jesus' baptism (Lk 3:23-38). It reverses the normal order, beginning with Jesus and going back not only to Abraham but to "Adam, the son of God." Unfortunately the most striking fact about these genealogies is that they are not the same. According to Matthew the line of Jesus' descent from David ran through Solomon and the whole succession of the kings of Judah; according to Luke it was David's son Nathan (2 Sam 5:14) who was Jesus' ancestor. Both lists include Shealtiel and Zerubbabel about midway between David and Joseph, but the lines from David to Shealtiel and from Zerubbabel to Joseph are entirely different.

Both pedigrees cannot be correct. If either one of them is right, the other is wrong; and there is no way to tell which is the right one. I have heard an eminent preacher say, "One is the genealogy of Joseph, and the other is the genealogy of Mary; but they are both genealogies of Jesus." The fact is that both are explicitly presented as genealogies of Joseph (Mt 1:16; Lk 3:23). For Christian faith, or for knowledge of Jesus' life, character, and teaching, it is immaterial whether he was a descendant of Solomon or of Nathan. The disturbing fact is that here, at the beginning of the New Testament, a serious question arises concerning the accuracy of the records. Many equally perplexing instances will be encountered as we proceed.

Matthew's genealogy exemplifies also another source of difficulty, the fact that the text of the Gospels has not come down to us entirely unaltered. In the course of copying manuscripts, the scribes inevitably made mistakes. In the mass of manuscripts that have been preserved we have not one uniform text but innumerable variant readings.

An example of such errors in copying, unimportant in itself but instructive, occurs in this genealogy. According to verse 17 the list consists of three series of generations, with fourteen generations in each. The first group has fourteen names, counting both Abraham at the beginning and David at the end. The second has fourteen without counting David again. The third, however, has only thirteen unless Jechoniah is counted again. Moreover the

20

son of Josiah was not Jechoniah (*i.e.*, Jehoiachin) but his father, Jehoiakim (2 Kings 24:6; 1 Chron 3:16-17); Matthew's list as we have it therefore skips a generation. The original reading (cf. 2 Kings 23:30, 34) was probably: "and Josiah was the father of Jehoiakim and his brothers, and Jehoiakim was the father of Jechoniah at the time of the deportation to Babylon."

More important than such questions of detail are differences of purpose and plan. The question of the relationship of each of the Synoptic Gospels to the others, including their agreements and differences, is called *the Synoptic problem.* The investigation of this problem proceeds by several distinct but related methods: source analysis, form history, redaction history, and literary criticism, including structuralism. Insofar as all these are concerned with questions of historical fact, they may be subsumed under the general head of *historical criticism.* Using all available means, they examine the ways of living and thinking, the customs and institutions, and the life-situations of the people originally addressed by the ancient writers in order to determine the intended meaning.

The ultimate purpose of our study of the Gospels, however, is not to find what they meant long ago but to find what they mean now, for us. Consequently much is now being said about *hermeneutics,* the branch of theology that deals with interpretation and tries to establish principles and rules for interpreting Scripture. Strictly speaking, interpretation includes both what the text meant for the first readers and what it means for us today; but the former belongs to historical criticism, and it is the latter that is now usually considered the sphere of hermeneutics.

Unfortunately, historical criticism and hermeneutics combined seem still not to have brought us closer to Jesus, but rather to have drawn us away from him, focusing attention more and more on the church of later generations, in which and for which the Gospels were composed. New Testament scholars can even calmly refer to a time when it used to be thought that accurate knowledge of Jesus' life and teaching was important. Some of us still think so. We are not greatly concerned about how many times Jesus visited Jerusalem, just where and when each event in his life occurred, or even the exact word he spoke. We are very much

21

interested in the kind of person he was, in whom all generations of Christians have seen a revelation of God. We consider what he taught about God and his will for man immeasurably more important than what any other person in human history has said or done.

CHAPTER I

JESUS' ANCESTRY, BIRTH, AND EARLY LIFE

The earliest expressions of Christian faith lay much stress on the point that Jesus was the Messiah, the king promised by the prophets. The word Messiah means "anointed." The decisive act in the enthronement of a Hebrew king was anointing his head with oil; therefore "the Lord's anointed" was a traditional title of the kings from the beginning of the Hebrew monarchy (1 Sam 16:6 and often). The Greek equivalent of Messiah is Christ; therefore in the Greek Old Testament (Septuagint) "the Lord's anointed" becomes "the Lord's Christ" (cf. Lk 2:26).

According to the Messianic prophecies of the Old Testament, the coming king would be a descendant of David (*e.g.*, Is 11:1; Jer 23:5). To call Jesus the Christ, therefore, implied that he was a descendant of David. The New Testament strongly attests his Davidic ancestry. Even the apostle Paul, who shows very little interest in the earthly life of Jesus, says that he "was descended from David according to the flesh" (Rom 1:3). One way to establish this was to trace the line of his descent, with such results as the genealogies given by Matthew and Luke (Mt 1:1-17; Lk 3:23-38). Neither evangelist is content to show merely that Jesus was a descendant of David. The genealogy in Matthew bears the title "The book of the genealogy of Jesus Christ, the son of David, the son of Abraham," and begins with Abraham, the father of the chosen people. Luke, in keeping with his interest in the Gentile mission and the universality of the gospel, treats the Davidic ancestry of Jesus as incidental and emphasizes instead his kinship with all mankind.

The first two chapters of Luke put more stress on Jesus' Davidic ancestry than the genealogy does (1:27, 32, 69). Joseph is introduced as a man "of the house of David." Gabriel tells Mary that her son will be given "the throne of his father David." And Zechariah praises God for raising up "a horn of salvation for us in the house of his servant David."

Mark and John say nothing about Jesus ancestry or his birth.

Matthew and Luke have accounts of his birth and infancy, covering almost entirely different ground. Luke's narrative is more extensive and circumstantial than Matthew's. It begins (1:5-80) with the events leading up to the birth of John the Baptist: the appearance of the angel Gabriel to John's father Zechariah and to Mary, Mary's visit to Elizabeth, and John's birth and circumcision. Luke then continues with the census decreed by Augustus, Joseph's trip with Mary to Bethlehem to be enrolled, and the birth of Jesus (2:1-7). Matthew has nothing of the parentage and birth of John the Baptist or of the annunciation to Mary. He tells briefly (1:18-25) of Mary's becoming pregnant by the power of the Holy Spirit, Joseph's assurance by an angelic message in a dream that Mary's conception fulfilled Isaiah 7:14, and the birth of her son.

The virgin birth of Jesus has become for many Christians a touchstone of faith in him and in the Bible. The modern scientific view of the universe, however, has made it a serious problem. One's position on this question depends inevitably upon the presuppositions he brings to it. One view can no more be demonstrated than another. If Jesus was a unique being, different from any other person ever born, the process of his conception and birth could have been unique also. Not being accessible to scientific observation, it cannot be proved or disproved scientifically.

Those whose understanding of the Bible is accompanied by a modern world-view, however, find it easier to understand how the belief in the virgin birth may have arisen than to accept it as historical fact. Many of the people who encountered Jesus in the flesh were probably convinced that he was no ordinary man. Without attempting to explain or formulate the idea, they may have felt that in meeting him they had somehow met God. It was inevitable that stories and beliefs about him should grow up and multiply, and in the thought-world of that day they might easily include the idea of a miraculous birth.

Equally dedicated Christians differ so widely and feel so strongly on this subject that a closer look at the biblical evidence is advisable. There is no explicit reference to the virgin birth, or even any clear allusion to it, anywhere in the New Testament outside of the first chapter of Matthew, the first chapter of Luke, and the words "betrothed" in Luke 2:5 and "as was supposed" in 3:23. Possibly it was taken for granted; yet even so it would surely have been mentioned somewhere if it had been considered a vital point of Christian faith. It does stand, however, in Matthew and Luke; and the two accounts are so different that they evidently follow independent lines of tradition. In neither Gospel, moreover, can the story be plausibly explained as a later addition to the original text of the Gospel. There are, however, some features of both narratives that call for explanation.

Both Matthew and Luke tell of other marvelous events accompanying Jesus' birth, but again they are not the same events. Luke's account (2:8-20) includes the appearance of angels to shepherds in the fields and their visit to the baby born to be "a Savior, who is Christ the Lord." Here, as in what goes before, there are echoes of Old Testament phraseology and ideas. The song of the angels (which would have to be sung in Hebrew or Aramaic to be understood by Judean shepherds!) has a distinctly Jewish flavor with its poetic balance of glory to God in the highest and peace among men on earth. The last words of this proclamation are commonly misunderstood because of a slight mistake in the manuscripts used for the KJV. Instead of "peace, good will toward men," the best manuscripts read literally "peace among men of good will" (or "favor"). Even this is often misinterpreted. The meaning is not men who have good will toward others, but men who have God's favor or approval.

The story of the shepherds is perhaps the most beautiful and most cherished part of the nativity stories. As history it is not subject to verification. It may be taken on faith or regarded as a legend embodying the simple trust and adoration of the common people to whom the child of Bethlehem brought assurance of salvation. Either way, it remains a beautiful story, beautifully told.

The chief importance of these first two chapters of Luke lies in the fact that they put the whole story of Jesus' life in its Palestinian Jewish setting, connecting it with the Old Testament and picturing vividly Israel's Messianic expectation. The fact that Zechariah was a priest and Elizabeth one of the "daughters of

Aaron'' (1:5) connects this story with the temple and the law. Prophecy is involved also (vv 41, 67).

Matthew has none of this, but tells (2:1-12) of the coming of the wise men from the East and the star that guided them. It is Matthew who tells also (2:13-23) of Herod's slaughter of the children of Bethlehem, the flight of Joseph and Mary to Egypt with their child, and their return to Palestine and settlement at Nazareth. All these are presented as further instances of the fulfillment of prophecy. Matthew's way of using prophecy is not what a modern scholar could call historically accurate, but it is in accord with a type of interpretation customary in New Testament times, and for that matter still practiced now. According to this way of thinking, it is assumed that the text refers to events and persons in the present or the immediate past or future.

Sometimes, indeed, one can hardly avoid a suspicion that prophecy, understood in this way, led to imagining events that never occurred. Did Joseph and Mary really take their child to Egypt for a while, or did some early Christian infer that they must have done so because God says in the book of Hosea (11:1), ''Out of Egypt I called my son''? Was Jesus really born in Bethlehem, or was it assumed that he must have been because the prophet Micah (5:2) had predicted that the Messiah would come from Bethlehem? More probably, the known fact of Jesus' birth at Bethlehem was felt by his followers to confirm their conviction that he was the Messiah.

How should we understand and judge these familiar narratives? The whole Christmas story, mingled as it is now with Santa Claus and other more or less pagan additions, seems much like a fairy tale for children. Even so, to raise questions about the truth of the record is painful. A good deal of the story, however, is undoubtedly legendary.

Matthew and Luke agree that Jesus was born in Bethlehem, the city of David. Matthew, however, says nothing of coming to Bethlehem from anywhere else, and he seems to imply that Joseph would have gone back to Bethlehem from Egypt if he had not been warned in a dream not to return to Judea (2:22-23).

Just where in Bethlehem Jesus was born is not known. Matthew says that when the wise men came to ''the place where the child was'' they entered the house (vv 9, 11). Luke says that Mary laid her newborn babe in a manger (2:7). Conceivably Joseph found lodging in a house at some time between the visit of the shepherds and the arrival of the wise men. It is also possible that the manger was in a house, for to this day it is quite common to keep domestic animals in the lower part of the house. The traditional birthplace under the Church of the Nativity is in a cave. There is nothing to prove or disprove the authenticity of the site.

When Jesus was born is unknown also. The choice of December 25 for the observance of Christmas was arrived at by faulty calculations and was probably influenced by the fact that the Jewish feast of Dedication (Hanukkah) and the Roman festival of Saturnalia, celebrating the winter solstice, came at about that time. Even the year of Jesus' birth cannot be determined. It would be 1 A.D. if our calendar were based on accurate historical knowledge, but that is not the case. A date within the years 6–4 B.C. seems to be as close as we can get to the time when Jesus was born.

Only Luke has anything to say about Jesus' early years. After the visit of the shepherds the story continues with the circumcision of the child on the eighth day of his life, as required by the law (Lk 2:21; cf. Gen 17:9-14; Lev 12:3). At this time he was formally given the name Jesus. This was not an uncommon name: It was especially appropriate, however, for the child born to be the Savior of men (Mt 1:21). It means "He will save" or "He saves," or in its full form "Yahweh will save" or "Yahweh saves."

According to Leviticus (12:1-4, 6) the mother of a boy is "unclean" for forty days after his birth, and at the end of that time must present an offering and be "purified." Luke apparently combines the mother's purification with the presentation and redemption (i.e., buying back) of the first son.

In the temple, Luke goes on to say (2:25-35), Joseph and Mary encountered a righteous and devout man named Simeon. Recognizing in the infant Jesus the Messiah for whom he was waiting, Simeon took him in his arms, praised God, and blessed the parents, but predicted also that division, opposition, and suffering would be involved in the Messianic deliverance. There was also in the temple (vv 36-38) an aged widow named Anna

27

(Hebrew, Hannah), a prophetess, who recognized what the baby was, and with thanksgiving to God "spoke of him to all who were looking for the redemption of Jerusalem." Is all this history or legend? It is not impossible that these incidents took place as recorded; it is equally possible that the stories are popular legends typifying the fervent Messianic hope of Judaism at the time of Jesus' birth and the fact that there were devout souls in Israel who found in him the answer to their hopes.

Having complied with the requirements of the law, Luke says (2:39), Joseph and Mary went back to Galilee "to their own city, Nazareth." Matthew gives no hint that Joseph and Mary had lived in Nazareth before Jesus was born. When they returned from Egypt, he says, they were warned not to go back to Judea, so they went to Galilee (Mt 2:22). The choice of Nazareth seems to have been governed only by the prophecy, "He shall be called a Nazarene" (v 23). But who were "the prophets" who predicted this? The word "Nazarene" does not appear in the Old Testament. The nearest approach to this statement is the angel's command to the parents of Samson (Judg 13:5, 7), "the boy shall be a Nazirite to God." "Nazirite" and "Nazarene" are not the same word. They are derived from different Hebrew roots, and could only have been confused in the Greek.

The whole tradition of Nazareth as the home of Joseph and Mary could have been derived from Matthew's elusive prophecy. More probably the fact of their residence in Nazareth came first, and the allusion to prophecy was a result of the general search for prophecies supporting the Messiahship of Jesus. All four Gospels agree that Nazareth was Jesus' home. Some scholars have been disturbed by the fact that no such town is mentioned in Jewish literature of the period or in the Old Testament. That must be true also, however, of many Palestinian villages that did exist.

Now begin "the hidden years." We really know nothing of Jesus' youth and early manhood, though much of what appeared later in his brief public life and in his teaching must have been the result of his experience and thinking during those years. Constructive imagination is indispensable in historical research, but a genuine concern for truth demands that the imagination be used with restraint.

Of Joseph we know very little. His fairness, considerate kindness, and quiet integrity are suggested by Matthew (1:19), and his devout observance of the law is repeatedly indicated by Luke (2:22-24, 27, 39, 41). The fact that Jesus so naturally thought of God as the heavenly Father may indicate the kind of fatherhood he had seen exemplified by Joseph. The last we hear of Joseph is at the time of the Passover trip to Jerusalem when Jesus was twelve years old. It is not unlikely that he died at some time during Jesus' adolescence, and the responsibility of being head of the family fell upon Jesus.

The personality of Mary has been so overlaid with legend and adoration that a lifelike picture of her as a real woman is hard to come by. Her innocence, faith, and dedication as a girl at Nazareth and her pondering and cherishing in her heart later what she saw or was told about her son are noted by Luke (1:26-38; 2:19, 33, 51). His statements may rest on an authentic tradition going back possibly even to Mary herself. Later there is a suggestion—hardly more than that—of misunderstanding between Mary and Jesus (Mk 3:31-35); but there is no reason to doubt that her faith in him survived the strain. According to John she was present at the crucifixion (19:25-27), and in Acts she appears with the disciples in the upper room at Jerusalem (1:14). That is the last mention of Mary in the Bible.

Luke gives us a glimpse of the boy Jesus at the age of twelve (2:41-51), when his parents took him with them to Jerusalem for the Passover, and apparently left him much to himself in the city. On the way home they discovered after a day's journey that they had left him behind at Jerusalem. Mary's reproach when they found him in the temple is very human. She was too relieved to be inhibited by the presence of the learned teachers of the law. Jesus' reply, too, may be taken as a reproof; but it may equally well be the answer of a lively boy, spoken with twinkling eyes and a smile: "Why, Mother, you know me! You might have known I'd be here." Of course the whole story may be dismissed as a devout legend, told to show how Jesus excelled the rabbis in wisdom. Stories of precocious wisdom are told about founders of other religions. I know of none, however, that is so humanly natural as Luke's story of the boy in the temple. It has none of the

29

extravagant supernatural coloring characteristic of such legends. It might even be true.

There were other children in the household while Jesus was growing up. Four brothers are named (Mk 6:3; Mt 13:55): James, Joses (or Joseph), Judas, and Simon. Sisters are also mentioned, but we are not told their names or how many of them there were. Some interpreters suppose that these brothers and sisters were either Joseph's children by a previous marriage (in which case Jesus would not have been Joseph's eldest son) or not really brothers and sisters of Jesus but his cousins. There is nothing in the record to support either of these assumptions.

Clearly the household in which Jesus grew to manhood was a large one, and presumably lively. No doubt there was much for the growing boy to do to help his parents. It was an excellent training for life, very different from that of John the Baptist. If Luke's account of Mary's visit to Elizabeth (1:36, 39-56) has a factual basis, the two families may also have exchanged visits at other times. If so, we may be sure that the boys would have discussed religious questions together. Quite possibly such spiritual communion during boyhood was the foundation of their later relationship.

How much formal education Jesus had, if any, is not known. We do not know whether there was a school attached to the synagogue at Nazareth during his lifetime, or, if so, whether he attended it. According to Luke he read the Scripture lesson in the synagogue service when he visited Nazareth later (Lk 4:16-20). In his teaching he sometimes assumed that his hearers had read or should have read texts in the Bible. "Have you not read . . . ?" he would ask (Mk 2:25; 12:10, 36; Mt 12:5; 19:4; 21:16, 42). The keen and active mind exhibited later by his sayings and parables must have absorbed the Bible stories and the teachings of the lawgivers and prophets, and with characteristic penetration and independence he combined and interpreted them in his own way. That he could both read and write is thoroughly probable, but of no consequence for history because he did not commit his words to writing.

Certainly during his boyhood and youth he learned much by observation of the life around him. When he spoke to his disciples

30

later (Mt 6:26, 28; Lk 12:24, 27) about the lilies of the field, clothed more gloriously than Solomon, and the birds that lived by God's loving care and did not store up goods for the future, it was surely not the first time that these thoughts had come to him. He knew also that birds fell to the ground, but he did not doubt that God knew and cared. He saw that sunshine and rain were not distributed according to what men deserved. God treated friends and foes alike, and men should do the same.

That is about all we know—indeed more than we know—about Jesus' boyhood and youth. The eighteen vitally important years between the ages of twelve and thirty are completely blank in the record. A few hints may be found in the accounts of later events. According to Mark, when Jesus spoke in the synagogue at Nazareth, the townsfolk said (6:3), "Is not this the carpenter?" In Matthew the people say (13:55), "Is not this the carpenter's son?" In Luke they say (4:22), "Is not this Joseph's son?" As the son of a carpenter, Jesus probably learned his father's trade. Serving the common daily needs of his neighbors would give him an understanding of human nature and of the concerns and problems of the people.

Among the subjects discussed in the streets and shops of Nazareth, current events must have played a part. During Jesus' boyhood, and not far from his home, there was a tragic demonstration of the futility of rebelling against Rome. The insurrection of Judas the Galilean (Acts 5:37) occurred when Jesus was about twelve years old. In order to prevent the registration of the Jews by the Romans, Judas seized control of the city of Sepphoris, only about six miles north of Nazareth. The revolt was quickly put down, Sepphoris was destroyed, Judas was killed, and his followers were dispersed. A few years later Herod Antipas, then ruler of Galilee, rebuilt Sepphoris and made it his capital. These events help to explain Jesus' subsequent attitude toward "that fox" Antipas (Lk 13:32), and to the Roman rulers whose vassal he was.

What else may have happened to Jesus and what he did during these years we do not know. It is hardly surprising, therefore, that speculation has run wild concerning his activity during these hidden years. Legends in the apocryphal Gospels, for example, tend to exalt displays of miraculous power in ways quite inconsistent with his character. Medieval legends took him as far from Palestine as Britain. Such naïve stories are more easily condoned than the outright impostures of modern times. Of these, perhaps the most notorious was the *Unknown Life of Jesus Christ,* published in French in 1894. It was ostensibly a translation of an ancient manuscript discovered in a monastery in Tibet, telling of travel, study, and preaching by Jesus in India and Persia.

Somewhat more plausible are the many attempts to make Jesus in his youth a member of the Essenes, a Jewish monastic order that had its center near the Dead Sea, with local chapters in other places in Palestine. This theory has at least the advantage of keeping Jesus nearer home. It has also some objective basis in striking similarities between the New Testament and the documents commonly called the Dead Sea Scrolls. I can only summarize here what seem to me the most essential points in this matter. The question is not as important as it seems to some. No thoughtful Christian would suppose that Jesus' gospel had no connection with the spiritual heritage of his people. According to Matthew, he said (5:17) that he had come not to destroy but to fulfill the law and the prophets. The whole history of the revelation of God in the Old Testament was a preparation for the gospel. What we call the Old Testament was the Bible of the Jews, and Jesus accepted it as such.

After the completion of the Old Testament, various parties and schools of thought arose among the Jews. It should not be surprising that Jesus shared beliefs with one or more of them. On several points he agreed with the Pharisees against the Sadducees. If he also agreed with the Essenes on some points, why should that be disturbing? Whether he learned these ideas from the Essenes is a question of historical fact, without theological implications unless one assumes that the validity of the gospel depends on its being wholly new. There are in fact points of agreement between Jesus and the Essenes, both in ideas and in language. There are also important differences; indeed, the disagreements are greater than the agreements. So far as I can see, there is no evidence at all of any direct contact between Jesus and the Essenes.

CHAPTER II

JOHN THE BAPTIST: THE BAPTISM AND TEMPTATION OF JESUS

Whatever other events or persons may have influenced Jesus' career, one of the most important was the appearance and work of John the Baptist. Mark begins his Gospel with it (1:4). In Matthew, John's appearance is related immediately after the return of Joseph and Mary from Egypt (3:1). Luke considers John's mission so important that he gives the date of the prophetic experience that inspired it (3:1-2). In the fifteenth year of the emperor Tiberius (A.D. 28/9), he says, "the word of God came to John the son of Zechariah in the wilderness" (cf. Jer 1:2, etc.). The rulers of Judea, Galilee, and the adjacent regions, as well as the Jewish high priests in office at that time, are named also. For Luke they serve merely to date an event that to them would have seemed insignificant.

All three Synoptic Gospels quote Isaiah 40:3 as referring to John the Baptist. In the Fourth Gospel John the Baptist himself says, "I am the voice of one crying in the wilderness" (1:23). Mark quotes also Malachi 3:1, which Jesus cites later with reference to John (Mk 1:2; cf. Mt 11:10; Lk 7:27). According to Matthew, Jesus identified John with Elijah, who was expected to come just before the Messiah (Mt 11:14; cf. Mal 4:5).

All the Gospels associate John's ministry with the Jordan River. The Fourth Gospel says (Jn 1:28) that John baptized at "Bethany beyond the Jordan." Where this was is unknown.

John's work consisted of preaching and baptizing. His preaching is briefly described by Mark and Luke as "preaching a baptism of repentance for the forgiveness of sins" (Mk 1:4; Lk 3:3). Instead of this, Matthew gives the same summary that he later gives for the message of Jesus (Mt 3:2; cf. 4:17): "Repent, for the kingdom of heaven is at hand." Matthew and Luke also report more of John's preaching. Scornfully denouncing the Pharisees and Sadducees who came to be baptized, he demanded that they produce fruit to show that their repentence was genuine

(Mt 3:7-10; Lk 3:7-9). Their proud reliance on being descendants of Abraham, he declared, was of no avail.

Luke adds (3:10-14) words spoken in response to questions from the people, who ask what producing good fruit means specifically for them. All, John tells them, must share what they have with those less fortunate; tax collectors must not extort more from the people than the law allows; soldiers must be satisfied with their wages and not rob the people.

Baptism, as John preached and practiced it, was thus a sign of repentance and forgiveness. It did not bring about either the repentance or the forgiveness; repentance had to come first and prove itself genuine by its fruit. John's baptism has been compared with similar Jewish rites, which included proselyte baptism, a symbolic bath taken by converts to Judaism. There is some uncertainty, however, as to the exact significance of the Jewish rite and just when it began to be practiced. In any case, John's baptism was one not of conversion to Judaism but of repentance within Judaism. Since the discovery of the Dead Sea Scrolls, the lustrations of the Qumran community have received much attention (IQS ii. 25; iii. 4-9; vv 13-14). There is no indication that they performed sprinkling or washing once and for all upon entrance into the order. It seems rather to have been repeated more or less regularly. Both ritual and moral cleansing were involved, but the moral and spiritual aspect was more prominent.

A further element in John's preaching, the most important of all for the Christian church, is given by Mark and repeated with additional matter by Matthew and Luke (Mk 1:7; Mt 3:11-12; Lk 3:15-18). John's baptism with water is to be followed by a baptism with the Holy Spirit—Matthew and Luke add "and with fire." This has been compared with a passage in the Qumran Manual of Discipline (1QS iv. 20-21): at the end of the present world order, "God will refine in his truth all the deeds of a man, . . . cleansing him with a holy spirit from all wicked deeds. And he will sprinkle upon him a spirit of truth, like water for impurity." Here God himself, not the Messiah, will do this. Judgment by fire is not an unnatural or uncommon idea. The idea of a baptism by fire, however, may reflect the Zoroastrian conception of a river of fire that will consume the world on the day of judgment. This is echoed in one of the Thanksgiving Psalms of Qumran (1QH iii. 29-32).

Nothing more is said in the Gospels of baptism with the Holy Spirit; but in the first chapter of Acts, Jesus tells the apostles that they will soon be baptized with the Holy Spirit (1:5). Their experience on the day of Pentecost (2:4) is regarded as the fulfillment of that promise, though they are said to have been not baptized but filled with the Holy Spirit, which was poured out (2:18, 33) as predicted in Joel 2:28. The prediction of John the Baptist is later connected with the gift of the Spirit at the house of Cornelius and at Samaria (11:15-16; 19:3-6). In the Fourth Gospel the risen Jesus breathes on the disciples and says, "Receive the Holy Spirit" (Jn 20:22).

The one who would administer the baptism of the Holy Spirit would be so great that John felt unworthy even to untie his sandal-thongs (Mk 1:7-8; Mt 3:11; Lk 3:15-18). Some of John's followers seem to have remained convinced that their master was greater than Jesus, but there is no reason to suppose that John shared their feeling (cf. Jn 3:27-30). The statements of his attitude in the Gospels are not necessarily mere Christian propaganda.

Jesus came to John with the others to be baptized (Mk 1:9-11; Mt 3:13-17; Lk 3:21-22). Christians have shied away from the thought that he needed to be forgiven. Perhaps the very strength of this feeling is the strongest evidence that his baptism actually occurred. The memory of it was preserved by those who handed down the tradition, and the evangelists recorded it, even though it was perplexing and even embarrassing for them. Matthew preserves evidence that the difficulty was felt very early. When Jesus presented himself for baptism, Matthew says (3:14), John protested. The Fourth Gospel avoids the difficulty by omitting Jesus' baptism altogether and having John testify that he has seen the Spirit descend on Jesus (Jn 1:29-34).

Matthew records also (3:15) Jesus' reply to John's protest: "Let it be so now; for thus it is fitting for us to fulfill all righteousness." This means more than doing what God requires. It means going beyond what is required. Matthew is particularly fond of this conception of righteousness, but he did not invent it.

35

Those least in need of forgiveness often have the keenest sense of sinfulness, because they aim at perfection and know they have not reached it. That Jesus should ask to be baptized "to fulfil all righteousness" indicates that he identified himself with his people and felt the weight of the nation's sin.

"And when he came up out of the water," says Mark (1:10), "immediately he saw the heavens opened and the Spirit descending upon him like a dove." This may refer to an inward experience of Jesus alone. Matthew too says (3:16), "He saw the Spirit of God descending." Luke, however, says (3:21-22) "The heaven was opened, and the Holy Spirit descended upon him in bodily form, as a dove." This apparently implies that not only Jesus but also John and the bystanders saw the descent of the Spirit.

The idea of the Holy Spirit is an important part of the conception of God that was inherited and assumed by Jesus. It is misunderstood, or not understood at all, by many Christians as well as others. The confusion is compounded by the use of the word "Ghost" for "Spirit" in the King James Version. When I was a child I thought that the Holy Ghost was the ghost of Jesus. Three and a half centuries ago, however, "ghost" meant simply "spirit." It is no longer used in such a broad sense and should be abandoned in this connection.

The greatest source of difficulty, however, is not in the Bible but in a misunderstanding of the doctrine of the Trinity. We may unravel some of the confusion by going back to the roots of the matter in the Old Testament. The Hebrew word for spirit is, from our point of view, ambiguous. At the very beginning of the Bible (Gen. 1:2), where the KJV has, "And the Spirit of God moved upon the face of the waters," the RSV also reads "Spirit," but with a footnote, "Or *wind*." Other recent versions have "wind" in the text (NEB, NAB, NJV), with footnotes recognizing "spirit" as an alternative. The Anchor Bible reads "an awesome wind." In Hebrew the same word means both "wind" and "spirit." This is important for understanding the Hebrew conception of spirit. The same ambiguity is found also in Greek. It is well illustrated by a verse in the Gospel of John (3:8): "The wind [*pneuma*] blows where it wills, and you hear the sound of it,

36

but you do not know whence it comes or whither it goes; so it is with every one who is born of the Spirit [*pneuma*]." No translation into English can reproduce this play on meaning. The basic conception of the Spirit of God in the Old Testament is a mighty but invisible force emanating directly from God.

The same Hebrew word also means breath, as in the expression "the breath of life" (Gen 6:17; 7:15) or "the breath of his nostrils" (2 Sam 22:16; Ps 18:15). Akin to this is the idea of spirit as that which leaves the body at death, as in the common expression rendered by the KJV (Job 3:11 etc.) "gave up the ghost" (RSV "expire"—*i.e.*, *ex-spire*, breathe out). The word also comes to mean disposition, attitude, or self. Sometimes (Prov 16:18-19, 32) "his spirit" may mean simply "he." The inspiration (in-breathing!) of the prophets is ascribed to the Holy Spirit (Num 11:24-29; 1 Sam 10:10; 19:23; 2 Chron 20:14; Is 61:1; Ezek 2:2), as is also the ability to govern wisely (Hag 2:4-5). Joel promises that when God restores the prosperity of Zion he will pour out his Spirit on the whole people, and all will prophesy (Joel 2:28-29; cf. Acts 2:17).

The thought of the Holy Spirit as a permanent possession of chosen and approved individuals appears later and more rarely, if at all, in the Old Testament. When David was anointed (1 Sam 16:13), "the Spirit of the Lord came mightily upon David from that day forward"; but whether it remained with him or came upon him repeatedly is uncertain. Isaiah says of the coming righteous king (11:2), "And the Spirit of the Lord shall rest upon him." This idea underlies the descent of the Holy Spirit upon Jesus and his later appropriation of the prophet's words, "The Spirit of the Lord is upon me" (Is 61:1; Lk 4:18).

When the Spirit came upon Jesus a voice from heaven was heard (Mk 1:11; Mt 3:17; Lk 3:22). In Mark and Luke, Jesus is addressed directly: "Thou art my beloved Son." In Matthew the words are apparently addressed to John and the people: "This is my beloved Son." In all three accounts the voice adds, "with thee [or with whom] I am well pleased." This heavenly acclamation consists of two free quotations from the Old Testament: Psalm 2:7, "You are my son"; and Isaiah 42:1, "in whom my soul delights."

For the evangelists and the other writers of the New Testament, "Son of God" summed up all that faith in Jesus implied, including his divine origin and nature. How and when it acquired this full meaning is a difficult question. It could hardly have had that significance for the first Jewish disciples. That the Messiah was ever called God's Son in first-century Judaism is not attested by contemporary Jewish literature. The Gospels themselves show that it was not unknown, but what it would have meant to a Jew is another question. The Messiah was not thought of as being anything but a man, or as differing from other men by nature. Conceivably the title "Son of God" for the Messiah was discontinued in Judaism precisely because of the meaning it acquired in Christianity. For the first Jewish followers of Jesus, it would have had simpler implications.

Two main elements seem to have entered into the earliest Christian usage. One was Jesus' own sense of an intimate filial relationship with God. This, however, did not set him apart from his disciples. God was both "my Father" and "your Father" to Jesus, and he taught the disciples to address God as Father (Mt 6:9; Lk 11:2). He told them to love their enemies and pray for their persecutors so that they might be sons of their heavenly Father (Mt 5:44-45). The idea of a sonship unique in kind may have grown out of the unique degree to which Jesus realized what for others was an ideal to be pursued.

The origin of the use of "Son of God" as a Messianic title is evident in Psalm 2:7. Originally this psalm was an ode for the coronation of a king, to whom God says, "You are my son, today I have begotten you." The word "today" shows that "begotten you" must mean here "made you my son"—that is, "adopted you"—indicating that at the time of his coronation the king became officially, so to speak, God's son. By the mouth of Samuel, God had promised to David concerning Solomon, "I will be his father, and he shall be my son" (2 Sam 7:14). Accordingly the reigning king was called son of God. He was also called the Lord's Anointed, or Messiah; and when this title was applied to the hoped for, righteous king, such royal psalms as Psalm 2 were interpreted as referring to him.

In the baptism narrative, Psalm 2:7 is not quoted exactly.

38

Instead of "my Son," all three accounts have "my beloved Son." The Greek reads literally, "my Son the beloved," or (NEB, RSV margin) "the Beloved." So taken, it recalls the passage quoted in the rest of the verse (Is 42:1): "Behold my servant, whom I uphold, my chosen, in whom my soul delights." Matthew quotes this later (12:18) in a form even closer to the words spoken by the voice at Jesus' baptism, reading "my beloved" instead of "my chosen."

In Matthew's account of the Transfiguration (17:5) the voice from the cloud uses exactly the same words that Matthew has in the baptism narrative. Here Mark (9:7) does not have the last clause. Many manuscripts of Luke (9:35) agree with Mark, but the reading with the best attestation is even closer to Isaiah: "This is my chosen Son," or "my Son, the chosen one."

Unquestionably, for Jesus his baptism was a profound and crucial experience. Whether for the first time he was then convinced that he was the Messiah, whether he had already come to this conviction or had been coming to it and now felt that he had received the seal of God's approval, or whether he did not believe that he was the Messiah at all but considered himself only a prophet and forerunner of the coming one, his baptism was the turning point between his previous life of preparation and waiting and the active ministry in which he would henceforth be engaged. No doubt he was praying, as Luke says, when the rite was finished.

Before his public work could begin, however, there was still a period of struggle and testing before him. "The Spirit immediately drove him out into the wilderness," says Mark (1:12-13). Somewhat more gently, Matthew (4:1-11) says that Jesus was "led up by the Spirit into the wilderness," while Luke (4:1-13) says literally that he was "led in the Spirit in the wilderness." The last two statements may have had a common Aramaic original, in which the same preposition could mean into, in, or by.

The wilderness undoubtedly means here the steep, barren slope of the central Palestinian plateau, west of the Dead Sea and the lower part of the Jordan River. In the Old Testament this arid and desolate region is called "the wilderness of Judea." It is the same wilderness in which the community of Essenes at Qumran strove to prepare the way of the Lord, and in which the word of God came to John the Baptist. Tradition identifies a rugged hill west of Jericho as the place where Jesus met the Tempter. Nothing in the record, however, points to a particular spot or precludes wandering about in the area.

Mark's account (1:13) is very brief: "And he was in the wilderness forty days, tempted by Satan; and he was with the wild beasts; and the angels ministered to him." The statement that Jesus was with the wild beasts may mean merely that he spent the days of his temptation in wild country without human companionship. In Mark the temptation continues for forty days; Matthew and Luke put it after forty days of fasting, when he was hungry (Mk 1:13; Mt 4:2; Lk 4:2). The ministration of angels referred to by Mark is not mentioned by Luke; Matthew puts it after "the devil left him." Fasting in the sense of living with a bare minimum of nourishment would be practically inevitable in the wilderness of Judea for one absorbed in solitary spiritual struggle. After forty days (a traditional round number) Jesus would certainly have been hungry. Luke even says that he ate nothing.

Then, with the heavenly voice at his baptism still ringing in his ears, Jesus heard an insidious whisper, "If you are the Son of God." This is the point of the experience as Matthew and Luke understood it. "You think you are God's Son?" the Tempter seems to say; "Prove it!" Both Matthew and Luke tell of three successive temptations, the same three though not told in the same order: the temptation to turn stones into bread, the temptation to throw himself down from the pinnacle of the temple, and the temptation to worship Satan in return for world dominion. It is a strange story, surely not meant to be taken as a literal record of an actual encounter with Satan in bodily form. Is it a myth of the divine Redeemer, who by his insight and fidelity thwarts the cosmic powers of evil? Is it a legend like those of other religions, in which demonic powers try to prevent the founder of the religion from undertaking his mission? Or is it a symbolic representation of real temptations met and overcome by Jesus, either as he faced his mission or in the course of his ministry? Probably in these narratives we have reminiscences of an experience that would be no less real if the form in which it was told was symbolic.

So understood, the story fits the situation in which Jesus began his ministry. Severe temptations may very well have assailed him as he faced his mission, and he may have told his disciples about them later. The elaborate narratives of Matthew and Luke may be the result of legendary or literary development; but that Jesus could speak of his own inner experiences in figurative or perhaps visionary language is shown later by his exclamation when the disciples reported their success in casting out demons (Lk 10:18): "I saw Satan fall like lightning from heaven." We cannot hope to get beyond a "perhaps" on such questions as these.

Once, Satan quotes Scripture to support his proposal, but Jesus rejects all three temptations with quotations from Scripture. In his inner struggles Jesus may have found strength and guidance in familiar verses that came to mind when he needed them.

Along with the effort to satisfy himself that he was indeed the beloved Son, the temptations seem to involve a misinterpretation of Jesus' mission. Perhaps he was tempted to conform his ministry to current expectations of what the Messiah would do, or to devote himself to a kind of service that was clearly needed but not what God intended him to do. Turning stones into bread might then signify using his powers and his position for his own benefit. Such a temptation would have some relevance for the early church (Acts 8:18-19); but judging by all we know about Jesus, we may be sure that no such interest would have presented any temptation to him at all. Much more likely to be tempting to him would be an impulse to devote his life to alleviating physical misery. When he saw the crowds of sick, hungry, aimless, or misguided people, he had compassion for them (*e.g.*, Mt 9:36; 14:14; 15:32). He healed many of the sick and on one or two occasions is said to have fed the hungry. All his time and strength might have been spent in ministering to the bodily needs of the people about him. But he knew also that there was a deeper need, which he alone could meet. "Man shall not live by bread alone" (Mt 4:4; cf. Deut 8:3), he replied to the Tempter, "but by every word that proceeds from the mouth of God."

The second temptation, following Matthew's order, was to

41

throw himself down from the pinnacle of the temple, counting upon God to preserve him from harm. This pinnacle is commonly supposed to mean a tower at the southeast corner of the temple enclosure, overlooking the Kidron valley, which was then much deeper than it is now. This time the devil quoted a psalm (91:11-12) as authority for such presumptuous reliance upon God. But Jesus answered scripture with scripture, using again a verse from Deuteronomy (6:16): "You shall not put the Lord your God to the test." The KJV says, "Ye shall not tempt the Lord your God," but God cannot be tempted. What is meant is putting God's power and goodness to a test, acting rashly and expecting him to extricate us from the results of our folly, as the Israelites did on the occasion referred to in the verse Jesus quoted (Deut 6:16; cf. Ex 17:1-7; Ps 95:8-9): "as you tested him at Massah."

If anything more were needed to prove that the account is symbolic, surely this temptation would be sufficient. Quite apart from the problem of transportation from the desert, a challenge to leap from the pinnacle of the temple, taken literally, would hardly deserve a serious reply. Putting God's care to the proof, however, is a very real and very common temptation. During his ministry Jesus was repeatedly challenged to authenticate his mission by some miraculous act (Mk 8:11-13; Mt 12:38-39; 16:1, 4; Lk 11:16, 29). He was ready to help when moved by compassion, but he consistently refused to respond to demands for a sign as proof of his authority.

The third temptation was to seek worldwide political power by worshiping Satan. Again the symbolic nature of the account is obvious: there is no "very high mountain" (Mt 4:8) in the wilderness of Judea; there is no mountain anywhere from which all the kingdoms of the world are visible. The traditional Mount of Temptation, just west of Jericho, does not afford a view beyond the limits of the Jordan valley. The temptation assumes that Satan holds the kingdoms of the world in his power and can give them away as he pleases. The proposal was therefore that Jesus should use Satanic power to further God's ends. If this reflects a real experience, it must have been rooted in the circumstances and requirements of Jesus' ministry. The subjugation of the Jewish nation by the Romans was a ground of bitter resentment among the people, and what many expected from the Messiah above all was to throw off this alien yoke, "that we, being delivered from the hand of our enemies, might serve him without fear" (Lk 1:74).

Some of Jesus' followers expected him to do this. Possibly there were times when he felt that there was no other way to achieve freedom and security for his people. The temptation to adopt Satanic means to gain God's ends, to seek peace by making war, to use force to accomplish what can never be accomplished by anything but persuasion and love, is always with us. But Jesus saw that while the way of political power and compulsion might seem shorter, it was Satan's way, not God's. "It is written," he said to the Tempter, "you shall worship the Lord your God, and him only shall you serve."

Matthew's and Mark's accounts of the temptation end with the statement that angels ministered to Jesus. Luke's conclusion is quite different: "And when the devil had ended every temptation, he departed from him until an opportune time."

Interpreting the temptation narratives as symbolic does not dispose of a deeper question: what are we to think of the assumed source of the temptations? Is Satan a real personal being, the author of evil impulses and acts? In the temptation story, of course, we are not dealing with sayings of Jesus, but it is quite certain that for him Satan was terribly real and possessed frightful power in the world. And, let it be said at once, there is no reason to feel apologetic about the fact that Jesus accepted such beliefs. He was talking not to us but to first-century Palestinians, and he was one of them. Not only did he have to speak in terms of what his hearers knew or believed in order to be understood, he thought in the same terms himself. To imagine him, with divine omniscience, deliberately translating his message into the language of a world-view he knew to be false would make him a figure so artificial and unreal as to be neither credible nor attractive. At any rate, it is profoundly significant that Jesus frankly recognized and boldly faced the reality and power of evil. This fact plays a very large part in the story of his life and in his teaching.

43

CHAPTER III

THE FIRST PART OF THE GALILEAN MINISTRY

In speaking of "parts" of the Galilean ministry we refer not to successive phases of Jesus' work but merely to more or less distinct portions of the narrative, sometimes marked by the insertion of collections of sayings and sometimes arbitrarily divided for convenience in presentation.

After the temptation Mark continues (1:14), "Now after John was arrested, Jesus came into Galilee." The story of John's arrest is not told, however, until considerably later (Mk 6:27-29), in connection with his death. Matthew (4:12) follows Mark's procedure. Luke has already told of John's arrest (3:19-20) at the end of his report of John's preaching. Here he therefore (4:14) says simply, "And Jesus returned in the power of the Spirit into Galilee."

How much time had elapsed between the temptation and the return to Galilee, and what Jesus had been doing in the meantime, the Synoptic Gospels do not say. The Fourth Gospel, which ignores both the baptism and the temptation, says that on the day after John's testimony to Jesus at the Jordan he repeated it in the hearing of two of his disciples (Jn 1:35-42), one of whom was Andrew of Bethsaida in Galilee, and that Andrew thereupon brought his brother Simon to Jesus, who named him forthwith "The Rock." The narrative continues (vv 43-51), "The next day Jesus decided to go to Galilee." The calling of Philip as a disciple and the conversion of Nathanael follow, still apparently at the Jordan; then chapter 2 begins with the wedding at Cana in Galilee (Jn 2:1-11). Thus both the Synoptic Gospels and the Gospel of John, though in quite different ways, bring Jesus back to Galilee after his meeting with John the Baptist.

With regard to what he did when he got there, however, there is a notable difference between John and the other Gospels. In John the sojourn in Galilee lasts only a few days, with no action except the rather casual "sign" of turning water to wine. After that, Jesus spent a few days in Capernaum "with his mother and his brothers and his disciples" and then returned to Jerusalem (vv

44

12-13). According to Mark, however (1:14), Jesus "came into Galilee, preaching." Matthew says that Jesus moved from Nazareth to "Capernaum by the sea, in the territory of Zebulon and Naphtali" (4:13-17), fulfilling a prophecy of Isaiah (9:1-2), and continues, "From that time Jesus began to preach." Luke says (4:14-15) that when Jesus returned to Galilee "a report concerning him went out through all the surrounding country," adding, "And he taught in their synagogues."

This period in Galilee can hardly be the one referred to in John. The trip to Jerusalem for the Passover is in John the occasion of the cleansing of the temple (2:14-22), which in the Synoptic Gospels occurs near the end of Jesus' life. The nocturnal visit of Nicodemus is related in the next chapter (3:1-15). Then, we are told, Jesus and his disciples spent some time in Judea baptizing. Meanwhile John was baptizing at Aenon; and the evangelist adds "For John had not yet been put in prison" (vv 22-24). This activity in Judea belongs therefore in the gap left by the first three Gospels between the temptation and the beginning of Jesus' work in Galilee. If there was such a period of work in Judea before the Galilean ministry, it does not follow that the particular events related in John occurred at this time. The cleansing of the temple, at least, is surely out of place. From now on the Synoptic Gospels record only preaching and healing in Galilee until, after a brief excursion into Gentile territory, a turning point is reached in the vicinity of Caesarea Philippi. Jesus then takes his final journey to Jerusalem, and the last part of his ministry is accomplished there.

Like the sources and traditions back of them, the Synoptic Gospels are largely composed of items handed down separately or in small collections and arranged by the evangelists according to their own individual purposes and interests. For the order of presentation Mark has set a pattern that by and large, with important exceptions, is followd by Matthew and Luke. Within this broad framework the items are arranged more by subjects than by sequence in time or place. It is therefore impossible to reconstruct a consecutive narrative of Jesus' life and work. About all that we can be sure of in that respect, it would seem, is that his public ministry began in Galilee and ended at Jerusalem, with the journey to Jerusalem connecting the two major divisions.

Even this framework is now treated by some scholars as an artificial theological construction; but the overall division into a Galilean ministry, a journey to Jerusalem, and the culmination of the whole story at Jerusalem, I am convinced, stands firm. There were witnesses of Jesus' ministry still living when the Synoptic Gospels were written. Their recollections would differ at many points and indeed would both fade and change as time went by. Many of them, however, would surely remember not only isolated incidents and sayings but the broad outlines of Jesus' ministry.

With the statement that Jesus returned to Galilee after the arrest of John the Baptist, Mark and Matthew give brief summaries of his message. "Jesus came into Galilee," says Mark (1:14-15), "preaching the gospel of God, and saying, 'The time is fulfilled, and the kingdom of God is at hand; repent, and believe in the gospel.'" Matthew, as already noted, reports the proclamation in the same words he has used to summarize John the Baptist's preaching (4:17; cf. 3:2). Luke (4:14-15) omits the summary.

What is the time to which Jesus refers in Mark, and in what sense was it fulfilled? The prophet Habakkuk, in a time of distress and disappointment, had said (2:3), "For still the vision awaits its time." The Greek translation (Septuagint) has here the same word for "appointed time" (*kairos*) that is translated "time" here in Mark. Similarly Daniel (8:17; cf. 8:26; 10:14; 11:27, 35) says the vision is for "the time of the end," and here too the same Greek word is used. Evidently the idea of a great change at the end of a divinely appointed period was not unfamiliar in Jesus' day. He said that this period had been completed and the awaited change was about to take place. What would then come about he called the kingdom of God, and he said it was at hand. What he meant by the kingdom of God is a question we shall have to keep in mind as we proceed.

Jesus' proclamation of the kingdom was not merely a warning to "flee from the wrath to come," as with John the Baptist (Mt 3:7; Lk 3:7). He came, says Mark (1:14-15), "preaching the gospel of God"; and the proclamation ends with an exhortation to "repent, and believe in the gospel," that is, the good news (Anglo-Saxon *godspel*). This name for Jesus' message echoes a word used often in the latter half of the book of Isaiah, a verb

46

which means "bring good news." It refers there to proclaiming to Jerusalem that God, in spite of present appearances, is still in control, that he still reigns as King (*e.g.,* Is 52:7; 61:1).

The Hebrew verb translated "bring good tidings" is used also in Aramaic; so too is the noun meaning "good news." I see no adequate reason to doubt that Jesus himself originated this way of speaking of his message. All three of the Synoptic Gospels, in one form or another, represent him as calling his proclamation good news. One of the passages in Isaiah mentioned above is said by Luke to have been read by Jesus in the synagogue at Nazareth; it is also alluded to in Jesus' reply to the disciples of John the Baptist (Is 61:1-2; Lk 4:18-19; 7:22; Mt 11:5). This and other places where the Hebrew verb appears probably suggested the term "good news" to Jesus. Later, of course, it was used for "the gospel about Jesus" instead of "the gospel of Jesus."

From the statement that Jesus returned to Galilee and taught in the synagogues Luke proceeds (4:16-30) to the visit to Nazareth, which Mark and Matthew record later. That it was Luke who changed the order of events is shown by a passing reference to miracles performed at Capernaum (v 23), of which nothing has yet been said. The reason for the rearrangement is obvious. The allusions to the widow of Zarephath and the Syrian Naaman (vv 25-27) reflect Luke's interest in the Gentile mission, which no doubt he wished to stress at the beginning of Jesus' ministry.

Mark and Matthew report at this point the calling of the first four disciples to follow Jesus (Mk 1:16-20; Mt 4:18-22). Simon Peter and his brother Andrew, while fishing in the Sea of Galilee, are invited by Jesus to follow him and become fishers of men; and they at once leave their nets and follow him. A little farther along the shore another pair of brothers, James and John, hear the same summons while mending their nets with their father Zebedee, and they too respond with alacrity, leaving their father with his hired helpers to carry on their trade.

According to Luke, Jesus came upon Simon and the sons of Zebedee, who were his partners, washing their nets together beside their boats (5:1-3). (Andrew is not mentioned at all here or anywhere else in Luke except in the list of the twelve apostles.) Jesus got into Simon's boat, had it moved out a little way from the

47

shore, and sat in it while he spoke to the people (cf. Mk 4:1; Mt 13:2). When he had finished speaking, he told Simon to move out to deeper water and let down his net. Simon did as Jesus told him and caught so many fish that he had to call James and John to help him, and together they filled both boats with fish, so that they began to sink. Thereupon Simon fell down before Jesus and said, "Depart from me, for I am a sinful man, O Lord." The summons to become fishers of men followed and was promptly obeyed (Lk 5:4-11). This is the first of the "nature miracles" attributed to Jesus, as distinguished from the miracles of healing. It has no parallel in the other Synoptic Gospels, but in John there is a similar incident (21:4-8) in connection with an appearance of Jesus to his disciples after his resurrection. The two incidents, though differing in detail and placed at opposite ends of Jesus' ministry, must have been originally the same.

Perhaps this is a good place to make some comments on the miracles in general. Something has been indicated by what was said about Jesus' birth, but there is more to say. The miraculous element is one of the most characteristic features of the Gospel story, and the one with which a modern student of the Gospels finds it hardest to come to terms. Our distinction between the natural and the supernatural is of course relatively new and quite foreign to the thinking of ancient peoples. They felt a difference between the usual and the unusual, but extraordinary things happened now and then. Nothing was thought of as merely natural in the modern sense. Most educated people today, however, though aware that there is much we cannot yet explain, are so conditioned by the world view of modern science that they find it hard to accept anything that runs counter to the normal processes of nature.

Science itself, to be sure, seems to have gone beyond a purely mechanistic conception of the universe. The whole concept of natural law, we are told, now needs and is undergoing revision. Exponents of the philosophy of science question the very idea of causality and speak of an element of uncertainty in the universe. But water still does not run uphill. The amazing achievements of applied science in our day are based on the assumption that if all the factors in a situation are recognized and the right steps are taken, the results can be counted on. These modern miracles are accomplished not by any suspension or contravention of natural law but by fulfilling the conditions on which it will operate in the direction and way we desire.

What is reported as a miracle may sometimes have been in fact a quite natural event. If we knew all the facts of the case we might be able to explain many things that, to those who saw them, seemed explicable only as direct acts of God. It does not follow, however, that all the miracles recorded in the Gospels or elsewhere in the Bible can be explained as natural events. Well-meaning interpreters have sometimes gone too far in trying to defend the accuracy of the Bible by natural explanations of supernatural events.

Some of the miracles related in the Bible—perhaps most of them—were not actual events at all, but legendary acts and manifestations whose real significance is their testimony to the impression made by an extraordinary personality on the people who encountered and observed him. Any man in the ancient world who strongly impressed his contemporaries was almost sure to have miracles attributed to him. Indeed, in our society legends grow up about exceptional persons even during their lifetime.

Speaking of Jesus in this way may seem to make him merely one of many great men, exceptional but not superhuman, not the divine being he is believed by Christians to be; but however his person and nature are understood, I for one cannot believe that even in him God acted in any way inconsistent with the same natural laws and operations by which he works today. This does not mean that he could do nothing that any man might not have done. Whatever Jesus was, he was not ordinary.

It does not mean, either, that God cannot or does not intervene in human affairs, as though the universe was a sealed machine, set and started by the Creator ages ago and running ever since in ways immutably determined at the beginning. That would not only eliminate any possibility of human freedom and so render meaningless such concepts as sin and salvation, it would also make impossible any kind of special providence and any hope of direct answers to prayer. We do not yet know enough to justify the sacrifice of these beliefs. We cannot set limits on what God can or will do. But whatever truth there is in the traditions of Jesus' miracles must have been within the same order by which the universe is governed now.

This still leaves open the question how much and just what historical fact there is in the particular miracle stories of the Gospels. There is a tendency at present to disparage concern with that question and to concentrate rather on the theological significance of the miracles. That is all very well if one is more interested in the faith of the early church than in the search for the real Jesus. It is not essential that all or any one of the miracles in the Gospels be demonstrably historical. It is, however, essential that a credible and fairly probable kernel of historical fact be discernible in the narratives taken all together, if they are to be anything more to us than relics of ancient thought.

Only a partial and tentative answer at best can be given to this question. In each instance we can only try to judge, with such knowledge as we have, what is most probable. Luke's story of the miraculous draft of fish, like the one in John, seems to be best characterized as a devout legend, exalting Christ as Lord of both man and nature, in obedience to whom man's needs are satisfied. Matthew's and Mark's accounts of the calling of the first disciples show the legendary nature of Luke's narrative.

The concise story of Mark and Matthew gives the impression that the four fishermen had never seen Jesus but were impelled by an immediate sense of divine authority. Curiously enough, by placing the event after the Sabbath in Capernaum, Luke implies (4:38-39) that at least one of the four already knew Jesus, for Jesus had gone to Simon's house from the synagogue at Capernaum. The story of his meeting Andrew and Simon at the Jordan in the Gospel of John (1:35-42) suggests that Jesus may have met the men before, won their allegiance, and told them to be ready to follow him whenever he called them.

Mark now presents (1:21-34) a series of miracles performed at Capernaum on the Sabbath. Whether he received the tradition of these acts as all occurring on the same day is not certain. Perhaps he brought them together to give the impression of a typically busy day in Jesus' ministry. That impression is enhanced by the frequent use of the adverb "immediately."

50

"And they went into Capernaum," says Mark (1:21), "and immediately on the sabbath he entered the synagogue and taught." Jesus had previously appeared as a prophet proclaiming good news and summoning the people to repentance; here we see him as a sage or rabbi giving instruction (cf. Mt 5:1-2). His teaching is referred to and quoted in the Gospels even more often than his preaching. Teaching in the synagogue is often mentioned (Mk 1:21; 6:2), sometimes together with the proclamation of the kingdom (Mk 1:39; 6:2; Mt 4:23; 9:35; Lk 4:44). Jesus is often addressed as "Teacher" or "Rabbi." The teaching expanded and clarified the proclamation.

Jesus' teaching was not like what the people were used to hearing. "And they were astonished at his teaching," says Mark (1:22), "for he taught them as one who had authority, and not as the scribes." The scribes were the successors of the wise men of the Old Testament. They shared with the priests the task of interpreting and applying the law (Ezra 7:6, 11-12, 21). They found their authority in the law of Moses, and cited for its interpretation "the tradition of the elders" (Mk 7:3, 5; Mt 15:2; cf. Mk 7:4, 8, 9, 13; Mt 15:3, 6), a long chain of pronouncements by a succession of leaders going back to Ezra. Jesus said, "Truly, I say to you (Mk 3:28 and often), or even, "You have heard that it was said . . . But I say . . ." (Mt 5:21, 27, 33, 38, 43).

"And immediately," Mark continues (1:23), "there was in their synagogue a man with an unclean spirit," which Jesus proceeded to exorcise. (The term "unclean spirit" is frequently used in the Gospels for demons; in fact Mark often has "unclean spirit" where Matthew or Luke, if not both, has "demon" (e.g., Mk 1:26; Lk 4:35). The afflicted man cried out, "What have you to do with us, Jesus of Nazareth? Have you come to destroy us? I know who you are, the Holy One of God." Jesus commanded the demon to be silent and come out of the man; and it obeyed, "convulsing him and crying with a loud voice," to the amazement of the congregation (Mk 1:27; Lk 4:36). "What is this?" they cried; "A new teaching! With authority he commands even the unclean spirits, and they obey him." The connection between teaching and exorcism seems strange. Presumably it lies in the demonstration of authority by the miracle.

This is the first of the healing miracles. It raises questions that apply to this kind of miracle in general, concerning both the historical reality of the cures and the understanding of them as casting out demons. If the nature miracles may be regarded as devout legends, the healing miracles cannot be disposed of so easily. Some of them too may be legendary, but we do not have to accept or reject them in a lump as they stand. The real issue is whether Jesus really healed sick people.

In nine of the twenty healing miracles, faith is explicitly stressed as a condition of healing or even as accomplishing it. Recent studies of the miracle stories in the Gospels in comparison with those told of Jewish and pagan saints and sages or "divine men" have brought out the fact that the emphasis on faith as a condition of healing is a distinctive element in the Gospel narratives. I see no reason to doubt that it goes back to Jesus himself. This suggests that Jesus healed the sick by what would now be called faith-healing, aided by the confidence inspired by his exceptional personality. If so, his cures were not miraculous in the modern sense of the word; they were extraordinary, but not supernatural, instances of psychosomatic healing. What kinds of physical and mental trouble might be amenable to such treatment we are unable to say; medical science seems much more open-minded now than it used to be. Whether leprosy, for instance, or blindness would ever yield to such "authority" as Jesus demonstrated may be open to serious doubt, though hardly to arrogant denial. Well authenticated cures of even such a dread disease as cancer in our own day remind us that "more things are wrought by prayer than this world dreams of." But even if not all the cures recorded in the Gospels actually occurred, it is altogether probable that Jesus healed many people afflicted with various ills of body and mind. To call this faith-healing only underlines the fact that he inspired such faith.

If such a suggestion seems to detract from the significance of the miracles as demonstrating his divine nature, it should be remembered that Jesus himself testified to the performance of such cures by others as well as himself: "And if I cast out demons by Beelzebul," he said to those who brought this charge against him (Mt 12:27-28; Lk 11:19-20), "by whom do your sons cast

52

them out?'' The meaning he saw in the expulsion of the demons was not that it certified his own unique nature but that it confirmed his proclamation of the nearness of the kingdom of God.

The reality of the cures does not stand or fall with the interpretation put upon them. The disorders were real, whether they were caused by demons or not. In discussing Jesus' temptation we have noted that he unquestionably believed in the reality and power of Satan. There is no hint that he ever questioned the belief in demons or the practice of exorcism. To recognize that is to recognize that he was a real man, subject to the limitations of living in the real world at that point in history.

The afflictions and evils that in antiquity were attributed to demons are still with us. Whatever we may call them, there are still legions of unclean spirits to be cast out—not only physical and mental disorders but also moral, social, economic, and political evils. Among them, sad to relate, is an alarming recrudescence of superstition. School and church have failed to communicate to large segments of our population a clear and convincing modern understanding of the universe. Science and technology, in spite of their amazing achievements, have not made life happy or free or decent or even safe. True devotion to Jesus in our world requires the translation of his teaching and example into the best thought and action possible today. The compassion that moved him to relieve suffering must find expression in earnest and competent efforts to eradicate the ills that afflict humanity.

The demoniac at Capernaum called Jesus "the Holy One of God" (Mk 1:24; Lk 4:34). At his baptism, Jesus had been declared to be the Son of God, and under temptation he had vindicated his right to the title. The term "Holy One of God" presumably had the same meaning, though it is used elsewhere in that sense only once (Jn 6:69). For the early church, and probably already for the Jews of Jesus' time, the many terms used for the Messiah had lost any differences or distinctions of meaning.

The result of the impression made by Jesus' teaching and the healing in the synagogue was that "at once his fame spread everywhere throughout all the surrounding region of Galilee" (Mk 1:28; Lk 4:37).

From the synagogue Jesus went with his four disciples to the home of two of them, the brothers Simon and Andrew (Mk 1:29-31; Mt 8:14-15; Lk 4:38-39). There he found Simon's mother-in-law in bed with a fever. "And he came and took her by the hand and lifted her up, and the fever left her; and she served them." Matthew's account of this incident is condensed and placed later in his narrative, after the Sermon on the Mount and two other miracles of healing.

When the sun set that evening, the Sabbath with its restrictions on carrying burdens being over, the people of the city thronged about Jesus, bringing "all who were sick or possessed with demons" (Mk 1:32-34; Mt 8:16-17; Lk 4:40-41). There are interesting variations in the three accounts of this episode. Matthew, like Mark, begins "That evening," but his change in the order of events makes this mean a later evening. All three evangelists distinguish between the sick and those possessed by demons, but Matthew and Luke bring out the distinction more sharply. Mark and Luke have an important detail that Matthew omits. Mark says that Jesus "would not permit the demons to speak, because they knew him." Luke is more specific: the demons, he says, cried, "You are the Son of God!" and Jesus "rebuked them, and would not allow them to speak, because they knew that he was the Christ." Here, confirming what has been said about the equivalence of various Messianic expressions, "Son of God" and "Christ" are clearly identical in meaning.

This is the first occurrence of the term "Christ" in the narratives of Jesus' ministry in the Synoptic Gospels. It has been used in titles, genealogies, and infancy stories; and Luke's account of John the Baptist says that the people wondered whether he was the Christ (Lk 3:15; cf. Jn 1:20, 25). In the Gospel of John (1:35-37, 40-42), when Andrew hears John call Jesus the Lamb of God, he finds his brother Simon and says, "We have found the Messiah." For the benefit of Greek readers who do not know Hebrew, the evangelist explains, "which means Christ."

When the word Christ is applied to Jesus in the Gospels it usually has the definite article, "the Christ," showing that it is still felt as a title rather than a personal name. The chief exception is in combination with the name Jesus. Soon, however, the term came to be practically a surname, and eventually it was regularly used as a name without the article. Jewish sources also frequently say "Messiah son of David" or "King Messiah" without a definite article.

Instead of the demonic cry and its suppression, Matthew (8:17) characteristically cites a prophecy: "This was to fulfil what was spoken by the prophet Isaiah, 'He took our infirmities and bore our diseases.'" The quotation is from the description of the suffering servant of the Lord in the fifty-third chapter of Isaiah (v 4), where more than anywhere else in the Old Testament the early church saw a portrait of Jesus. Usually the connection is found in his rejection and suffering; here the mention of infirmities and diseases brings the prophecy to mind, though Jesus did not literally take upon himself the afflictions of those whom he healed.

The silencing of the demons introduces us for the first time to one of Mark's most characteristic ideas, commonly called "the Messianic secret." According to Mark, Jesus made no claim to be the Messiah during his ministry, was not recognized as such by the people, and was even careful not to let the fact of his Messiahship be known. Even Peter's confession at Caesarea Philippi was not welcomed and praised as in Matthew (Mk 8:30; cf. Mt 16:17-19). Only at the end, and in answer to a direct question from the high priest, according to Mark, did Jesus acknowledge his Messiahship (14:62). The explanation of this distinctive conception, scholars have suggested, is that Mark, fully convinced that Jesus was the Messiah, could find no clear evidence that he had presented himself as such to the Jewish nation; and the reason for this silence, Mark decided, could only be that Jesus was not yet ready to claim his Messiahship publicly and did not want the fact divulged prematurely.

A further inference is often drawn, that Jesus did not in fact claim to be the Messiah because he did not believe that he was. Only after his resurrection, it is thought, did the disciples come to believe this. It is possible, however, and to me seems more likely, that Jesus discouraged public acclamation of him as Messiah because he knew that it would be misunderstood. It would arouse false hopes in his followers and false fears in the religious and civil authorities, and thus would hinder his work instead of promoting it. To be the Messiah was one thing; to be the kind of Messiah the people expected and wanted was something quite different.

Luke follows Mark in the belief that only the demons recognized Jesus as the Christ, and he would not allow them to make him known (4:35, 41). Matthew, here and elsewhere, passes over the demonic acclamation (12:16). Once he says that Jesus "ordered them not to make him known," but by omitting the recognition by the demons he makes "them" mean the people who were healed.

The next morning after the busy Sabbath at Capernaum, according to Mark and Luke, Jesus arose early and sought solitude outside the city in "a lonely place," not necessarily a desert but a place where he could be alone (Mk 1:35; Lk 4:42). He was not left to himself very long, however. The people "sought him and came to him," says Luke, "and would have kept him from leaving them." Mark says that "Simon and those who were with him" found Jesus and told him that everyone was seeking him; but he said that other cities, too, must be given the good news of God's kingdom, adding, "for that is why I came out" (Mk 1:38). This apparently means that he had come out of Capernaum to carry his message to other cities; in Luke, however, he says (4:43), "for I was sent for this purpose."

According to Mark and Matthew the mission of preaching and healing now proceeded throughout "all Galilee" (Mk 1:39; Mt 4:23). Luke says he preached "in the synagogues of Judea" (4:44). The apparent discrepancy is resolved if we recognize that Luke used the name Judea for Palestine as a whole. More difficult to explain is Luke's omission of any reference to healing or exorcism. Matthew (4:23-25; cf. 9:35) elaborates Mark's statement, specifying the varieties of afflictions healed as well as the regions from which the people came, including not only Galilee, but Syria, the Decapolis, Transjordan, and Judea (cf. Mk 3:7-8; Lk 6:17).

CHAPTER IV

THE SERMON ON THE MOUNT AND THE SERMON ON THE PLAIN

At this point Matthew inserts the Sermon on the Mount (Mt 5–7), the first of his five major discourses. Seeing the crowds that had gathered, he says, Jesus went up on a mountain and sat down, and his disciples came to him (5:1). "And he opened his mouth and taught them." The "sermon" is thus addressed to the disciples, not to the crowds. What we have here, however, is obviously not a stenographic record of a particular sermon, but a collection of sayings spoken on various occasions and transmitted separately or in other connections. Luke (6:17) presents some of the same material, with notable differences, as spoken when Jesus "came down" from the hills where he had appointed the twelve apostles, "and stood on a level place." Luke says that Jesus "healed them all," and then proceeds with the Sermon on the Plain (6:20-49), addressed, like Matthew's Sermon on the Mount, to the disciples. Both discourses are clearly compilations of materials from two or more sources. Luke's is much shorter than Matthew's and contains very little that is not in the Sermon on the Mount. Matthew, however, has much that Luke uses in other connections, and much also that is found nowhere else and exhibits features characteristic of other unique material in Matthew.

In both Gospels the sermon begins with what are commonly called the Beatitudes (Mt 5:3-12; Lk 6:20-23), short sayings that begin, "Blessed are . . ." The Greek adjective translated "blessed" represents a Hebrew word used often in the Old Testament, especially in Psalms and Proverbs. It means fortunate, well off, to be congratulated, or the like. The person pronounced blessed may not feel at all happy; in fact, those whom Jesus called blessed would appear to most people to be decidedly unhappy.

There are four striking differences between the Beatitudes given by Matthew and those given by Luke. First, Matthew has nine Beatitudes, Luke only four. The sayings concerning the meek, the merciful, the pure in heart, the peacemakers, and those

57

persecuted for righteousness are lacking in Luke. Second, whereas Matthew's Beatitudes are stated more generally in the third person ("the poor in spirit," "those who mourn," and so on), shifting to the second person only in the last Beatitude, Luke's are all addressed directly to the hearers in the second person ("you poor," "you that hunger now"). A third and very important difference is that Luke understands and phrases the Beatitudes in a more literal and material sense than Matthew does. It is not "the poor in spirit" who are called blessed in Luke but "you poor," not "those who hunger and thirst for righteousness" but "you that hunger now." Instead of "those who mourn" Luke has "you that weep now," and instead of "they shall be comforted" he has "you shall laugh." The fourth difference is even more emphatic. Luke's four Beatitudes are followed by four corresponding Woes (6:24-26): "But woe to you that are rich, . . . Woe to you that are full now, . . . Woe to you that laugh now, . . . Woe to you, when all men speak well of you, . . ."

In the last Beatitude Luke retains "your reward is great in heaven." If he is thinking of physical hardships in this life, the compensations he has in mind are not limited to this world. The contrast he stresses involves not merely a social revolution but the establishment of the kingdom of God. This is clear from Luke's whole account of Jesus' teaching.

Which version of the Beatitudes is correct, Matthew's or Luke's? What did Jesus really say and mean? Granted that he might have uttered similar sayings, with verbal variations, at different times and places, we have here a radical difference in points of view. The only way to resolve it is to compare these sayings with the rest of Jesus' recorded teaching. Meanwhile a few observations can be made on these particular texts.

In some parts of the Bible, especially some of the Psalms, poverty and piety are considered practically inseparable. A more ancient view, still apparent at many points in the Old Testament, had been that righteousness was rewarded by prosperity and long life in this world, and misfortune was a punishment for sin; but as Israel suffered more and more adversity, and the most faithful individuals and groups were the most oppressed and afflicted, it came to be felt that the humble, the meek, the devout, the poor were the righteous people of God, and the mighty and prosperous were the proud, wicked oppressors. Only in humbly waiting for God to act was there any hope. The later portions of the Old Testament are full of this assurance. Psalm 37, for instance, is echoed in the third Beatitude in Matthew (Ps 37:11; Mt 5:5). Matthew's "poor in spirit" and Luke's "you poor" were thus actually the same people.

It was to the poor, humble, oppressed common people that Jesus promised the blessings of the kingdom of God. But they were not only grieving and longing for righteousness. They were also merciful, pure in heart, peacemakers, persecuted for righteousness' sake. They were Jesus' disciples, reviled and persecuted for his sake. Clearly the people whom Jesus considered fortunate were not those commonly called successful, then or now.

The last Beatitude (Mt 5:11-12; Lk 6:22-23) must have been spoken at a later time in Jesus' ministry, when the disciples had begun to encounter persecution. In fact, the experience of the church in the following generation or two has colored the tradition of this saying, especially in Luke's expression, "when they exclude you . . . and cast out your name as evil." The later condemnation of Christians as heretics and the separation of church and synagogue are reflected here. Before the end of his life, however, Jesus, facing rejection and death himself, must have warned his followers of the violent opposition they would meet if they remained loyal to him. This final Beatitude, in short, is an instance of the dislocation of a saying through being combined editorially with others as though they had all been spoken at the same time. The sayings about salt and light that follow in Matthew (5:13-16) illustrate this further. In Mark and Luke they appear at other points; Luke gives one of them twice (Mk 4:21; 9:50; Lk 8:16; 14:34-35).

Another fact illustrated by the saying about salt is that the most familiar things in the Bible are not always the best understood. Only in Matthew is the salt identified with the disciples. In Mark the saying is preceded by the cryptic statement (9:49), "For every one will be salted with fire," which immediately follows the stern warning (vv 47-48) that it would be better to lose an eye than to be thrown into hell. Matthew and Luke omit the sentence about being salted with fire. What does it mean? A tempting explanation was offered by a great scholar who perceived that in Aramaic the phrase "with fire" would be spelled and pronounced exactly like a word that meant "going bad" or "putrifying." He therefore read the verse, "Everything that is going bad is salted." After this Jesus says in Mark, "Have salt in yourselves, and be at peace with one another." At least for Mark, the salt is not the disciples themselves but something they should have in or among themselves.

Luke attaches the whole saying about salt to the end of his section on renunciation as necessary for discipleship (14:25-33). Like Matthew, Luke says "lost its taste" instead of Mark's "lost its saltness," suggesting that the ordinary use of salt for seasoning is in mind; but instead of Matthew's "It is no longer good for anything except to be thrown out and trodden under foot" Luke has "It is fit neither for the land nor for the dunghill; men throw it away." How any salt could be good for soil or the manure pile is not clear. In Old Testament times land captured in war was sometimes sown with salt to make it useless (*e.g.,* Judg 9:45; Deut 29:23; Jer 17:6; Zeph 2:9; cf. Ezek 47:6-12).

As often, we cannot tell just what Jesus said or what he meant by it. The saying about salt means at least that to render the service required of them Jesus' disciples must be morally and spiritually qualified.

After this saying Matthew has one about light (5:14): "You are the light of the world. A city set on a hill cannot be hid." Many of the oldest towns in Palestine are situated on hilltops and visible from a distance. The disciples must not hide themselves from the world. The next saying (v 15) points out that to do so would defeat the purpose for which they were chosen: "Nor do men light a lamp and put it under a bushel, but on a stand, and it gives light to all in the house." In Mark and Luke this appears later as a question (Mk 4:21; Lk 8:16). In another connection Luke repeats the saying, but reads (11:33), "puts it in a cellar or under a bushel." Mark adds the phrase, "under a bed," a vivid touch that enhances the absurdity of the picture. This illustrates a characteristic feature of Jesus' teaching. He could gently

60

disparage or sometimes scathingly denounce an idea or activity by making it appear ludicrous.

Matthew reports next (5:16) a sentence of exhortation, which points the moral of the saying about salt and light: "Let your light so shine before men, that they may see your good works and give glory to your Father who is in heaven." The disciples' ability to do good is to be so used that those who see the good works will praise not the doers but God.

Now comes the first extended section of Matthew's unique teaching material (Mt 5:17-48; 6:1-8). It includes several sayings found also in Luke and one in both Mark and Luke, but so much of it is peculiar to Matthew and distinctive in content and language that the use of a special written source seems probable if not certain. Wherever he got this material, however, Matthew has manifestly arranged and edited it to bring out his understanding of Jesus' relation to the law.

The section is introduced by Jesus' statement that he has come not to abolish but to fulfil the law and the prophets (5:17). The coupling together of law and prophets is characteristic of the first Gospel. It does not appear in Mark; Luke has it in this form only once (16:16; cf. Mt 11:13), but in the last chapter of his Gospel the risen Christ speaks of "the law of Moses and the prophets and psalms" (Lk 24:44). This way of referring to the Scriptures reflects the stage in the formation of the Old Testament canon that had then been reached. The five books of the law had been accepted as sacred Scripture for four or five centuries, and for two or three centuries the books of the prophets had been recognized as a second body of sacred literature; but the rest of the Old Testament (known to this day simply as Writings or Scriptures) had not yet been "canonized." It was therefore natural to speak of the Law and the Prophets as comprising the whole body of revealed literature, with the Psalms and other writings still on a somewhat lower plane. Jesus would naturally follow current usage in this respect; this item of Matthew's Jewish coloring is thus probably an authentic reflection of Jesus' practice.

The Gospels are full of references to the fulfillment of prophecy by Jesus. Relatively few direct quotations of prophecies are attributed to Jesus himself, but there are many allusions to the

61

prophetic books in his sayings. There are also references to unspecified prophecies by such expressions as ''what is written,'' ''as it is written,'' or ''as it was said.''

In using prophecy as he did, Jesus did not necessarily imply that the prophets had consciously referred to him in particular. As he read Isaiah 53 (Lk 22:37) or Zechariah 13 (Mk 14:27; Mt 26:31) he might have thought, ''This is just what is happening to me,'' or ''This is what my Father has sent me to do,'' without assuming that the prophet was thinking specifically of him. The way similar references are made in contemporary documents leaves one wondering sometimes how far those who quoted prophetic texts meant that the precise fulfillments they saw or expected were intended by the prophets themselves. One of the Dead Sea Scrolls, the commentary on Habakkuk, says, ''And God told Habakkuk to write the things that were to come upon the last generation, but the consummation of the period he did not make known to him'' (1 Q Hab vii. 1-2). In other words, what was spoken by the prophets meant more than they themselves knew.

It was not long, of course, before the church came to believe that the prophets and Moses (and also David) were speaking directly and specifically about Jesus. If he thought so himself, he would be interpreting Scriptures in a way that would not have seemed strange to his hearers. We cannot determine whether this was what he believed. He was clearly convinced that he was carrying out God's will as revealed in the Scriptures (Mk 14:21, etc.).

The major emphasis in the paragraph about fulfillment in the Sermon on the Mount is not on prophecy but on the law. ''For truly, I say to you,'' Jesus continues (Mt 5:18), ''till heaven and earth pass away, not an iota, not a dot, will pass from the law until all is accomplished.'' This is the only sentence in the paragraph that has a parallel in one of the other Gospels. Luke gives it (16:17) in connection with a saying that contrasts the law and the prophets with the gospel. The iota (KJV jot) and the dot (KJV tittle) represent the smallest details. *Iota* is the smallest letter in the Greek alphabet, corresponding to *yodh,* the smallest letter of the Hebrew and Aramaic alphabet. The dot (literally ''horn'') is the tiny projection that in the Hebrew alphabet distinguishes a *d* from an *r* or a *b* from a *k*.

The idea of fulfillment, in the sense that something that has been predicted happens, is applied to the law in the post-Resurrection saying in Luke (Lk 24:44) which has already been quoted. So here in Matthew (5:18) Jesus says, "until all is accomplished," or more literally, "until everything happens." There is a predictive element in the books of the law. It consists largely of conditional promises and warnings, but there are also unconditioned predictions.

With reference to the law, however, fulfillment had also another meaning. The law is fulfilled when it is fully obeyed, when what it demands is fully carried out. The next verse brings this out (v 19): "Whoever then relaxes one of the least of these commandments and teaches men so, shall be called least in the kingdom of heaven." This seems to imply that a person who breaks the law and teaches others to do so may nevertheless be in the kingdom of heaven. Here and elsewhere Matthew evidently regards the kingdom as practically the equivalent of the church.

The disciples must have been as puzzled as Christians are today by the demand that they be more righteous than the scribes and Pharisees (Mt 5:20). We have met the scribes in the synagogue at Capernaum (Mk 1:22). The Pharisees have not hitherto been mentioned, except that Matthew includes them (3:7) among those whom John the Baptist denounced as a brood of vipers. The expression "scribes and Pharisees" is very common. Once Mark speaks of "the scribes of the Pharisees," and Luke uses the same expression once in Acts (Mk 2:16; cf. Acts 23:9). In general, with a rough oversimplification, it may be said that the Pharisees were a movement or an unorganized party; the scribes were more like a profession though not paid. Apparently most of the scribes, but not all, were Pharisees.

The Pharisees were the successors of the Hasidim, the loyal devotees of the law who had resisted the encroachment of Greek ideas and customs in the second century B.C. They developed their own interpretations of the law, which were passed on by word of mouth from generation to generation. This oral tradition was supposed to have been inspired on Mt. Sinai together with the written law, though it often actually adjusted the requirements of the ancient laws to new circumstances and customs by rather free interpretations. Its purpose was to work out precisely what the law required, so that one could be sure he was doing the revealed will of God. This was no burden; it was an expression of joyful devotion.

Inevitably, however, the Pharisees' method of interpretation tended to produce a legalistic emphasis on the letter of the law. Their elaborate casuistry was the very opposite of Jesus' direct penetration to the basic spirit and principle of the law. He repudiated the tendency of the scribes and Pharisees to become absorbed in trifles, their failure to put first things first.

In the Gospels the Pharisees are often called hypocrites. That charge we shall consider later. Here they appear as models of rectitude and respectability. What is called in question is their whole approach to the interpretation of the law. Jesus was no less devoted to the law of Moses than they were. He rejected the oral law, however, as a mere "tradition of men" (Mk 7:8-9; Mt 15:3). The Pharisees and scribes were actually, he told them, "making void the word of God" by their tradition (Mk 7:13; Mt 15:6).

What Jesus meant by a righteousness exceeding that of the scribes and Pharisees (5:20) was a thoroughgoing effort to obey the revealed will of God according to its inmost intent, not because every item was explicitly commanded or could be logically deduced from the sacred text, but because one's own conscience and judgment responded to the underlying principle of it all. The paragraphs that follow this verse in Matthew illustrate the implications of such radical obedience.

The principle is first applied (Mt 5:21-22) to the sixth commandment of the Mosaic decalogue (Ex 20:13; Deut 5:17), "You shall not kill." The clause, "and whoever kills shall be liable to judgment," is not part of the commandment, but may have been familiar as an inference added when the commandment was quoted. At any rate, it affords a link with what follows about anger and insults. Even presenting an offering at the altar, Jesus says (Mt 5:23-24), must be postponed until any unforgiven offense against a fellow man has been made right.

The saying about being quickly reconciled with an accuser (vv

64

25-26) sounds like a bit of prudent advice. It appears in a different light in the context in which Luke reports it (12:54-57). There Jesus asks the multitude why they cannot interpret the signs of the times for themselves, and why they cannot decide for themselves what is right. The advice to seek speedy reconciliation with an accuser means then, "Do what is right on your own volition; don't wait until you are compelled to do it." That goes well with what comes a few verses later in Matthew (5:38-42): turning the other cheek, giving up the cloak when deprived of the coat, going the second mile. Thus the saying about the accuser is an illustration of the righteousness that exceeds that of the scribes and Pharisees.

The same principle is next applied (vv 27-28) to the seventh commandment, "You shall not commit adultery"; and again Jesus goes back of the overt act to the inner desire of the heart. These two verses, like the previous treatment of the sixth commandment, are recorded by Matthew only; but nothing could be more characteristic or more true to the spirit of Jesus' whole life.

The next two verses (vv 29-30; cf. 18:8-9; Mk 9:43-48) enforce the strict demand just made with a saying found at a later point in Mark, where Matthew repeats it. It is the stern saying about plucking out an eye or cutting off a hand that causes one to sin. Such a sacrifice, Jesus says, is better than being cast into hell. The word here translated "hell" is not, as in some places in the KJV (Mt 11:23; 16:18; Lk 10:15; 16:23), "Hades." That name corresponds to Hebrew "Sheol," denoting a shadowy underworld to which all the dead went, righteous and wicked alike (cf., *e.g.*, Ps 16:10; Acts 2:27, 31). The word used here is "Gehenna," a Hebrew name taken over bodily into Greek. Originally the name of a valley just south of Jerusalem where child-sacrifice to the god Moloch was practiced (2 Kings 23:10; cf. Jer 7:31-32; 32:35), by the time of Jesus it had come to symbolize what our word "hell" signifies. In this sense it is used in Jewish literature. Elsewhere in the New Testament it occurs only in James 3:6.

There is no reason to question the authenticity of these sayings, or to doubt that Jesus accepted the current belief in the punishment of the wicked by everlasting fire in Gehenna. It need not be supposed, of course, that the worm and fire were understood literally, or that Jesus thought of the dead as suffering bodily torment (Mk 9:48, quoting Is 66:24).

The third of Matthew's six antitheses (Mt 5:31-32) contrasts the Mosaic law of divorce with Jesus' unequivocal condemnation of divorce and remarriage as amounting to adultery. This appears in Mark and is repeated by Matthew in a fuller context, where it can be more adequately discussed (Mk 10:11; Mt 19:9). Luke (16:18) has it at still another point without any connection with its context. Matthew includes it here with the other items in the series to show how Jesus' requirements go beyond those of the Pharisees.

Next the contrast, "You have heard . . . but I say to you," is applied to taking oaths to confirm statements or promises (Mt 5:33-37). What was said formerly is in Leviticus (19:12), "And you shall not swear by my name falsely." Its positive counterpart is added in an abridged quotation from Deuteronomy (23:23), "You shall be careful to perform what has passed your lips, for you have voluntarily vowed to the Lord your God what you have promised with your mouth." Jesus forbids his disciples to use oaths to confirm what they say. The unsupported statement, yes or no, is sufficient. Jesus was not prescribing a legal procedure but describing the speech and conduct to be expected of his disciples.

The incidental reference to Jerusalem as the city of the great King (v 35) is the only place in Jesus' recorded teaching where the noun "king" is applied to God, and it is a quotation from Psalm 48:2. If Jesus ever used the expression common in Jewish prayers, "King of the universe" (or "of eternity"), there is no record of it. God's sovereignty is of course involved in the idea of the kingdom of God, and it is implied here in the designation of heaven as his throne, an echo of the last chapter of Isaiah (66:1).

Some of the most widely quoted sayings in the Sermon on the Mount, and the ones most consistently violated, are the commands (Mt 5:38-42) to turn the other cheek, to give the cloak when deprived of the coat, to go two miles when compelled to go one, to refuse no request for a gift or a loan, to offer no resistance to an evil man, as recent translations read where the KJV says "resist not evil." Luke's version of this group of sayings (6:29-30) is shorter than Matthew's, and there are differences that do not affect the meaning of the paragraph as a whole. What Jesus had in mind was clearly a personal insult or slight. The specific mention of the right rather than the left cheek should not be unduly stressed, but a right-handed person striking a heavy blow with his fist would hit not the right cheek but the left. A blow on the right cheek would ordinarily be a slap with the back of the hand, an insult rather than an injury.

How far Jesus himself would have extended this to wrongs done to others, to violence against others, or to political, economic, and social injustice is debatable. Any effort to prevent violence or harm, to heal or prevent disease, to alleviate poverty and misery, any protest against wrongs of any kind, is resistance to evil. But he who healed the sick, who denounced in scathing language injustice and oppression, who drove the money changers from the temple, certainly did not mean that his followers should do nothing and say nothing against wrong. He did mean that hatred and violence are not the way to deal effectively with evil men or evil institutions.

For the people of Palestine, suffering under the Roman regime, it must have been as hard to believe this as it is today in the United States of America for people struggling to achieve economic and political equality of opportunity, or as it is for the native people of Palestine or Vietnam who are exiled from their homes and dependent upon the scanty bounty of the United Nations and charitable organizations. But if Jesus was right in his attitude to the evil in the world and in people, the only way that in the long run can overcome evil is the way of nonviolence and love, followed intelligently.

What love means and what it does not mean in this connection must be considered in light of the next paragraph of the Sermon on the Mount, with its parallel in Luke's Sermon on the Plain (Mt 5:43-48; Lk 6:27-28, 32-36). Once more we find considerable verbal differences along with an identity of major content that shows that both Gospels depend ultimately on the same original material. Similar variations may have existed already in Jesus' own repeated utterance of these sayings.

Again Matthew begins, "You have heard that it has been said"; but what follows occurs nowhere in the Old Testament or in the intertestamental or rabbinic literature. The Old Testament says (Lev 19:18), "You shall love your neighbor." It does not say, "and hate your enemy," though there are such protestations as "I hate the company of evildoers" (Ps 26:5) in the Psalms. Initiates into the Qumran community undertook to love all the sons of light and hate all the sons of darkness (1QS i. 9-10). The Old Testament commandment in Leviticus is what Jesus called the second greatest commandment in the law (Mk 12:31; Mt 22:39; cf. Lk 10:27). Here he even goes beyond it. "But I say to you, Love your enemies and pray for those who persecute you" (Mt 5:44). Luke has a somewhat fuller version of this saying (6:27-28). This is like what has been said about turning the other cheek; in fact it simply carries the same theme a little further. Loving your enemies means praying for them, blessing them, doing good to them; in short, returning good for evil. It is the positive, active aspect of the attitude that finds negative expression in nonresistance.

Conscientious Christians often wonder how love can be a matter of voluntary obedience to a command. If we do not spontaneously love our neighbors, to say nothing of our enemies, can we make ourselves love them by an act of the will? Evidently the love of which Jesus speaks (and Leviticus too, for that matter) is not falling in love with a person. It is not even necessarily liking him. It is not primarily a way of feeling about a person at all, but a way of treating him. Sympathy, liking, even affection and devotion may lead to the action or follow it. They may grow out of gratitude. The feeling, however, is of secondary importance.

In the rest of the paragraph in the Sermon on the Mount, Jesus gives a reason for loving enemies and persecutors (Mt 5:45-46): "so that you may be sons of your Father who is in heaven; for he makes his sun rise on the evil and on the good, and sends rain on the just and on the unjust. For if you love those who love you, what reward have you?" Luke has this a little later (6:32-33) and in a slightly different form. The reference to rewards here and elsewhere seems at first sight to be inconsistent with disinterested goodness for the sake of God's kingdom, but the problem is more apparent than real. Jesus, like the great rabbis of his time, taught that men should do right not because it pays (Lk 6:35) but because it is God's will; but at the same time he recognized, as the rabbis did, that righteousness has incidental, secondary rewards. The best, most direct reward is in being sons of God.

The New Testament abounds in references to Christians as sons or children of God. Some of them reflect a theological development that goes beyond the meaning of the saying quoted by Matthew and Luke. Since Jesus' disciples are taught to pray to God as their Father (Mt 6:9; Lk 11:2), they are already his sons; one does not have to become a son of his own father. What Jesus must mean here is therefore, "that you may be *true* sons of him who is your Father," or in other words, "that you may be worthy to be called God's sons" (cf. Lk 15:21; 1 Jn 3:1).

The idea of being sons of God recalls the ancient Semitic idiom used in the Old Testament to indicate belonging to a particular species or group of any kind (Ps 8:4; 90:3). Just as a human being is a son or daughter of man, so a divine being is a son of God or of the gods (Gen 6:4; Ps 82:6). When Jesus, however, speaks of his disciples as sons of God, he neither affirms nor denies that man as such is divine. He is not speaking of human nature or of men in general. He implies rather a special kind of sonship by adoption, more like the divine sonship of the Hebrew kings already referred to in connection with Jesus' baptism. The relationship, in short, is one of voluntary consecration on man's part and acceptance on the part of God. In this sense it is a disciple's first and highest aim to be a son of his Father in heaven.

Being God's child means being like him. That is the reason for loving one's enemies: "for he makes his sun shine on the evil and on the good, and sends rain on the just and on the unjust." For Jesus the equal treatment of good and evil did not cast doubt on God's goodness but confirmed it. To me this is one of the most extraordinary points in Jesus' teaching. Many people still regard life from an early Old Testament point of view. If they are good, they expect to be prosperous and happy; if misfortune strikes them they say, "What have I done to deserve this?" Seeing sunshine and rain meted out to good and bad alike, they take this as

69

evidence that God is unfair or indifferent. To Jesus the same facts demonstrated God's goodness.

But what amazing spiritual audacity! If Jesus was right, this is no less than a revelation of the deepest reality of our existence. If not, he was a tragically deluded wishful thinker. There is no more searching criterion of faith in him than our decision on that question. Early one morning many years ago I was walking along the shore of the Sea of Galilee, and Whittier's familiar lines kept running through my head:

> O sabbath rest by Galilee!
> O calm of hills above,
> Where Jesus knelt to share with thee
> The silence of eternity,
> Interpreted by love!

Suddenly the full impact of the last two lines struck me with the force of a revelation. Eternity, I thought, is indeed silent to man's deepest questions. With our finest and most powerful instruments we may search in vain for the meaning of existence. There is good in the world and also evil; there is love and there is hate, beauty and ugliness. Trying to see life steadily and see it whole, we have to select those facts that seem to us decisive, and interpret the whole in the light of them. Jesus interpreted it by love. We cannot know that his interpretation is true; we can only commit ourselves to it and live by it. He lived and died by it, "endured the cross, despising the shame" (Heb 12:2). In that life and death Christians see a sublime demonstration of God's love (Rom 5:8; 2 Cor 5:18-19), breaking down our indifference and estrangement and impelling us to commit ourselves to the way of the cross.

If we fail to love our enemies, Jesus continues (Mt 5:46-47; Lk 6:32-35), we are no better than the tax collectors and the Gentiles, the two kinds of people most despised by his hearers. Anybody can love those who love him. Luke's Sermon on the Plain presents this idea at greater length. The command to love one's enemies undoubtedly looks like a counsel of perfection; and indeed in Matthew the paragraph ends (5:48), "You, therefore, must be perfect, as your heavenly Father is perfect." Instead of this, however, Luke has (6:36), "Be merciful, even as your Father is merciful.'' There is only one other place in the Gospels where Jesus speaks of being perfect, and this too is in Matthew. In the account of the rich man who expresses dissatisfaction with obeying the commandments as the way to eternal life, Jesus says, according to Mark and Luke, ''You lack one thing''; in Matthew he says, ''If you would be perfect'' (Mk 10:21; Lk 18:22; Mt 19:21).

A Hebrew word sometimes translated ''perfect'' in the KJV (''blameless'' in the RSV) is applied in the Old Testament (*e.g.,* Gen 6:9; 17:1; Deut 18:13) to righteous men without any implication of absolute perfection. Jesus could have used the Aramaic equivalent of this word. If he did it would mean in this connection something like thoroughgoing, unbounded, not limited by prejudice or personal interest; that is, the sentence must mean, ''Your love must be all-inclusive, as God's is.'' That is quite possible.

The fact that only Matthew uses the word ''perfect,'' however, and he uses it twice, makes it more probable that he altered the saying that Mark and Luke report correctly. Whatever the decision should be concerning this word, the demand for a righteousness that goes beyond strict obedience to precepts, and includes love of enemies, is an essential and distinctive element of Jesus' own teaching. It is most prominent and explicit in Matthew, but it underlies and pervades all the Gospels and is expressed in many ways. It was by no means unknown, for that matter, in Judaism.

The nearest approach in the Old Testament to the saying about being perfect or merciful is the basic principle of the Holiness Code of Leviticus (19:2 etc.): ''You shall be holy, for I the Lord your God am holy.'' The word ''holy'' is never applied to God in Jesus' recorded sayings, and the noun ''holiness'' does not occur at all; but the holiness of God is everywhere presupposed. It is implied in the petition (Mt 6:9; Lk 11:2), ''Hallowed be thy name,'' and in the passage (Mt 5:34-36; 23:16-22) about things by which one must not take oath.

The practical implications and specific applications of the law of love cannot be reduced to rules and precepts. They must be decided in particular situations and relationships by each individual for himself. According to Luke (12:57), Jesus once said, "And why do you not judge for yourselves what is right?" The insistence on independent personal decision is closely related to Jesus' determination of God's will by a few basic principles rather than detailed rules.

The next section of the Sermon (Mt 6:1-8) consists of warnings, found only in Matthew, against ostentatious piety. The first sentence contains a slight textual difficulty. Most of the best manuscripts read, literally, "Take care not to practise your righteousness before men"; but instead of "righteousness" some excellent manuscripts have "charity" (KJV "alms"), while the famous Codex Sinaiticus and a few of the ancient versions have "giving." This may very well be an instance of variant translations of the same Aramaic word. In the Jewish literature of that time the common Hebrew and Aramaic word for righteousness was coming to be used in the special sense of charity. It could have been understood by a translator in either way. The interpretation as charity would be encouraged by the fact that the next few sentences (vv 2-4) deal with almsgiving. The more general meaning fits the sayings about prayer that follow (vv 5-8). The point throughout is that acting to be seen forfeits the reward given by God to sincere, unheralded action and prayer.

People who do this are called hypocrites. This is the first appearance of a word frequently applied to those whom Jesus condemned, especially in Matthew. We have noted its application to the Pharisees. It occurs in the New Testament only in the Synoptic Gospels, and always in sayings of Jesus. The Greek word, of which "hypocrisy" is a transcription rather than a translation, means playing a part; and a "hypocrite" is an actor. Theaters had become familiar to the Jews in the Greek and Roman settlements in Palestine, but they were regarded as centers of pagan pollution. To call a man a hypocrite, therefore, was like calling a minister an actor in a Puritan community.

That there were people in Jesus' day who literally sounded a trumpet before them in the streets and synagogues may be questioned. The expression is probably a case of Jesus' characteristic use of hyperbole. Public praying at street corners or in the synagogues, however, may not have been unknown. One recalls the public praying of Muslims wherever the established time of prayer finds them. Such a practice may become mechanical; but it often expresses an entirely sincere devotion quite devoid of self-consciousness. The instruction to go into one's room and shut the door (v 6) is not to be taken literally. The concrete way of speaking emphasizes the necessity of inner privacy, but the most intense and most personal prayer may be made silently in the midst of a crowd.

Sincerity in prayer requires that it be direct and simple. God is not impressed by verbosity (vv 7-8). Nor is the purpose of prayer to give him information. Prayer is a child's expression of his hopes, fears, and aspirations to his Father, who already knows what the child needs, but wants the communion of spirit with spirit.

Matthew gives here (6:9-15; cf. Lk 11:2-4) what we call the Lord's Prayer, introduced with the simple direction, "Pray then like this." Luke puts it after the story of Mary and Martha. Both settings may be artificial; it is the prayer itself that matters. Mark does not report it at all.

It begins in Matthew, "Our Father who art in heaven." Luke has simply, "Father." Matthew (or his special source) favors the expression "Father who is heaven" or its equivalent "heavenly Father," both in prayer and in speaking of God (*e.g.*, Mt 16:17; 18:10, 19). It is a Jewish form of address that Jesus himself may very well have used. In one form or another, Jesus' most characteristic word for God was "Father." With the possessive pronoun "my" or "his" or only the definite article (Mk 8:38 and parallels; 13:32 and parallels) it refers to God as the Father of Jesus himself or of the coming Son of Man or Messiah. According to Luke, Jesus even as a boy spoke of God as "my Father" (2:49). It is Luke also who reports that Jesus twice called upon God as Father from the cross (23:34, 46), and after his resurrection spoke to the troubled disciples of "the promise of my Father" (24:49). But Jesus spoke not only of God as his own Father; he spoke also of "your Father" (Mt 6:15 and often) and taught the disciples to address God as "our Father" or simply "Father."

In Judaism it was by no means unusual to speak of God and to him as Father, both of individuals and of the whole people of Israel. Some prayers in the Jewish Prayer Book begin, "Our Father, our King." A famous rabbinic saying is, "Who is there for us to lean on? On our Father who is in heaven." A prayer in the apocryphal book of Sirach begins, "O Lord, Father and Ruler of my life" (Sir 23:1); and in another place (51:10) the reading of the Greek text, "the Father of my lord," represents a Hebrew text that was probably intended to be read, "my Father, my Lord."

For Jesus the term "Father" meant not only Creator, though that was a part of the meaning. It meant not only the supreme authority whom we must obey, though it did mean that. It meant also Provider, Protector, loving Parent, with all that human parenthood at its best implies. It meant far more, indeed, than the most perfect human parenthood could mean. "If you then, who are evil," Jesus said (Mt 7:11; cf. Lk 11:13), "know how to give good gifts to your children, how much more will your Father who is in heaven give good things to those who ask him."

In Matthew the Lord's Prayer consists of seven petitions, of which Luke has five. The first three are requests not for anything for ourselves but for God's glory and his purposes on earth. The first petition is typically Jewish: "Hallowed be thy name." The idea of the hallowing of the name has a long history behind it. Among the early Semites the name represented fame or reputation; indeed it expressed and embodied the very existence and identity of a person. So God's gracious acts were said to be done for his name's sake (*e.g.*, Ps 23:3); blasphemy or any speech or conduct reflecting discredit upon him was said to profane his name (*e.g.*, Lev 22:32); while reverence for him as holy, praising him as holy, and so acting as to reflect credit upon him were called (*e.g.*, Is 29:23) hallowing or sanctifying his name (literally, making it holy). This must be the first concern of Jesus' disciples.

The second petition in both Matthew and Luke is "Thy kingdom come"(Mt 6:10; Lk 11:2). Jesus had proclaimed when he first came back into Galilee after his baptism (Mk 1:15 and parallels): "The kingdom of God is at hand." Near as it was, it had obviously not yet arrived when he gave the disciples this prayer. It still has not come. Its coming depends upon God.

"Thy will be done," whether or not it corresponds to our own desires, is the ultimate wish of every dedicated heart. It was the prayer of Jesus himself in Gethsemane. What God's will requires must be accepted with sincere submission. This is the passive aspect of the petition. Actively it means that he who prays wishes to do God's will himself, and wants every group of which he is a member to do God's will.

The phrase "on earth as it is in heaven" applies not only to the third petition but to all three. Critical editions of the Greek text make this clear by their arrangement of the lines, but our English translations obscure or ignore it. Literally the phrase reads, "as in heaven, also on earth." In heaven, this implies, God's name is hallowed, his kingdom is present and manifest, his will is done. But what does "in heaven" mean? Jesus, as a child of his time, may have thought of heaven in simple terms of time and space. Rabbinic Judaism believed in several heavens, sometimes three, sometimes as many as seven. How much meaning such ideas had for Jesus we cannot tell. His statement that those who participated in the resurrection of the dead would be like angels, not marrying or giving in marriage (Mk 12:25 and parallels), implies a kind of incorporeal existence. All we can be sure of is that he believed in a real world in which was already realized what could only be hoped and prayed for here. However that may be, there can be no getting away from the plain meaning of "also on earth."

Luke's shorter form of the Lord's Prayer omits both "Thy will be done" and "as in heaven, also on earth." Possibly this omission merely reflects the liturgical practice of a different group of churches. Possibly Luke has preserved the original prayer, and Matthew presents a liturgical expansion. The same question applies to the form of address at the beginning of the prayer. There is no way to determine the right answer to it. What the disciples are to pray for is not vitally affected. Matthew's form has a clear structure, but this may be a result of the use of the prayer in public worship.

The four remaining petitions are for our own benefit, but only the first has to do with bodily needs. "Give us this day our daily bread" (Mt 6:11; Lk 11:3) is a request for physical sustenance, perhaps intended to cover not only food but all the necessities of everyday life. Instead of "this day" Luke has "each day"; in either case provision is asked only for one day at a time. Whether "daily bread" is the right translation is a question on which scholars disagree. The Greek adjective occurs nowhere else. To me "our bread for the coming day" seems the best translation. In the morning this would refer to the day just beginning; in the evening it would mean the following day. That the petition has anything to do with the Messianic banquet of the coming age seems to me improbable.

In the next petition the words "debts" and "debtors" bother some people, who prefer "trespasses" and "those who trespass against us." The latter reading goes back all the way to the pioneer work of Tyndale (1535). The English Prayer Book perpetuated this rendering, which is still used in many churches. All the standard English versions after Tyndale, however, have "debts" and "debtors"; and this is what the Greek actually says. In Aramaic, sins are regularly called debts and sinners are called debtors. Luke reads "sins" instead of "debts" (11:4). Probably this is simply a different translation of the same Aramaic word. The idea of debt is preserved in Luke's "every one who is indebted to us" where Matthew has "our debtors." Several recent translations read "the wrong we have done" and "those who have wronged us" or the like.

The petition (Mt 6:13; Lk 11:4), "And lead us not into temptation," has troubled sincere Christians perhaps more than anything else in the Lord's Prayer. It seems unworthy and cowardly to ask to be spared temptation, and the idea that God would ever tempt anyone to sin seems incongruous (cf. James 1:13). The word "temptation," however, was not always so limited in meaning as it is for us now. The Bible refers often to tempting God (cf. Mt 4:7) in the sense of putting him to the test. The Greek word translated "temptation" means testing or trial of any kind, including persecution.

"But deliver us from evil." Perhaps, with recent versions (JB, NEB, TEV, NAB), we should translate "from the evil one." The Greek is ambiguous (cf. Mt 5:39). The connection with the preceding clause suggests a special reference to the temptation or trial from which the disciples ask to be spared. Thus the double petition may mean, "Lead us not into temptation, but deliver us

76

from the Tempter''; or, since "evil" in the Bible has a wide range
of meanings, "Do not cause us to be tried too severely, but
deliver us from harm." Since we cannot tell precisely what Jesus
had in mind, it would seem justifiable to use the prayer in any of
these senses.

The whole prayer is couched in the plural. Even if Luke's
simple "Father" is more authentic than Matthew's "Our
Father," both Luke and Matthew read "give us," "our daily
bread," "forgive us our debts," and "our debtors," "Lead us
not . . . but deliver us." Even in the privacy of his own room with
the door shut, a Christian cannot leave his brother out of his
prayers.

Obviously this model prayer was not meant to exhaust all the
things for which the disciples might pray. Everything in the
Gospels bearing on the subject warrants the assumption that
anything worth asking for or desiring would be a worthy object of
prayer, subject always to Jesus' "Nevertheless, not as I will, but
as thou wilt" (Mt 26:39).

At the end of the prayer in Matthew (6:13) some manuscripts
have, "For thine is the kingdom and the power and the glory, for
ever. Amen." The parallel in Luke (11:4) and some manuscripts
of Matthew omit this. It seems clearly to have been added in the
liturgical use of the prayer in some churches. There is a tendency
in liturgy to multiply words (cf. Mt 6:7-8), though in this instance
the language is by no means redundant or inappropriate. It is less
prolix than the prayer of David (1 Chron 29:10-11), which
probably afforded a pattern for it.

After the prayer, Jesus adds in Matthew (6:14), "For if you
forgive men their trespasses, your heavenly Father also will
forgive you; but if you do not forgive men their trespasses, neither
will your Father forgive your trespasses." This is one of only
three sayings in the Sermon on the Mount (5:29-30, 32-33) that
have parallels in Mark (9:43-48; 10:11-12; 11:25-26). In all three
instances Matthew has a doublet later.

Now the Sermon on the Mount moves on to the subject of
fasting (Mt 6:16-18). Apparently it is assumed that the disciples
do fast, the only question being how they should do it. An
incident, however, which comes a little later and is related by all

77

the Synoptic Gospels (Mk 2:18-20; Mt 9:14-15; Lk 5:33-35), raises the question whether this was so. That Jesus would have instructed his disciples about something that they did not do until after his death is possible but unlikely. It is possible that this is not an authentic saying of Jesus' but a later pronouncement, uttered perhaps by a prophet who believed that he was speaking under the inspiration of the spirit of Jesus. But if Matthew himself put the Lord's Prayer in its present position, and what are now verses 16-18 immediately followed verse 8 in Matthew's source, the saying about fasting is probably authentic but addressed to a general audience. Like almsgiving and prayer, fasting must not be done to attract attention and make an impression.

The futility of laying up treasures on earth is the next subject in the Sermon on the Mount (Mt 6:19-21; Lk 12:33-34). Here Matthew uses a group of sayings that appears in a quite different form in Luke and in a somewhat more logical connection. The section on anxiety, which comes a few verses later in Matthew, immediately precedes these sayings in Luke (Lk 12:22-32). After them, Luke has the ones about constant watchfulness, which are given near the end of Matthew's Gospel (Lk 12:35-46; Mt 24:43-51; 25:1-13).

The difference in arrangement corresponds to a difference in tone. In Matthew the sayings sound like wise advice for the ordinary conditions of life: earthly treasures are subject to destruction by moth and rust or to loss by theft; but treasures in heaven are indestructible, and where one's treasure is his heart will be also. Luke begins the paragraph with a direct command and seems to have a note of more immediate urgency: "Sell your possessions, and give alms; provide yourselves with purses that do not grow old, with a treasure in the heavens that does not fail, where no thief approaches and no moth destroys," ending with the comment about heart and treasure. One gets the impression here that the situation is overshadowed by the expectation of the end of the age, whereas in Matthew what is contemplated is the certainty of the individual's death sooner or later. There is no room for doubt about Jesus' attitude toward the pursuit of wealth. How far it was affected by the impending crisis is hard to define, but material possessions did not stand high in his scale of values.

The next saying is obscure: light within a person depends on the soundness of his eye, which is the lamp of the body (Mt 6:22-23; Lk 11:34-36). Luke's version agrees closely with Matthew's, but he adds another sentence: "If then your whole body is full of light, having no part dark, it will be wholly bright, as when a lamp with its rays gives you light." It can hardly be said that this makes the meaning clearer. Instead of "sound" and "not sound" the KJV reads "single" and "evil." These are the literal meanings of the Greek adjectives but they make no sense here. The word meaning "single" was sometimes used at that time in the sense of "generous," and an evil eye signified stinginess (cf. James 1:5). These meanings also, however, do not fit here. The rendering of the RSV is no doubt correct, or as the NAB puts it even more plainly, "If your eyes are good" and "if your eyes are bad."

Having the body full of light obviously means a spiritual state of inner light, that is, clear perception and true understanding, right ideas and attitudes. Such an inner light depends on sound organs of vision. The unhealthy or injured eye then indicates such spiritual conditions as prevent the perception of truth in general or the gospel in particular.

Next Matthew has the familiar saying about serving two masters (Mt 6:24; Lk 16:13, cf. vv 9, 11). Luke gives this in exactly the same words along with other sayings on the same subject following the parable of the Unjust Steward. This time the moral is explicitly stated: "You cannot serve God and mammon." The word "mammon" is a common Aramaic word for wealth found often in the Jewish literature of the period, including the Dead Sea Scrolls. Wealth is a jealous master, and so is God (Ex 20:3-6). Mammon can be enslaved and made to serve the will of God, but it has many subtle ways of making itself the master instead of the slave. This subject comes up so often in the sayings of Jesus that he must have considered it of crucial importance. Only wholehearted devotion to God, uncorrupted by "the deceitfulness of riches" (Mk 4:19; Mt 13:22 KJV), could satisfy him.

What is perhaps the most beautiful portion of the Sermon on the Mount, and the hardest to believe, now follows in Matthew (Mt 6:25-34; Lk 12:22-31). In Luke it comes after the parable of the

79

Rich Fool and is followed by the saying about treasure in heaven. "Do not be anxious," Jesus says. As God feeds the birds and clothes the lilies, he will feed and clothe you. "For the Gentiles seek all these things"—for us this means, "These things are what the world seeks"—but your Father knows your needs and will supply them if you "seek first his kingdom and his righteousness." What is meant by seeking the kingdom of God depends on what is meant by the kingdom. If it is thought of as God's sovereignty, seeking it means accepting and obeying him as Ruler of one's own life. If the kingdom is thought of as still to come, seeking it means being prepared for it and fulfilling the conditions for admission to it.

According to Matthew but not Luke, Jesus adds, "and his righteousness." What is meant by seeking God's righteousness? It is endeavoring to do his will and please him. The word for righteousness often means justice. Seeking God's justice should include trying to promote justice in social and civic as well as personal relations, though how far Jesus had this in mind, if he used these words, is open to question. The same word also, as we have seen (cf. Mt 6:1), may mean "charity." This too, as an expression of love, is involved in seeking the righteousness of God.

Both Matthew and Luke have the concluding clause: "and all these things shall be yours as well." Jesus can hardly have meant that one who puts God's kingdom first can expect to be exempt from the troubles and trials that others suffer. Jesus himself was put to death as a criminal. He foresaw that it would be so; and he said that no one unwilling to sacrifice everything that life offered, or even life itself, could be his disciple (Lk 14:26-27).

For humanity at large it is certain that devotion to the kingdom and righteousness of God would bring about a vast amelioration of our lot. Natural catastrophes would still occur, though eventually some kind of protection even from them might be found. The conquest of disease, the prevention of tragic accidents, the adequate production and distribution of food and other necessities, and the solution of the problem of overpopulation would be very much easier and more rapid if all people sincerely and unselfishly sought the good of others. All these things might

80

indeed be ours if we sought together God's kingdom and his righteousness.

For most individuals, however, Jesus' assurance can be accepted only in the sense that God gives his children all it is possible to give them as members of the whole interdependent body of mankind in this world of very limited possibilities; that strength to endure what cannot be avoided is available; but that happiness, prosperity, health, safety, and life itself are not guaranteed.

At the end of the paragraph Matthew has a verse that does not appear in Luke: "Therefore do not be anxious about tomorrow, for tomorrow will be anxious for itself. Let the day's own trouble be sufficient for the day." There is enough trouble to bear each day as we go along without augmenting it by anxiety about what has not happened. The KJV translates the first clause, "Take therefore no thought for the morrow"; but the Greek word does not refer to forethought and planning. Jesus did not encourage a casual irresponsibility that makes one a burden to others. The story of Mary and Martha has no such implication, as we shall see when we come to it (Lk 10:38-42). What Jesus disparaged was worrying about one's own welfare or security.

Luke too has in this context a verse (12:32) not found elsewhere: "Fear not, little flock, for it is your Father's good pleasure to give you the kingdom." This combines the three major images by which Jesus conveyed his understanding of God: Shepherd, Father, and King. As a corollary of this conception of God, the disciples were given an exalted idea of what they were themselves. They were helpless sheep, tenderly cared for and protected; but they were also subjects of the Supreme Ruler of the universe; indeed they were the King's sons, with whom it was his sovereign will and fatherly pleasure to share his own royal authority and power.

In this sublime assurance Jesus lived and died. Was he right, or was he pathetically and tragically mistaken? However much we admire his moral grandeur and accept the way of life he presented, are we in the last analysis merely temporary inhabitants of a world that offers us much that helps and much that hurts, but a world that cares nothing about us one way or the other? Or are we truly

81

sons of the Most High God, Maker of heaven and earth, and heirs of his kingdom?

"Judge not, that you be not judged," the next paragraph in the Sermon on the Mount begins (Mt 7:1-5; Lk 6:37-38, 41-42). Luke includes the same material in the Sermon on the Plain, combined with other sayings given elsewhere in Matthew (Lk 6:39-40; Mt 15:14; 10:24-25). Here we are again in the atmosphere of the wisdom literature of the Old Testament, the atmosphere of wise counsel for daily living. These and many other sayings of Jesus resemble proverbs; in fact, some of them may have been popular proverbs that he simply quoted. The art of salting one's discourse with appropriate proverbs, often with a touch of humor, is still hugely appreciated by the Arabs of Palestine. Nothing could better promote real communication with such people as those to whom Jesus spoke. But, alas, how many otherwise good Christians are guilty of uncharitably judging others! No sin is more prevalent, and it causes untold suffering and harm.

The next saying, about giving what is holy to dogs and casting pearls before swine (Mt 7:6), has the same tone of popular wisdom and the same crisp, concise quality. Charitable judgment of others need not be exercised to the point of blindly entrusting to them what they are unable to appreciate or respect. The reference to dogs recalls Jesus' remark to the Syrophoenician woman about throwing the children's bread to the dogs (Mk 7:24-30; Mt 15:22-28). That the dogs represent Gentiles here as they do there is possible but unlikely.

The next paragraph (Mt 7:7-11; Lk 11:9-13) returns to the subjects of prayer and providence. He who asks, Jesus says, will receive; he who seeks will find; the door will be opened to him who knocks. This is supported by the analogy of a human father, who would not give his son a stone if asked for bread, or a serpent if asked for a fish, or (Luke adds) a scorpion if asked for an egg. If men, who are evil, give their children good gifts, their heavenly Father, who is good, will surely do no less. This "how much more" argument is a recognized form of reasoning in the rabbinical literature, where it is known as "light and heavy," *i.e.,* arguing from the less to the more important. Other examples appear in Jesus' sayings and parables.

In Matthew it is said that God will give "good things." In Luke he will give "the Holy Spirit." To some this appears more probably authentic than Matthew's reading, because it makes the promise more spiritual; but for that very reason others consider it a change made to prevent unjustified confidence that anything prayed for will automatically be received. A much broader assurance is implied by the preceding sentences. The Holy Spirit, moreover, is a subject in which Luke is especially interested. Jesus was confident of God's concern for all human needs, and he was not given to cautiously guarded and qualified statements.

The Golden Rule, which Matthew gives here, is placed by Luke with the sayings about nonresistance and love for enemies (Mt 7:12; Lk 6:31). In Matthew Jesus adds, "for this is the law and the prophets"(cf. Mt 5:17; 22:40). Neither the principle nor its use as a summary of the law was new. The Talmud relates that the great rabbi Hillel (who was still living during Jesus' boyhood) was once challenged by a pagan to teach him the whole law while he stood on one foot. Hillel replied, "What is odious to you, do not do to your neighbor. This is the whole law; everything else is commentary. Go and learn it." Similar statements are attributed to Confucius and other teachers.

In the last division of the Sermon on the Mount (Mt 7:13-14; Lk 13:23-24) practical instruction gives way to warnings of the dangers and difficulties of the path to the kingdom of heaven. Over against the wide gate and easy way to destruction, followed by many, Jesus points to the narrow gate and hard way to life, which few find. Luke's condensed version of this saying presents a somewhat different picture. Being asked whether those who were saved would be few, Jesus replied, "Strive to enter by the narrow door; for many, I tell you, will seek to enter and will not be able." Here, instead of careless throngs passing down the broad way to destruction, we see the narrow door besieged in vain by an anxious, pushing crowd. The setting given by Luke for the saying seems artificial. Both evangelists probably received the saying without context or framework, but Jesus may have expressed the same idea on various occasions.

Both forms of the saying indicate that the way to the kingdom is not easy, and not many find and follow it. This is not a doctrinal pronouncement, but a statement of observed fact: Jesus is pointing out the way to life, but few of his hearers heed his counsel.

Now he warns the disciples against false prophets, whom he describes as ravenous wolves disguised as sheep (Mt 7:15). Only Matthew preserves this saying. That there were men in Palestine in Jesus' day and later who claimed the gift of prophecy and led many astray is shown not only by the Gospels (cf. Mk 13:22; Mt 24:24) but also by the works of the historian Josephus. These false prophets can be recognized by their fruit, for a bad tree bears bad fruit (Mt 7:16-20; Lk 6:43-45). Jesus must have used this comparison often. It appears in other connections in the Gospels (cf. Mt 12:33). According to both Matthew and Luke it was used also by John the Baptist (Mt 3:8, 10; Lk 3:8).

The Sermon on the Mount ends with stern warnings of the difference between profession and performance (Mt 7:21-23; Lk 6:46; 13:26-27). Saying to Jesus "Lord, Lord," is not enough to gain entrance to the kingdom of heaven; what is essential is doing the will of the heavenly Father. This is the first place where Jesus speaks of God as "my Father" instead of "the Father" or "your Father." The expression appears nineteen times in Matthew, only four times in Luke, and never in Mark.

This is also the first reference in Matthew to the use of the word "Lord" in addressing Jesus. Luke has reported it (5:8) in his account of the calling of the first disciples, and again in the question (13:23), "Lord, will those who are saved be few?" Mark has it only once (7:28), in the story of the Syrophoenician woman. The wide-ranging meanings and implications of this word must be examined when we have more instances before us. The repetition, "Lord, Lord," seems to express urgent entreaty, if not protest, as also in the parable of the foolish bridesmaids (Mt 25:11).

Jesus says that many will so address him "on that day," which can only mean the day of judgment. That the judge will be Jesus himself is obviously presupposed. We are now in the realm of things to come at the end of the present age. Doing the will of God now is bound up with being accepted then and entering the kingdom of heaven.

As the ground of their hope of acceptance, the protestors urge, according to Matthew, that they have prophesied and done mighty works in Jesus' name. In Luke they say that they have eaten and drunk in his presence, and he has taught in their streets. Which of these is what Jesus said can only be guessed. Both are suggestive. Neither conspicuous religious activities nor a superficial knowledge of Jesus and his teaching will be accepted on the day of judgment. Those who depend on such qualifications will not be recognized. Their rejection will be sealed with words from a psalm: "Depart from me, all you workers of evil" (Ps 6:8).

Both the Sermon on the Mount and the Sermon on the Plain end with what may be called the parable of the two builders (Mt 7:24-27; Lk 6:47-49). Its point is not affected by an interesting difference between the pictures drawn by Matthew and Luke. In Matthew one house is founded directly on rock and the other on sand; and the test to which they are subjected consists of rain, floods, and wind. In Luke the wise builder digs deep and lays a foundation on the rock; the foolish one builds on the ground without a foundation; and what causes the second house to fall is that a flood rises and the stream breaks against the house. Somewhere along the line of tradition the story was apparently not copied or repeated word for word, but retold as a whole. The details were thus adapted, perhaps unconsciously, to the type of soil and mode of building familiar in the speaker's and hearers' environment. It is possible that the adaptation was made deliberately, but this seems less likely. Jesus would not have been concerned about the details of the story. He was interested only in driving home the necessity of putting his teaching into practice.

What Jesus is talking about in the Sermon on the Mount is not doctrine; it is a way of life. Is it a practical, possible way of life in the world as it is? Was it intended as a program for individuals and society in this world, or was it a pattern only for the short time that might elapse before the coming of the kingdom of God? These questions cannot be answered here, but three brief statements may be made. First, the atmosphere of the Sermon on the Mount is not that of feverish apocalyptic expectation. The situation presupposed is that of ongoing everyday life. Second, Jesus was not legislating for a body politic and all its citizens. He was teaching how people must live to be eligible for the kingdom of God. Third, this way of life will not accomplish ends for which it was not intended. It is the way of those who seek first the kingdom of God and his righteousness.

Matthew marks the conclusions of the discourse (7:28-29) with his usual formula ("And when Jesus finished these sayings"), completing the sentence with the statement made by Mark and Luke about Jesus' teaching in the synagogue at Capernaum (cf. Mk 1:22; Lk 4:32): "the crowds were astonished at his teaching, for he taught them as one who had authority, and not as their scribes."

CHAPTER V

THE SECOND PART OF THE
GALILEAN MINISTRY

After the Sermon on the Mount, Matthew returns to Mark's narrative with the sentence (Mt 8:1), "When he came down from the mountain, great crowds followed him." Luke also, after inserting his account of the call of the first disciples, rejoins Mark at this point. Now follows the third of the healing miracles recorded in the Synoptic Gospels (Mk 1:40-45; Mt 8:2-4; Lk 5:12-16), one of the eight reported by all three. As Jesus moved on from Capernaum, he was approached by a leper, who knelt before him and said, "If you will, you can make me clean." Jesus touched him and said, "I will; be clean." Although charged to tell no one of his cure, but to go to a priest and fulfil the rites of cleansing (Lev 14:2-32), the man spread the news so widely that people flocked to Jesus and made it impossible for him to enter a town openly. (Matthew omits this last detail; Luke says simply, "But he withdrew to the wilderness and prayed.")

Before continuing further with Mark, Matthew presents six incidents that appear at various other points in Mark or Luke or both. First Matthew relates the fourth of the healing miracles (Mt 8:5-13; Lk 7:1-10). When Jesus returned to Capernaum, we are told, a Roman centurion appealed to him to heal a sick slave. According to Matthew the slave was paralyzed; Luke says he was "sick and at the point of death." In Matthew the centurion is said to have come directly to Jesus; but according to Luke he sent a delegation of Jewish elders, who told Jesus that the centurion was friendly to the Jews and had built them a synagogue.

Jesus agreed to come and heal the slave, but the centurion said he was unworthy to have Jesus enter his house and suggested that the cure might be accomplished at a distance by a word of command. In Luke the suggestion is made by friends sent to meet Jesus. The centurion cited the military discipline to which he was accustomed: he obeyed his superiors and was obeyed by his soldiers. Jesus expressed amazement at such faith, surpassing any he had found among his own people. He did as he was asked, and the slave immediately recovered. Luke says that the friends who had been sent to Jesus found the slave well when they got back to the house.

Jesus' expression of surprise is followed in Matthew by a statement given by Luke in a different connection (Mt 8:11-12; Lk 13:28-29). Using the familiar image of the Messianic banquet, Jesus says that in the kingdom of heaven many from east and west will join Abraham, Isaac, and Jacob at the table; but "the sons of the kingdom will be thrown into the outer darkness," where "men will weep and gnash their teeth." Matthew's incorporation of this saying in the story of the centurion's servant brings out its unavoidable implication, the extension of salvation to the Gentiles and the rejection of the chosen people as heirs of the kingdom. Usually it is Luke who shows most interest in the Gentiles, and Matthew who preserves sayings that seem to restrict the gospel to Israel (cf. Mt 10:5-6, 23; 15:24).

Jesus' attitude toward the Gentiles and his teaching concerning their place in the divine plan of salvation pose a problem that will come up again. For the present I may acknowledge a suspicion that in personal contacts with Gentiles Jesus found his own convictions profoundly affected. Theories of development in Jesus' thinking during his brief ministry are precarious. In this case, however, it seems entirely credible that, with his sympathy and understanding, wider human contacts stimulated broader ideas and attitudes.

Next Matthew reports the healing of Peter's mother-in-law and the exorcisms and healings in the evening, which he omitted from his account of the Sabbath in Capernaum (Mt 8:14-17; Mk 1:29-34; Lk 4:38-41). Characteristically Matthew adds, "This was to fulfil what was spoken by the prophet Isaiah, 'He took our infirmities and bore our diseases'" (Is 53:4).

Matthew now gives Jesus' replies to two men who volunteered to follow him (Mt 8:18-22; Lk 9:57-60). Matthew introduces these incidents with a statement similar to one that Mark and Luke make on another occasion (cf. Mk 4:35; Lk 8:22): "Now when Jesus saw great crowds around him, he gave orders to go over to the other side." By inserting the encounters between Jesus' command to cross the lake and his embarkation, Matthew makes

88

it appear that they occurred just as Jesus was about to step into the boat.

The first man, whom Matthew calls a scribe, addressed Jesus as "Teacher" and said, "I will follow you wherever you go" (Mt 8:19-20; Lk 9:57-58). Jesus warned him of what this would involve: "Foxes have holes, and birds of the air have nests; but the Son of man has nowhere to lay his head." This is the first occurrence of the term "Son of man" in the Gospels. It is Jesus' favorite way of referring to himself and occurs only in his sayings. Simple as this appears, the implications of the expression and Jesus' use of it involve serious problems, which we shall have to consider later.

The second man who spoke to Jesus (Mt 8:21-22; Lk 9:59-60) said, "Lord, let me first go and bury my father." Jesus' reply to this request appears in Matthew as, "Follow me, and leave the dead to bury their own dead." Luke has it, "Leave the dead to bury their own dead; but as for you, go and proclaim the kingdom of God." Such a response seems severe, even harsh. It is easier to understand if the incident occurred where Luke places it (9:51), after Jesus had "set his face to go to Jerusalem." There is reason to believe that Jesus' most stringent demands were directed only to those who would go all the way with him to danger and possible death.

After these incidents, Matthew inserts two that come later in both Mark and Luke (Mt 8:23-24; Mk 4:35-41; 5:1-20; Lk 8:22-39), the calming of the storm on the Sea of Galilee and the exorcism of the Gadarene demoniac, who, with Matthew's curious propensity for doubling, becomes two demoniacs in his account. These incidents will be discussed where Mark and Luke report them.

Now Matthew resumes Mark's order of events, and the three Gospels proceed together with the next three items (Mk 2:1-12; Mt 9:1-8; Lk 5:17-26). The first is the healing of a paralytic. Mark's account of this, following the tour through Galilee, begins, "And when he returned to Capernaum after some days." Matthew, having just told of a miracle on the eastern side of the lake, brings Jesus back to Capernaum with the sentence (9:1), "And getting into a boat he crossed over and came to his own city," which obviously cannot mean Nazareth here. Luke (5:17) does not say where the healing took place. These details are significant only because they show again that the evangelists were no more concerned about geography than they were about chronology. In this instance Mark explicitly, Matthew presumably, and Luke probably regarded the miracle as performed at Capernaum; but they got there at three different times and in three different ways.

The healing of the paralytic, the fifth healing miracle, is especially familiar because of the extraordinary measures taken to get the patient into the presence of Jesus, who was in a house, speaking to the crowd that had gathered there. So dense was the throng, says Mark, that "there was no longer room for them, not even about the door." Unable to get in through the crowd, the men who had brought the paralyzed man made a hole in the roof and lowered him through it on his pallet to the place where Jesus was. Luke says that they let him down "through the tiles," presupposing a tiled roof like those in the Greek cities. Mark, however, says literally, "and when they had dug (it) out," which implies a roof made of poles overlaid with branches or rushes and covered with earth. This picturesque incident reflects popular enthusiasm about Jesus and the faith of the sick and their friends in his ability to heal them.

The account is also the first of a series of "conflict stories" in Mark, recording the beginning of the opposition that eventually led to Calvary. Before healing the man, Jesus said to him, "My son, your sins are forgiven." At this "some of the scribes" said to themselves (or to one another), "It is blasphemy! Who can forgive sins but God alone?" Jesus proceeded to heal the paralytic, demonstrating "that the Son of man has authority on earth to forgive sins." This now becomes the point of the story. The man who was forgiven and healed had only to get up and go home, though Luke adds that he glorified God, as well he might.

The miracle is followed by the calling of a tax collector to be one of Jesus' disciples (Mk 2:13-17; Mt 9:9-13; Lk 5:27-32). Mark gives the man's name as Levi the son of Alphaeus, and Luke gives it simply as Levi; but in the Gospel of Matthew he is called Matthew. Possibly the church in which the Gospel of Matthew was composed had a tradition that identified the converted tax collector with the apostle Matthew.

To invite a tax collector to join the band of disciples was a daring act, comparable to making a U.S. Revenue agent one's companion in the Kentucky mountains. In the Roman empire the collection of taxes was farmed out to wealthy men who could pay well for the concession and then exact enough more from the people to make a high profit. The Latin word for such a man was *publicanus*; hence the word "publican" used in the KJV. Levi (or Matthew) would have been not one of these rich tax-farmers but an agent. Even so, he served the Roman oppressors, and any group that included him would not be popular. To follow Jesus he abandoned his odious occupation. This would make his conversion all the more impressive.

The calling of Levi affords an example of the attitude of Jesus and his followers toward people despised and cast out by the respectable segment of society. Levi did not turn his back on his former associates, but invited many of them to dinner to meet Jesus. This at least is how Luke understood the matter (5:29). Mark and Matthew are not so clear on this point (Mk 2:15; Mt 9:10). It is possible to understand them as meaning that the host was Jesus.

Again the teachers of the law object to Jesus' conduct. This time the criticism is directed against his eating and drinking with tax collectors and sinners. The sinners would not necessarily be criminals or immoral persons, but more broadly the common people who knew and cared nothing about the fine points of the law (cf. Jn 7:49). That a religious teacher should freely associate with such riffraff seemed to the scribes shocking. Jesus, however, said, "Those who are well have no need of a physician, but those who are sick; I came not to call the righteous, but sinners." This should not only have silenced the opposition, it should also have prevented forever the existence of similar attitudes among his own followers. In the midst of this saying Matthew has a quotation of Hosea 6:6, which he cites again a little later (Mt 9:13; cf. 12:7).

Now follows a discussion of fasting (Mk 2:18-20; Mt 9:14-15; Lk 5:33-35), in particular the question why John the Baptist's disciples and the Pharisees fasted but Jesus' disciples did not. Mark treats this as a distinct new incident: "Now John's disciples and the Pharisees were fasting; and people came and said to

91

him . . . '' Jesus replied, ''Can the wedding guests fast while the bridegroom is with them? As long as they have the bridegroom with them, they cannot fast. The days will come, when the bridegroom is taken away from them, and then they will fast in that day.'' In the last two and a half sentences it is tempting to see an addition made later to sanction the practice of fasting, which had meanwhile crept into the church. The whole story may have been created for this purpose, but that seems less likely.

As though part of the same conversation, the evangelists report the sayings about putting a new patch on an old garment and putting new wine in old wineskins (Mk 2:21-22; Mt 9:16-17; Lk 5:36-38). The idea in Mark and Matthew is that a piece of unshrunk cloth used as a patch will shrink and tear away from the old cloth. Luke thinks of tearing a piece from a new garment to repair an old one, thus both ruining the new garment and making a patch that does not match the old garment. If the new cloth and new wine refer to the gospel or the Christian life, the moral of the sayings seems to be that the old system of religious practices, of which fasting is a part, cannot assimilate the new teaching. A whole new set of institutions is required.

Luke appends here (5:39) a saying not reported by Mark or Matthew: ''And no one after drinking old wine desires new; for he says, 'The old is good.'''' This is a fine text for conservatives, but it does not go well with the other sayings, which imply that the new wine is better. Apparently this is another instance of combining sayings that have only a superficial connection, in this case a reference to new wine.

At this point Matthew introduces a large block of material (9:18-34), most of which appears later in Mark or Luke if not both. It includes four miracles, which we shall deal with when we reach them in Mark or Luke. Then Matthew tells of the healing and preaching mission of the twelve apostles. Mark's introductory statement that Jesus ''went about among the villages teaching'' is much expanded in Matthew (Mk 6:6; Mt 9:35-36); and a saying not reported by Mark but used later by Luke is added (vv 37-38), telling the disciples to pray for laborers to reap the abundant harvest. Before proceeding with the instructions to the twelve, Matthew lists their names (10:2-4).

Mark's brief report of the instructions now becomes the nucleus of Matthew's second discourse, which, however, begins (10:5) on an exclusively Matthaean note: "These twelve Jesus sent out, charging them, 'Go nowhere among the Gentiles, and enter no town of the Samaritans, but go rather to the lost sheep of the house of Israel.'" The expression "lost sheep of the house of Israel" occurs elsewhere only once, and only in Matthew (15:24).

Neither Mark nor Luke mentions such a limitation of the mission of Jesus or his disciples. Luke, as we have seen, is at pains to legitimize the Gentile mission and to root it in the ministry of Jesus from the beginning (Lk 4:24-27). Even in Matthew the limitation is annulled at the end, when the risen Lord tells the disciples to make disciples of all nations (Mt 28:19); and before that (21:43) Matthew announces the transfer of the kingdom from Israel to "a nation producing the fruits of it."

It has been suggested that the instructions to the disciples in Matthew's second discourse originated in a manual for early Christian evangelists in their efforts to be "witnesses in Jerusalem and in all Judea"(Acts 1:8). If so, the compiler used sayings found also in Mark and often in Luke, usually in other contexts. Moreover, comparison with Matthew's editorial procedure in the Sermon on the Mount indicates that he also made this collection to fit his scheme of five major discourses. That some of the material in the chapter originated in connection with a Judean mission after Pentecost is not improbable. Some recollection of this early enterprise survives in Acts (9:31-43; 10). In that case, it was the missionaries of the apostolic church who were told to go only to the lost sheep of the house of Israel (Mt 10:5-6). The warnings of persecution seem more suitable for this situation than for a brief tour of healing and teaching during Jesus' ministry.

Luke too has much of the material used in Matthew's second discourse but not found in Mark. As usual, he presents it in smaller portions and at different points in his outline. His account of the expedition of the twelve agrees with Mark's for the most part (Lk 9:1-6; cf. Mk 6:7-13); but he adds to the purpose of the mission that the disciples were "to preach the kingdom of God"; and where Mark says that they preached repentance, Luke uses his favorite verb, saying that they went through the villages "preaching the gospel" (literally, "evangelizing").

In Matthew the instructions for the mission of the twelve begin with preaching: "And preach as you go, saying, 'The kingdom of heaven is at hand'" (10:7; cf. 3:2; 4:17). The gospel is thus summarized again in the same words previously used for the message of John the Baptist and Jesus. The twelve are told also (10:8) to "heal the sick, raise the dead, cleanse lepers, cast out demons." Then comes a saying recorded by Matthew alone: "You received without paying; give without pay."

There is a curious, though unimportant, variation in the command concerning equipment (Mk 6:8-9; Mt 10:9-10; Lk 9:3, cf. 10:4). Mark says that the twelve are to "take nothing for their journey except a staff," but in both Matthew and Luke, Jesus tells them not to take a staff; and although Mark says that they must wear sandals, Matthew will not allow them even that much comfort (so also Luke in the mission of the seventy). All three evangelists say they must not carry money.

The brief command reported by Mark to lodge in only one house in each village is expanded in Matthew and in the directions to the seventy in Luke (Mk 6:10; Mt 10:11-13; Lk 9:4; 10:7). On entering the house where they intend to stay, the disciples are to salute it with a wish for peace. If the house is worthy, as Matthew says, or if a son of peace is there, as Luke puts it, the peace invoked will rest there. If not, it will return to the disciple who uttered the greeting. This reflects the age-old Semitic idea of blessings and curses as actually conveying the good or evil by an almost physical power (cf. Is 55:11).

To the command to remain in the same house in each town Luke adds (10:7-8), "eating and drinking what they provide, for the laborer deserves his wages," and again, "eat what is set before you." In the reference to a laborer Matthew reads "food" instead of "wages" (10:10). Apparently Matthew means that the disciples should feel no obligation to provide for their own sustenance; they are earning it. Luke seems to be thinking more of the hesitation they might feel in accepting food offered to them.

The instructions to the twelve in all three Gospels, and to the seventy also in Luke, include the symbolic act of shaking the dust from their feet when they leave a town that will not receive them (Mk 6:11; Mt 10:14; Lk 9:5; 10:10-11). Mark and Luke add "for a testimony against them"; and in the directions to the seventy Luke has the disciples say they are doing this and add, "nevertheless know this, that the kingdom of God has come near."

Both Matthew and Luke now report Jesus' statement that on the day of judgment it will be more tolerable for Sodom and Gomorrah than for a town that has rejected the disciples (Mt 10:15; Lk 10:12). Matthew puts here a saying that Luke uses at the beginning of the directions to the seventy (Mt 10:16; Lk 10:3): "Behold, I send you out as sheep in the midst of wolves"; and Matthew adds, "So be wise as serpents and innocent as doves."

After this, Luke quotes a pronouncement of woe against Chorazin and Capernaum for their failure to repent in spite of the mighty works Jesus had done there (Lk 10:13-15; cf. Mt 11:21-24). This includes a comparison of the doom of these cities with that of Tyre and Sidon, recalling the comparison with Sodom and Gomorrah. Matthew puts this paragraph after Jesus' tribute to John the Baptist.

The remainder of Matthew's second discourse includes several paragraphs of material used in other connections by Luke, beginning with one from Mark's apocalyptic discourse (Mt 10:17-22; cf. Mk 13:9-13; Lk 21:12-17). This reflects a situation more developed than that of the mission of the twelve; it speaks of being delivered to councils, flogged in synagogues, and dragged before governors and kings. I therefore defer discussion of it until we reach the point where Mark has this material.

The last sentence of Matthew's paragraph (10:23) is not recorded by Mark or Luke: "When they persecute you in one town, flee to the next; for truly, I say to you, you will not have gone through all the towns of Israel, before the Son of man comes." This can hardly mean merely that Jesus will catch up with the disciples. The Son of man here is not one who is present but one who is coming soon. Other sayings show that the reference is to a coming from heaven for judgment. The mission in view is therefore that of the church, which in spite of persecution must be pursued vigorously until the Son of man comes. Perhaps the saying was uttered first by a prophet who believed he spoke by the spirit of Jesus (cf. Acts 11:27-28; 21:10-11).

After this, Matthew has a proverb-like saying (10:24-25; cf. Lk 6:40): "A disciple is not above his teacher, nor a servant above his master; it is enough for the disciple to be like his teacher, and the servant like his master." This obviously refers to the rejection and persecution that the disciples must be prepared to endure. They cannot expect to be exempt from what Jesus himself has to suffer. A sentence found only in Matthew brings this out: "If they have called the master of the house Beelzebul, how much more will they malign those of his household" (cf. Mk 3:22-27 and parallels).

"So have no fear of them," Matthew's discourse continues (10:26); "for nothing is covered that will not be revealed, or hidden that will not be known." The paragraph that begins thus appears in Luke after a series of woes on the Pharisees and lawyers and is introduced there by a warning against the leaven of the Pharisees (Lk 12:1-9). Mark and Luke also have the declaration that everything hidden will be made known in connection with the saying about putting a lamp under a bushel (Mk 4:21-25; Lk 8:16-18). Here in Matthew it is followed by a command to utter in the light what Jesus has told in the dark, and proclaim upon the housetops what they have heard whispered (10:27). Luke gives this in that context (12:3) as a prediction instead of a command, and makes it refer to what the disciples have said instead of what they have heard.

Next in both Matthew and Luke the disciples are told not to fear men, who can kill the body but not the soul, or, as Luke has it, "who kill the body, and after that have no more that they can do" (Mt 10:28; Lk 12:4-5). Instead they are to fear him who "can destroy both soul and body in hell." Literally this implies that those condemned to future punishment are destroyed, body and soul. Luke does not mention the soul but says, "fear him who, after he has killed, has power to cast into hell; yes, I tell you, fear him!" The word translated "hell," here as elsewhere in the RSV, is Gehenna.

A familiar and cherished promise of God's concern for his children comes next in both Gospels (Mt 10:29-31; Lk 12:6-7).

96

Jesus assures the disciples that not even a sparrow falls to the ground unnoted by God, but they are worth far more in his sight than many sparrows. In Luke Jesus says of the sparrows, "not one of them is forgotten before God." In Matthew he says, "not one of them will fall to the ground without your Father's will" (RSV), literally "without your Father" (KJV). God cares about even the least of his creatures. A man, however, especially a disciple fearlessly doing his duty, is "of more value than many sparrows." "But even the hairs of your head are all numbered," Jesus assures his followers (cf. Lk 21:18).

Both Matthew and Luke end this paragraph with a saying about acknowledging Jesus before men (Mt 10:32-33; Lk 12:8-9; cf. Mk 8:38; Lk 9:26). Those who do so he will acknowledge before his Father who is in heaven but those who deny him before men he will deny before his Father who is in heaven. In Luke this reads, "And I tell you, every one who acknowledges me before men, the Son of man also will acknowledge before the angels of God." Here Jesus, or the Son of man, is not judge but witness, and the judgment is apparently in heaven.

Something of what may be involved in loyal acknowledgment of Jesus is made plain by the next paragraph in Matthew, a warning reported later by Luke (Mt 10:34-36; Lk 12:51-53). Jesus has not come to bring peace, he says, but a sword. The next sentence in Matthew echoes a verse from the prophet Micah (7:6), except that Jesus says he will bring about the divisions in families that Micah cites as characteristic of the social disorders of his day. Luke's report fills in the picture but is less like Micah. Both forms give unmistakable notice of the sacrifice of normal ties to which discipleship may lead, not because these relationships are incompatible with discipleship if all concerned are equally dedicated, but because that is not always the case.

Still stronger is the statement that follows in Matthew (10:37-38): "He who loves father or mother more than me is not worthy of me; and he who loves son or daughter more than me is not worthy of me; and he who does not take his cross and follow me is not worthy of me." Luke has this saying later (14:26-27) in even sterner language: one who comes to Jesus must "hate his own father and mother and wife and children and brothers and sisters, yes, and even his own life.'' Otherwise ''he cannot be my disciple''; and one who ''does not bear his own cross and come after me, cannot be my disciple.'' Matthew may have toned down the original harshness of the saying.

The statement that the disciple must take or bear his own cross is reported by Mark and Luke and repeated by Matthew as part of what Jesus said at Caesarea Philippi (Mk 8:34; Mt 16:24; Lk 9:23). Luke reads there, ''take up his cross daily,'' which, like his ''bear his own cross'' here, suggests a continuous life of sacrifice and endurance rather than a single act of dedication. This reference to a cross before the crucifixion seems to be a transparent allusion to Jesus' carrying his own cross to Calvary (Jn 19:17). The connection vanishes, however, if, as the Synoptic Gospels say, Simon of Cyrene carried Jesus' cross (Mk 15:21; Mt 27:32; Lk 23:26). The metaphor would be clear without such an allusion. Crucifixion was a familiar mode of execution, and references to a condemned criminal carrying his cross are found in both classical and rabbinic literature.

The saying is followed by a paradox (Mt 10:39; cf. Mk 8:35; Mt 16:25; Lk 9:24; 17:33): ''He who finds his life will lose it, and he who loses his life for my sake will find it'' (Mark reads, ''for my sake and the gospel's''). The Gospel of John applies this to the contrast between this life and the future life: ''He who loves his life loses it, and he who hates his life in this world will keep it for eternal life'' (Jn 12:25).

The word translated ''life'' in these places is often translated ''soul.'' The KJV uses both words for the same Greek noun in two consecutive verses (Mk 8:35-36; Mt 16:25-26). This noun (*psychē*), however, does not refer to the immortal part of man as distinguished from his mortal body. Neither does it, for that matter, designate life as contrasted with death; there are other Greek words for that concept. There is no English word that corresponds to it exactly. Sometimes ''self'' comes closest to its meaning. The Aramaic word that Jesus must have used covers much the same range as the Greek word. It is also frequently used in a reflexive sense. The Greek text of Luke 9:25, ''if he gains the whole world and loses or forfeits himself,'' probably represents this use of the Aramaic noun.

A famous and usually discerning commentator made a strange remark about this saying. By these words, he said, Jesus based his teaching on self-interest: the purpose of not seeking one's own life was merely to save it. But what Jesus meant was that only he who loses himself in devotion to something greater than himself really lives.

What all this has to do with the mission of the twelve disciples is by no means obvious. The place where Luke puts it, during the final journey to Jerusalem, is more appropriate, if indeed it does not reflect a still later time of persecution; yet Jesus may have said these things at any time and probably said them often.

Matthew now concludes his second discourse with three related sayings (10:40-42). Two of them are variations of sayings found in Mark, one of these being in Luke also. The first, "He who receives you receives me, and he who receives me receives him who sent me," refers in this context to the twelve disciples. In Mark and Luke it is a part of the story of Jesus' taking a child in his arms, and Matthew repeats part of it in that connection (Mk 9:37; Lk 9:48; Mt 18:5). There the reference is to the child. The converse of the statement appears in Luke, addressed to the seventy (10:16): "He who rejects you rejects me, and he who rejects me rejects him who sent me." A wider application follows in Matthew's discourse (10:41): "He who receives a prophet because he is a prophet shall receive a prophet's reward, and he who receives a righteous man because he is a righteous man shall receive a righteous man's reward." The expression "because he is," literally "in the name of" (cf. KJV), might refer either to the receiver or to the one received, but the meaning is probably that he who receives a prophet or a righteous man because that man is a prophet or a righteous man will be considered as such himself and rewarded accordingly.

The third saying of the group (10:42) supports this interpretation but raises another question: "And whoever gives to one of these little ones even a cup of cold water because he is a disciple, truly, I say to you, he shall not lose his reward." Here "because he is a disciple" surely refers to the one who receives the cup of water; but, if so, the "little ones" are the disciples.

The reward of one who gives a cup of water is mentioned

elsewhere in Mark (9:41). The expression there is, "whoever gives you a cup of water to drink because you bear the name of Christ." That presents a difficulty that will be dealt with in the appropriate place, but it confirms the understanding of the "little ones" as disciples. Why then does not Jesus say here, "whoever gives to one of you"? Conceivably it is because he has in mind not only the twelve but all his followers. We shall encounter other references to "little ones" (Mk 9:42; Mt 18:6, 10, 14; Lk 17:2).

The second discourse ends (Mt 11:1) with a variation of the usual formula: "And when Jesus had finished instructing his twelve disciples, he went on from there to teach and preach in their cities."

CHAPTER VI

THE THIRD PART OF THE GALILEAN MINISTRY

Matthew proceeds with an incident related later by Luke (Mt 11:2-6; Lk 7:18-23). As told by Matthew the story begins, "Now when John heard in prison about the deeds of the Christ." John's imprisonment has so far been barely mentioned by Matthew and Mark (Mk 1:14; Mt 4:12). Luke has briefly reported it (3:19-20); here he says only that John's disciples had "told him of all these things." Matthew's reference to Jesus simply as "the Christ" is unusual in the Gospels.

The question brought by John's disciples was, "Are you he who is to come, or shall we look for another?" Having performed many miracles "in that hour," according to Luke, Jesus replied, "Go and tell John what you have heard and seen," and reminded the messengers of the various kinds of maladies they had seen cured, adding "and the poor have good news preached to them." The list contains clear allusions to several verses in Isaiah (Is 29:18-19; 35:5-6; 61:1). "And blessed is he who takes no offense at me," Jesus concludes, as though rebuking John for his doubts.

John's question is often taken to indicate that he had not previously thought of Jesus as the Messiah. It is equally possible, however, that John had long believed Jesus to be the one mightier than he who would baptize with the Holy Spirit and fire. The reports that reached him in prison may have revived this hope, or may have aroused impatient doubt because Jesus was not doing what the coming one was expected to do.

Both Matthew and Luke continue with a tribute to John spoken when the messengers left (Mt 11:7-19; Lk 7:24-35). What did people expect, Jesus asked, when they flocked to the wilderness to see and hear John? Surely not a pliant seeker of popularity, "a reed shaken by the wind," nor a well-fed, well-dressed preacher—for such a man they would go to the court of a king. If they went to see a prophet, they saw one, "and more than a prophet."

John, Jesus continues, is the messenger promised by Malachi, sent to prepare the way for the Lord's coming in judgment (Mal 3:1). No man ever born was greater; "yet he who is least in the kingdom of heaven is greater than he." Did Jesus consider John excluded from the kingdom? I cannot avoid a suspicion that these words were added by some preacher or teacher who felt that he must avoid making John seem equal to a Christian. The quotation marks belong after "no one greater than John the Baptist."

This is supported by the saying that follows in Matthew (11:12-13). Luke has it later (16:16). In Matthew it reads: "From the days of John the Baptist until now the kingdom of heaven has suffered violence, and men of violence take it by force. For all the prophets and the law prophesied until John." Luke's form is shorter: "The law and the prophets were until John; since then the good news of the kingdom of God is preached, and every one enters it violently." If these are both derived from the same original text, we cannot recover it. Luke's favorite verb, "preach good news," and the fact that his version is clearer than Matthew's, indicate that he rewrote the saying. His form of it suggests a mass movement into the kingdom; Matthew may have in mind efforts to force God's hand by direct action (cf. Mt 21:31).

The important point here is that in both Gospels the saying, like the one before it, distinguishes two eras; but here the era of the kingdom begins with John the Baptist, not after him. He was not the last prophet of the old order but the first herald of the new. This agrees better with Jesus' tribute to John than the contrary implication of the preceding verse, and favors the authenticity of this saying in its original form.

At the end of Jesus' tribute to John the Baptist, according to Matthew, he adds, "and if you are willing to accept it, he is Elijah who is to come. He who has ears to hear, let him hear" (Mt 11:14-15). John the Baptist is here identified not only with the messenger of Malachi 3:1, but with the prophet Elijah, whose return "before the great and terrible day of the Lord comes" is predicted a little later in Malachi (4:5). (The identity of the messenger and Elijah is implied.) This is stated more fully later (Mk 9:11-13; Mt 17:10-13).

Now Matthew and Luke continue with Jesus' apt comparison of

102

the men of that generation with children in the marketplace, peevishly complaining that their companions will not play either a happy or a mournful game with them (Mt 11:16-19; Lk 7:31-35). This is significant for Jesus' positive attitude to life and his standard of right human relations. Highly as he valued John's place in the divine program, he sharply distinguished between John's way of living and his own. There will be more to say about this in the last chapter.

The last sentence reads in Matthew, "Yet wisdom is justified by her deeds"; Luke reads, "by all her children" (Mt 11:19; Lk 7:35). Perhaps the word "wisdom" should be spelled with a capital W. In the wisdom literature of the Old Testament and the Apocrypha God's wisdom is often personified and speaks in the first person (*e.g.*, Prov 1:20-33; 8; Sir 24). Here, however, recent translations are almost unanimous in avoiding any suggestion that wisdom is personified.

The verb translated "is justified" may mean "is vindicated, proved to be right." Matthew's reading, "deeds" (literally "works"), fits this meaning. "Justified," however, may mean "judged to be right, approved." This goes better with Luke's reading, "by all her children." According to a common Semitic idiom, just as sons of wickedness are wicked men, and sons of tumult are tumultuous ones, wisdom's children are people who have wisdom. Luke's form of the saying therefore means, "Wisdom is recognized by those who are wise." This was probably the original text and meaning.

Another passage not found in Mark comes next in Matthew; Luke has it at the end of the instructions of the seventy (Mt 11:20-24; Lk 10:13-15). "Then he began to upbraid the cities where most of his mighty works had been done," Matthew says, "because they did not repent." Chorazin and Bethsaida will suffer more severely on the day of judgment than Tyre and Sidon; and Capernaum will be brought down to Hades and judged more severely than Sodom. Matthew has already quoted the prediction that a town that rejects the disciples will be punished more than Sodom and Gomorrah; in Luke this immediately precedes the denunciation of the Galilean cities (Mt. 10:15, Lk 10:12).

103

This passionate outburst seems bitter, if not vindictive. Possibly, however, Jesus said these things out of grief for the cities he knew, rather than personal resentment, just as he is later reported to have wept over Jerusalem (Lk 19:41).

Matthew now records Jesus' thanksgiving to God for hiding the truths he is preaching from those who are "wise and understanding" and revealing them to "babes," the simple, unsophisticated common people (Mt 11:25-26; Lk 10:21). Between the denunciation of the cities and this thanksgiving Luke tells of the return of the seventy disciples, who reported joyfully, "Lord, even the demons are subject to us in your name!" (10:17-20). Jesus replied, "I saw Satan fall like lightning from heaven." Then, as in the Great Commission in the longer ending of Mark (cf. Mk 16:15-16), he announced that he had given the disciples "authority to tread upon serpents and scorpions, and over all the power of the enemy."

It was God's gracious will, Jesus says, that what was hidden from the wise should be revealed to babes. It is often so. Learning controlled by humility and reverence can mitigate the consequences of ignorance, but pride and presumption will keep the most brilliant thinker from seeing through the facts to the truth.

Next comes a saying (Mt 11:27; Lk 10:22) that sounds so much like the Gospel of John that commentators call it "Johannine." "All things have been delivered to me by my Father," Jesus says, and he claims a unique, exclusive understanding between "the Father" and "the Son." This is different from another passage where the expression "the Son" is used. In the apocalyptic discourse Jesus says. "But of that day or that hour no one knows, not even the angels in heaven, nor the Son, but only the Father" (Mk 13:32; Mt 24:36). To judge by the whole tone of Jesus' sayings in the Synoptic Gospels, this "Johannine" saying is much more likely to be an expression of the later theology of the church than of the teaching of Jesus. That does not necessarily make it less true. What the church came to believe about him may be as true as anything he said of himself.

After this Matthew has the familiar invitation, "Come to me, all who labor and are heavy laden" (Mt 11:28-30). Neither Mark nor Luke has this. In the book of Sirach (51:23, 26-27), Wisdom says:

> Draw near to me, you who are untaught,
>   and lodge in my school. . . .
>
> Put your neck under the yoke,
>   and let your souls receive instruction;
>   it is to be found close by.
> See with your eyes that I have labored little
>   and found for myself much rest.

These lines may or may not have suggested the similar references in the saying recorded by Matthew (cf. Mt 13:52). The rabbis spoke of "the yoke of the law" and "the yoke of the kingdom of heaven." It would therefore be quite natural for Jesus to say, "The yoke the scribes offer you is heavy and will exhaust you, but mine is easy to bear." I once heard an explanation of the easy yoke given by an old uneducated preacher. He had grown up, he said, on a farm where oxen were used, and he told how the yokes were fashioned so that they would fit without galling the animal's shoulders. When a young ox was to be trained, he was yoked with an older and stronger one and the yoke was so made that the end worn by the young ox was longer than the other, making the older ox pull a larger share of the load.

After this long section of matter found nowhere else or shared only with Luke, Matthew rejoins Mark with the story of the disciples plucking grain on the Sabbath (Mk 2:23-28; Mt 12:1-8; Lk 6:1-5). The law allowed going through a grainfield and plucking a few ears by hand on the way, but some of the Pharisees found fault with the disciples for doing this on the Sabbath. The basic issue was Sabbath observance. But Jesus reminded the critics that when David was fleeing from Saul he made the priest at Nob give him the consecrated bread of the Presence ("show-bread"), which the law reserved for the use of the priests (1 Sam 21:1-6; Ex 25:30; 39:36; 40:23; Lev 24:5-9).

In Mark, Jesus says that this occurred "when Abiathar was high priest." First Samuel 21:1 says that the priest at Nob at the time was Ahimelech, and the next chapter tells how he and his

105

family were slaughtered at Saul's command for helping David, the only survivor being Ahimelech's son Abiathar (1 Sam 22:9-22; 2 Sam 8:17; 1 Chron 18:16; 24:6, 31). Later, when David became king, he had "Zadok the son of Ahitub and Ahimelech the son of Abiathar" as priests at his court; yet at the end of his reign the chief priest was Abiathar. Since it was not uncommon in the ancient world to name boys after their grandfathers, it is quite possible that there were two Ahimelechs and two Abiathars.

Matthew and Luke and some important manuscripts of Mark do not have the troublesome clause. If we had to suppose that it was an exact record of Jesus' words, we should have to raise the question whether he made a mistake in a matter of history. The significance of the item is that it compels us to recognize the existence of textual and historical problems even in reported sayings of Jesus. As previously noted, such difficulties constitute a problem for faith only if one assumes a literalistic, mechanical view of inspiration.

After the reference to David, Matthew has three more verses apparently continuing what Jesus said on this occasion (12:5-7). Neither Mark nor Luke has them, and it seems doubtful that they belong here. The first one cites another way in which the Sabbath is profaned without incurring guilt, and Jesus asks his hearers whether they have not read about it "in the law." The reference may be to a passage in Numbers concerning a special burnt offering (28:9-10), but why the performance of a duty according to the law should be considered a profanation of the Sabbath is not clear.

The next verse, "I tell you, something greater than the temple is here" (Mt 12:6) resembles verses 41-42 of the same chapter and is more clearly relevant in that context than it is here. The only apparent reason for inserting it here is that, like the preceding verse, it refers to the temple.

The last of these three verses introduces the same quotation from Hosea used before (v 7; cf. 9:13; Hos 6:6): "I desire mercy, and not sacrifice." The fact that only Matthew has it in either place makes Jesus' use of the quotation on these occasions questionable. It is entirely probable, however, that he was known

106

to have used it sometimes. "Mercy" is not a good translation of Hosea's Hebrew word. It is what the Greek word used in Matthew means, and this word is used by the Septuagint in Hosea 6:6; but Jesus would either have quoted the Hebrew text or used an Aramaic translation, and the Aramaic word is the same as the Hebrew. The context in both places where the verse is quoted shows at least that Matthew understood it to mean that human welfare is more important than correct ritual. That this was the point of Jesus' defense of the disciples is indicated by another statement (Mk 2:27): "The sabbath was made for man, not man for the sabbath." Only Mark reports this.

The story ends with a Q.E.D., "so the Son of man is lord even of the sabbath." All three evangelists record this (Mk 2:28; Mt 12:8; Lk 6:5); yet its authenticity is uncertain. Involuntarily one thinks of an early Christian teacher or missionary telling the story and concluding, "So you see, the Son of man is greater than the law; his authority embraces even the Sabbath."

An instructive case study of Matthew's and Luke's ways of using Mark is afforded by the accounts of the healing of a man with a withered hand (Mk 3:1-6; Mt 12:9-14; Lk 6:6-10), which in all three Gospels follows the incident of plucking grain on the Sabbath. Whether it happened immediately after that incident is not clear. Mark begins, "Again he entered the synagogue," which might refer either to the same or to a different occasion. Matthew reads, "And he went on from there, and entered their synagogue." Luke, however, says distinctly, "On another sabbath, when he entered the synagogue and taught, . . . "

Luke expands Mark's account of this episode; Matthew condenses it. Mark alone has a characteristic human touch, perhaps too human for Matthew and Luke: "And he looked around at them with anger, grieved at their hardness of heart." The three agree that Jesus told the man to stretch out his hand; he did so, and the hand was restored. This concludes Mark's series of conflict stories. Again a miracle, a cure on the Sabbath, provoked the conflict.

After these demonstrations of Jesus' independence and authority, we are told, the Pharisees went out and began to discuss ways to get rid of him (Mk 3:6; Mt 12:14; Lk 6:11; cf. Mk 8:15;

12:13). Mark says that they "held counsel with the Herodians," the party that supported the sons of Herod the Great. Matthew and Luke omit this, although Matthew elsewhere retains a reference to the Herodians (22:16).

Mark continues with the statement that Jesus withdrew with his disciples to the sea (evidently meaning the Sea of Galilee); "and a great multitude from Galilee followed; also from Judea and Jerusalem and Idumea and from beyond the Jordan and from about Tyre and Sidon a great multitude, hearing all that he did, came to him" (Mk 3:7-8; cf. Mt 12:15; 4:25; Lk 6:17). Before this, Luke inserts the appointment of the twelve apostles, which follows it in Mark. So great was the press, Mark says (3:9), that Jesus "told his disciples to have a boat ready for him because of the crowd, lest they should crush him." Matthew and Luke omit this too. There is a similar reference later in Mark and Matthew (Mk 4:1; Mt 13:2), but Luke omits it there too, having used the same idea in his account of the calling of the first disciples (5:3).

Again the demons cause Jesus no little embarrassment by making the wretched people they have possessed cry out (Mk 3:11; cf. Mk 1:24; Lk 4:34), "You are the Son of God." Only Mark records this; Luke has reported the same acclamation with the healing of many sick people at Capernaum (4:41). Matthew says simply (12:15) that Jesus "healed them all, and ordered them not to make him known," but makes up for the condensation by again quoting in full the passage from Isaiah that was briefly echoed in the accounts of Jesus' baptism (Mt 12:17-21; Is 42:1-3).

Now Mark tells of the choice and appointment of the twelve apostles (3:13-19). Matthew nowhere records this but gives the names of the twelve (10:2-4) in connection with their preaching mission. Luke says that Jesus spent the whole preceding night in prayer (6:12). The purpose for which the twelve were appointed is stated only in Mark: "And he appointed twelve to be with him, and to be sent out to preach and have authority to cast out demons" (3:14). Personal association with Jesus himself is the first purpose. But this is only preparatory; "and to be sent out." They were also to be apostles, envoys, missionaries. As such they had a double mission, "to preach and have authority to cast out demons."

This is an admirable summary of the mission of the Christian church in the world. It exists to proclaim the gospel and to apply it to the alleviation of human distress. It cannot accomplish this double mission unless it fulfills its first purpose "to be with him." Being with Jesus means different things to different people. Whatever else it may involve, however, any separation from the real man who was crucified under Pontius Pilate, any dissolving of his historical person and gospel in theological abstraction, stultifies and nullifies the true purpose of the Christian church.

The lists of the twelve chosen disciples in the Gospels might be expected to agree, and on the whole they do, but there are some differences. Instead of Thaddeus, the tenth name in Mark and Matthew, Luke has "Judas the son of James." This Judas is not mentioned elsewhere, unless he is the man called in John (14:22) "Judas (not Iscariot)." The last member of the twelve (aside from Judas Iscariot) is another Simon (Mk 3:18; Mt 10:4). In Mark and Matthew he is called "the Cananaean." Luke calls him here "Simon who was called the Zealot," in Acts simply "Simon the Zealot" (Lk 6:15; Acts 1:13). "Cananaean" does not mean "Canaanite" (in the Greek the two words are quite distinct). It is a Greek transcription of the Aramaic word for Zealot, which Luke translates.

One of the twelve, therefore, was a member of the Zealots, the most aggressive advocates of rebellion against Rome. Simon must have been one of those who hoped Jesus would take up arms. Jesus' refusal must have been a bitter disappointment to Simon, and perhaps to Judas Iscariot.

The name or epithet Iscariot has occasioned much speculation. Three of the many proposed explanations deserve mention. It may represent Hebrew Ish-Kerioth, "man of Kerioth." It may be an Aramaic word meaning "deceiver" or "one who deals falsely." It may represent the Latin noun *sicarius,* that is, dagger-man or assassin, a term applied later to the most extreme Zealots.

According to Mark and Luke, Jesus had gone "up on the mountain" to appoint his inner circle of disciples (Mk 3:13; Lk 6:12). After doing this, Luke says, he came down, healed many who had unclean spirits (Lk 6:17-19; cf. Mk 3:7-8), and delivered the Sermon on the Plain, which we have considered together with

109

Matthew's Sermon on the Mount (Lk 6:20-49). This done, he then entered Capernaum. Luke relates here the healing of the centurion's servant, previously reported by Matthew (Lk 7:1-10; Mt 8:5-13). This is followed by a miracle recorded only by Luke, the restoration of a widow's son to life at Nain (7:11-17). The funeral procession was leaving the city when Jesus and his disciples arrived. Moved by compassion, Jesus told the man to get up, and he "sat up, and began to speak." Luke adds that Jesus "gave him to his mother," recalling similar statements about Elijah and Elisha (1 Kings 17:23; 2 Kings 4:36). What influence these Old Testament precedents may have had on Luke's story is anybody's guess, but the uncertainty today regarding a clinical definition of death suggests the possibility of a premature decision in this case.

The story ends with one of Luke's surprising references to Judea (Lk 7:17; cf. 4:44). Nain was in Galilee, about six miles southeast of Nazareth; yet Luke says that the report of the miracle spread through Judea. Only if Judea means all Palestine was Nain in Judea.

Luke now tells of Jesus' response to a question brought by two disciples of John the Baptist, and his public tribute to John; Matthew has this after his second major discourse (Lk 7:18-35; Mt 11:2-19).

After the paragraphs about John the Baptist, Luke gives his account of the woman with an alabaster flask of ointment, anticipating a much later incident in Mark (Lk 7:36-50; cf. Mk 14:3-9). He then concludes this section of his Gospel with an item reported by him alone (Lk 8:1-3). As Jesus went on, he was accompanied not only by the twelve but also by "some women who had been healed of evil spirits and infirmities." One of them was Mary Magdalene (i.e., Mary of Magdala, a town on the western shore of the Sea of Galilee). Seven demons had gone out of her, Luke remarks casually, though the story of this miracle is nowhere told. All four Gospels record her participation in events associated with the crucifixion and resurrection of Jesus. "Joanna, the wife of Chuza, Herod's steward," is no doubt the Joanna mentioned also by Luke among the women at the tomb (24:10). Susanna is not mentioned elsewhere, but Luke says there

110

were "many others." They provided for Jesus and his disciples "out of their means." Mark and Matthew mention this at the time of the crucifixion (Mk 15:40-41; Mt 27:55-56).

These items, not recorded by Mark, appear in Luke after the appointment of the twelve. After Mark's account of that event, the RSV and TEV say, Jesus went "home"; other versions read, more literally, "into a house" (Mk 3:19). This may or may not have been the house in which he lived while in Capernaum (v 20). In any case, "the crowd came together again, so that they could not even eat."

The next verse (v 21) is variously understood. The RSV says, "And when his family heard it, they went out to seize him, for people were saying, 'He is beside himself.'" The Greek expression rendered "his family" may mean "his friends" or "his relatives" (NEB, NAB, JB). Some take "they were saying" as impersonal, The words rendered "people were saying" (NEB, TEV) mean literally "they said." The opinion expressed here may have been that of Jesus' friends or relatives. This is one of the few things in Mark that Matthew and Luke both omit. Nothing is said of the success or failure of the attempt to seize Jesus.

Evidently there were people who questioned his sanity. Any person who ignored common assumptions ran the danger of being considered insane. Where skepticism was joined to bigotry and superstition, any extraordinary achievement might arouse a suspicion of alliance with evil powers.

That this happened to Jesus is attested by the charge brought against him by scribes from Jerusalem, as Mark reports next (Mk 3:22; Mt 12:24; Lk 11:15): "He is possessed by Beelzebul, and by the prince of demons he casts out the demons." In Matthew and Luke this is connected with the healing of a dumb demoniac ("blind and dumb," Matthew says) (Mt 12:22; Lk 11:14). Matthew has already reported the healing of two blind men (9:27-31), followed by the healing of a dumb demoniac (vv 32-34). In the latter instance the Pharisees said, "He casts out demons by the prince of demons." Again in the second discourse Jesus alludes to such hostile propaganda: "If they have called the master of the house Beelzebul, how much more will they malign those of his household" (Mt 10:25; cf. Jn 13:16; 15:20)—an

111

instance of the "how much more" argument. Now Matthew repeats the charge (12:22-24), and in so doing practically repeats the miracle also, except that this time the demoniac is both dumb and blind. Perhaps he innocently recorded as different incidents variant forms of the same tradition, but the result looks like careless editorial work. Luke's account of the healing of the dumb demoniac seems to combine two of Matthew's stories (Lk 11:14; cf. Mt 9:33). He repeats almost the same words used by Matthew earlier, but instead of ascribing to the Pharisees the accusation of Satanic power, he says that some of the people made it and others demanded a sign from heaven (Lk 11:15-16).

The title "Son of David" is used by the two blind men in the first of Matthew's stories and by "all the people" in the third (9:27; 12:23). In Mark and Luke it is applied to Jesus only in the healing of another blind man at Jericho, where Matthew also has it and again has two blind men (Mk 10:47-48; Lk 18:38-39; Mt 20:30-31). According to Matthew the "Canaanite" woman used it in appealing to Jesus (Mt 15:22; cf. Mk 7:26), and again it is Matthew who quotes it when Jesus enters Jerusalem and the children hail him in the temple (Mt 21:9, 15; cf. Mk 11:9-10). These are the only places where the expression is used of Jesus. It was familiar in Judaism, especially in the form, "Messiah Son of David."

Beelzebul (cf. 2 Kings 1:2-3) (KJV Beelzebub, following the Vulgate instead of the Greek manuscripts) is another name for Satan. Jesus uses the latter name in his reply to the charge. Mark says that he called the scribes and spoke to them "in parables," evidently meaning not a story but simply a comparison (3:22-26). "How can Satan cast out Satan?" Jesus asks. Any kingdom or family divided against itself cannot endure. If Satan is expelling his own subjects and agents, he is doomed.

The other evangelists (Mt 12:25-26; Lk 11:17-18) introduce Jesus' reply with the words, "knowing their thoughts." Matthew expands Mark's report, Luke condenses it, and both add the question, "how then will his kingdom stand?" The idea of a kingdom of Satan at war with the kingdom of God, and temporarily dominant in the world, appears in one Greek manuscript in an addition to the long ending of Mark: "The limit

of the years of the authority of Satan is fulfilled.'' In the Dead Sea
Scrolls the present age is called ''the dominion of Belial,'' using
another name for Satan that occurs once in the New Testament (2
Cor 6:15), but never in the Gospels.

Matthew and Luke have next an important paragraph not found
in Mark (Mt 12:27; Lk 11:19). ''And if I cast out demons by
Beelzebul,'' Jesus says, ''by whom do your sons cast them out?
Therefore they shall be your judges.'' Not only Jesus is exorcising
demons, but also ''your sons,'' which can only mean the sons of
those to whom he is speaking. He has given the apostles authority
to cast out demons (Mk 3:15; Mt 10:1). Possibly they are here
called ''your sons.'' The reference may, however, be to exorcists
who were not followers of Jesus. In any case, Jesus' question
implies that they are casting out demons by the power of God.

Jesus continues, ''But if it is by the finger of God that I cast out
demons, then the kingdom of God has come upon you'' (Lk
11:20; Mt 12:28). This is one of the four places where Matthew
has ''kingdom of God'' instead of ''kingdom of heaven''; no one
knows why. Instead of ''finger of God'' Matthew has ''Spirit of
God''; but Luke, being especially interested in the Spirit, would
hardly have substituted ''finger'' if his source had read ''Spirit.''
The expression is probably an allusion to the story of the plagues
of Egypt (Ex 8:19), where Pharaoh's magicians, unable to
duplicate the plague of gnats, say, ''This is the finger of God.''

That Jesus said this is fairly sure; but since he clearly taught that
the kingdom of God had not come, what does the statement that it
''has come upon you'' mean? The Greek verb here is found
nowhere else in the Gospels. Its meaning, however, is plain. It
appears four times in Paul's letters (Rom 9:31; 2 Cor 10:14; Phil
3:16; 1 Thess 4:15), and in the Greek Old Testament it is used to
translate an Aramaic verb that occurs eight times in the Aramaic
part of Daniel (Dan 4:11, 20, 22, 24, 28; 6:24; 7:13, 22). Jesus
tells his accusers that the kingdom of God has caught up with
them, not for salvation but for judgment. That is what the coming
of the kingdom meant to John the Baptist. Jesus too called for
repentance. The demonstration of God's supreme power in the
conquest of the demons both confirmed his assurance that the
kingdom was near and put to shame those who would not

113

recognize it. Which being interpreted means now: "You cynics, who suppose that self-interest rules the world, are convicted and condemned by countless acts of mercy and kindness, not perceiving that they manifest the power of God, which alone can prevail in the end."

Jesus' refutation of the charge against him is clarified and enforced by an illustration in all three Gospels (Mk 3:27; Mt 12:29; Lk 11:21-22): If a strong man's house is broken into, the robber must have overcome and bound the owner. In Luke the house is a palace, which the owner guards in full armor; he can be stripped of his armor and robbed only "when one stronger than he assails him." Since Satan is unable to prevent the expulsion of his agents from people possessed by them, he has evidently been bound and rendered helpless by "one stronger than he."

Matthew and Luke add here (Mt 12:30; Lk 11:23), "He who is not with me is against me, and he who does not gather with me scatters." In another connection Mark and Luke have the converse: "For he that is not against us is for us"(Mk 9:40; cf. Lk 9:50). The two forms together imply that Jesus considers every man either a friend or a foe. There is no neutral position.

Next, Mark and Matthew report Jesus' statement about blasphemy against the Holy Spirit (Mk 3:28-30; Mt 12:31-32; Lk 12:10). Luke has it, somewhat condensed, in another connection. Both contexts associate blasphemy against the Holy Spirit with rejection of Jesus. He was convinced that his work was inspired and accomplished by the Holy Spirit. To reject his proclamation of the kingdom of God and the proof of its nearness in his ministry of healing was to deny the manifest work of the Spirit of God.

Matthew includes here a statement (Mt 12:32; Lk 12:10) quoted later by Luke but not found in Mark; "whoever says a word against the Son of man will be forgiven." Here again Jesus uses the expression with which he contrasted his way of life with that of John the Baptist (Mt 11:19; Lk 7:34). As pointed out there, "a son of man" means in Hebrew and Aramaic simply "a man." "The son of man" indicates a particular man. Mark uses the term in the plural in this same passage (Mk 3:28; cf. Mt 12:31): "all sins will be forgiven the sons of men" (Matthew says "will be forgiven men"). Perhaps what Jesus meant here was not "against the Son of man" but "against a man." Even so, he would be referring indirectly to himself.

Many sensitive souls have worried about the unforgivable sin and wondered whether they might have committed it and incurred eternal damnation. What is meant by blasphemy against the Holy Spirit, however, is clear. In the Bible the Holy Spirit is the active power of God at work in the world. Jesus' adversaries, seeing God's work, ascribed it to Satan. This was blasphemy against God himself. It could never be forgiven because it bespoke a willfully blind spirit that made repentance impossible. Without repentance, which presupposes recognition of the need to be forgiven, there can be no forgiveness (cf. 1 Jn 1:8-9). When a person realizes that he needs forgiveness, that itself is proof that he has not committed the unforgivable sin.

An honest, conscientious error of judgment, made by a person who is willing and able to change his mind when shown to be in the wrong, is a very different thing from the sin that Jesus condemned. Over and over again he denounced hardhearted self-righteousness. That was what made the charge brought by his enemies unforgivable. There was no hope for people who saw what they saw and called it the work of the devil.

Matthew gives next a brief series of sayings (Mt 12:33-35; cf. 7:15-20; Lk 6:43-45), repeating in part what has already been used in the Sermon on the Mount and the Sermon on the Plain. The saying about knowing a tree by its fruit is followed by one about the good brought by a good man from his treasure and the evil brought by an evil man from his. Matthew introduces this with the denunciation of the Pharisees as a brood of vipers, which both he and Luke have previously reported as uttered by John the Baptist (cf. Mt 3:7; Lk 3:7). Matthew adds to the series a saying warning Jesus' hearers against careless speech (12:36). The charge of healing by demoniac power was just such a statement as people often make irresponsibly.

Now Matthew presents another important passage that Luke reserves for the final journey to Jerusalem (Mt 12:38-42; Lk 11:29-32). Some of the scribes and Pharisees, Matthew reports, asked for a sign. In the Old Testament a message from God is sometimes authenticated by a miraculous "sign" (*e.g.*, Judg

115

6:36-40; Is 7:10-16). Mark reports later that the Pharisees demanded of Jesus a sign from heaven, but he refused (8:11-13). In Matthew and Luke this is expanded and an exception is made: "An evil and adulterous generation seeks for a sign; but no sign shall be given to it except the sign of the prophet Jonah." Matthew repeats this (cf. Mt 16:4) where Mark has the unqualified rejection of the demand.

What the sign of Jonah means is explained in Matthew as follows (12:40): "For as Jonah was three days and three nights in the belly of the whale, so will the Son of man be three days and three nights in the heart of the earth." Instead of this, Luke says, "For as Jonah became a sign to the men of Nineveh, so will the Son of man be to this generation." A statement in both Gospels interprets this: the men of Nineveh, who repented when Jonah preached to them, will arise at the judgment and condemn the generation that has not repented at the preaching of Jesus. So the queen of Sheba, who came from afar to learn wisdom from Solomon, will condemn this generation. Matthew's first explanation is clearly not what Jesus intended but an insertion by a copyist or perhaps a reader.

Explaining the historical allusions Jesus says, "something greater than Jonah is here"; and "something greater than Solomon is here." (The Greek word for "greater" is in the neuter gender.) The "something greater" must be the manifestation of God's kingdom. The demand for a sign was needless and futile, because there were abundant signs already to convince and convict those who observed them.

Following this passage in Matthew, and almost immediately preceding it in Luke, is a paragraph (Mt 12:43-45; Lk 11:24-26) about what may happen when a demon that has been expelled from a man finds no other place to rest and comes back to his victim. If he finds his former home unoccupied, he will bring seven other demons to live there with him, and the possessed man's condition will be worse than before. The general meaning is plain: to get rid of evil influences—physical, mental, or spiritual—is not enough if their place is not filled with good influences.

In Mark the "Beelzebul controversy" fills the interval between the undertaking of Jesus' friends or relatives to seize him (3:21) and the arrival of his mother and brothers, with which Matthew now rejoins Mark's order (Mk 3:31-35; Mt 12:46-50; Lk 8:19-21). (Luke puts the coming of the family sometime before the debate about Beelzebul.)

Some think that the word "brothers" here means not sons of Mary but simply relatives. A cousin or even a more distant kinsman might be called a brother in Hebrew or Aramaic; but there is no reason to suppose that these brothers were not younger sons of Joseph and Mary. Later in Mark the people of Nazareth name the four brothers of Jesus and mention his sisters (Mk 6:3; cf. Mt 13:55).

CHAPTER VII

TEACHING BY PARABLES

The visit of Jesus' mother and brothers is followed in Mark and Matthew by a group of parables (Mk 4:1-34; Mt 13:1-52; Lk 8:4-18; 13:18-21), which with some additions constitutes Matthew's third discourse. Luke gives some of the same material earlier and some of it later in his "special section." The series begins with Jesus getting into a boat and speaking to the crowd on the shore (Mk 4:1; cf. 3:19). Mark says, "Again he began to teach beside the sea"; but in chapter 3 Jesus went to a house, and there has been no indication meanwhile of his leaving it. Matthew says: "That same day Jesus went out of the house and sat beside the sea" (13:1).

"And he taught them many things in parables" (Mk 4:2; Mt 13:3; cf. Lk 8:4). The distinction between parables and sayings cannot be drawn sharply. The Greek noun *parabolē* means simply a comparison. Once the KJV so renders it (Mk 4:30). In another place (Lk 4:23) our English versions translate it "proverb." It does not necessarily refer to a story, but is applied also to comparisons in the form of general statements.

Jesus' parables, however, are often brief narratives. Usually the story as a whole has one point. Special meanings in details are not intended. A story in which each character, place, or act stands for something is not a parable but an allegory. Jesus' parables are not allegories, though a few of them have significant details.

The parable of the sower (Mk 4:3-9; Mt 13:3-9) verges on allegory. The crop varies according to the kind of ground on which the seed falls. I have seen a Palestinian farmer sowing seed by hand on just such variegated ground as this story envisages. Jesus' parables reflect the everyday life of his country, which until recently had hardly changed from what it was in his day.

When the crowd had gone after hearing this parable, the disciples questioned Jesus about it (Mk 4:10-12; Mt 13:10-15; Lk 8:9-10). According to Matthew they asked, "Why do you speak to them in parables?" Such a question was actually unnecessary for Jesus' hearers or the disciples. There was nothing strange or new in his use of stories. The great Jewish teachers of his time used such stories much as he did. Experienced speakers know that there is no better way to make a point than to use an apt illustration, and a good story that fits the point is the most effective kind of illustration.

There is a strong reaction at present against this understanding of the parables on the ground that as "aesthetic objects" they are self-sufficient. The contention is not that they are art for art's sake, to be enjoyed with no thought of meaning, but that their meaning is to be found in their own form and content, not in anything outside of themselves. This seems fair enough; the applications of the principle that are offered, however, are generalizations that strangely resemble the "lessons" drawn from Scripture by an old-fashioned Sunday school teacher. At the same time they are sometimes so involved, not to say far-fetched, that one cannot imagine Jesus expecting his hearers to see them. In fact, it is explicitly stated that these stories mean more than Jesus meant by them.

Jesus' reply to the disciples, indeed, as the Gospels report it (Mk 4:11; Mt 13:11; Lk 8:10), suggests that the parables were intended not to elucidate but to obscure the truth. The gospel, it seems, is a mystery that the parables convey to the initiated without giving it away to the crowd. This is utterly contrary to the essential nature and obvious purpose of Jesus' parables. The language of the whole verse recalls Isaiah 6:9-10, where the prophet's mission seems to be represented as preventing Israel from being converted and healed. In Matthew, Jesus says explicitly, "With them indeed is fulfilled the prophecy of Isaiah which says"—and then quotes the two verses (13:14-15).

That Jesus spoke of the gospel of the kingdom as a mystery is not impossible. The Greek noun appears frequently in the epistles and in Revelation (Rom 11:25; 16:25; Eph 1:9; 3:9; Rev 1:20; 10:7; 17:5, 7), usually with reference to a secret purpose of God that has now been revealed. The Septuagint uses this word six times in Daniel 2 (vv 27-30, 47) to translate an Aramaic noun that Jesus could have used. It appears often in the Dead Sea Scrolls. The idea of a mystery was therefore familiar to the Jews of Jesus' day. The Greek word, however, appears nowhere else in the Gospels. That, together with the fact that it is associated with an idea that we can hardly attribute to Jesus, makes the authenticity of the whole passage doubtful.

Possibly, however, it originally had quite a different meaning, not incompatible with Jesus' purpose and attitude. What Jesus said may have been misunderstood by the Greek translator. Mark says that, "for those outside," parables are used "so that they may indeed see but not perceive," etc. (4:12). Luke too says "so that seeing they may not see," etc. (8:10). Matthew, however, says "because seeing they do not see," and so on (13:13), that is, Jesus used parables not to prevent people from understanding but because they did not understand. His reply to the disciples' question then amounted to this: "God has given you the ability to understand the secret of his kingdom; but these poor people cannot comprehend it unless it is put in the simplest possible form. I use stories to make things clear to them."

The Aramaic language expresses purpose and cause by the same conjunction, which also serves as a relative pronoun. The same words may mean "so that they may not understand," "because they do not understand," or "who do not understand." Mark and Luke have taken the conjunction in one sense, Matthew in another. Either rendering is literally correct, but Matthew's expresses the meaning Jesus probably intended.

Matthew's quotation of Isaiah makes the people's lack of understanding a matter of fact rather than purpose (Is 6:10). This is not actually what the Hebrew text says. What is really meant, however, is surely not that Isaiah's mission was to prevent repentance and healing. His bitterly ironical language reflects what proved to be the actual result of his preaching.

Mark almost refutes his own theory when he says at the end of his group of parables (4:33), "With many such parables he spoke the word to them as they were able to hear it." His misconception, however, leads him to add (v 34), "he did not speak to them without a parable, but privately to his own disciples he explained everything." The parables are thus regarded as riddles. Matthew also says, "Indeed he said nothing to them without a parable," but instead of mentioning private explanations to the disciples he gives his own view of Jesus' use of parables (13:34-35).

At this point Matthew introduces a saying that Luke gives much later (Mt 13:16-17; Lk 10:23-24). It follows naturally the quotation from Isaiah. "But blessed are your eyes," Jesus says, "for they see, and your ears, for they hear." Jesus goes on to remind the disciples that there have been many prophets and wise men (prophets and kings, Luke says) who desired to see what the disciples are seeing and to hear what they are hearing, but did not have that privilege. Obviously the reminder is intended to evoke not pride but humble gratitude.

Next in all the Synoptic Gospels there is an interpretation of the parable of the sower (Mk 4:13-20; Mt 13:18-23; Lk 8:11-15), explaining it as a picture of four different kinds of people who respond to the gospel in different ways. Those in the first group do not take it in at all; therefore Satan immediately snatches it away. Hearers of the second kind receive the word gladly but fall away as soon as the going gets hard. The third group consists of those who accept it but allow it to be overgrown and choked out by the concerns of everyday living. Only the hearers of the fourth kind—those who receive and retain the word—are fruitful.

Commentators have long questioned the authenticity and accuracy of this explanation, holding that it converts the parable into an allegory and changes its meaning to one relevant for the church in later generations. After accepting this argument for many years, I now find it unconvincing. The interpretation does describe the situation of the later church, and indeed of all generations of church history; but it describes also the situation that confronted Jesus himself.

The enthusiasm of the great crowds who heard him gladly was not shared by all his hearers, nor did it last long in all those who felt it. He faced a general failure of his own people to believe his proclamation and repent. The parable of the sower was his answer to questions that must have seemed like the voice of Satan saying, "If you are the Son of God." He could sow the seed, but he could not make it take root in poor soil or protect it from the things that made people unable or unwilling to receive it and nourish it to maturity.

121

It is true that a typical parable has just one point, to which everything else is subordinate. Scholars who insist that this must always be so take the first three kinds of soil together as indicating the obstacles encountered by the gospel. The abundant crop from the good soil then signifies that the word will prevail and accomplish its purpose (cf. Is 55:11), and this is taken to be the only meaning intended by Jesus. If that explanation is correct, the story itself was much expanded in the course of its transmission. A simpler assumption is that here, as in the parable of the prodigal son, Jesus used a more elaborate story than usual to convey a more elaborate idea. The moral, both for the disciples and for Jesus himself, was, ''Don't be discouraged; this is what we have to expect, but the good soil will produce a great harvest.''

After the interpretation of this parable, Mark and Luke have the saying used by Matthew in the Sermon on the Mount about putting a lamp under a bushel or a bed (Mt 5:15; Mk 4:21; Lk 8:16), followed by the statement, ''For there is nothing hid, except to be made manifest; nor is anything secret, except to come to light'' (Mk 4:22; Lk 8:17). Matthew and Luke also have this in another context (Mt 10:26; Lk 12:2). For Mark's ''except to be made manifest'' and ''except to come to light,'' Luke has here ''that will not be revealed'' and ''that will not be known.'' This is probably another reflection of the ambiguous Aramaic word that serves both as a conjunction and as a relative pronoun. Mark understands the saying to mean that anything now hidden will be made known sooner or later, but perhaps what Jesus meant was that everything that had hitherto been hidden would be revealed now.

Mark continues (Mk 4:24; Lk 8:18), ''And he said to them, 'Take heed what you hear.''' Matthew omits this; in Luke it becomes, ''Take heed then how you hear.'' The insertion of ''then'' and the change from ''what'' to ''how'' suggest that since everything secret will come to light, listening carefully to obscure sayings will be rewarded. Mark and Luke give here a saying that Matthew has already used (Mk 4:25; Lk 8:18; Mt 13:12): ''For to him who has will more be given; and from him who has not, even what he has will be taken away'' (Luke reads, ''even what he thinks that he has'').

122

Mark's second and third parables (4:26, 30) are introduced by
the words, "And he said," as though Jesus was still speaking to
the disciples; but what follows these parables (vv 33-34) shows
that they were delivered to the people. Matthew says explicitly
(13:34), "All this Jesus said to the crowds." The first of the two,
the parable of the seed that grows of itself (Mk 4:26-29), is the
only one recorded by Mark alone. A common interpretation of it
exemplifies the error of seeing meanings in details. The words,
"first the blade, then the ear, then the full grain in the ear," are
thought to indicate a gradual extension of the kingdom of God in
the world. The point of the parable, however, is that while man
sows the seed and reaps the harvest, the growth comes by a
process for which he can only wait. For those who look for the
kingdom of God, this is a word of both encouragement and
warning: God's power, not yours, will accomplish his will. The
kingdom is not yours but his.

Where Mark has this parable, Matthew gives the parable of the
weeds (KJV, tares), the first of five in this chapter that are not
found in Mark or Luke (Mt 13:24-30). The plant referred to is
more exactly darnel (so JB, NEB), which grows wild in wheat
fields and resembles wheat in appearance. To this day in Palestine
women and children go through the wheat fields before harvest
and pick it out by hand. In the parable, the owner of the field has
to contend not only with what has grown naturally. An enemy has
come by night and sowed darnel so thickly that it cannot be
weeded out without destroying the wheat. To save his crop the
owner must let grain and weeds grow together and have his
servants sort them out after the harvest. The meaning of this must
be considered together with the parable of the dragnet (Mt
13:47-48), which comes a little later.

Mark's third parable, the story of the mustard seed, is
somewhat condensed in the other Gospels (Mk 4:30-32; Mt
13:31-32; Lk 13:18-19). Its subject is the contrast between a small
beginning and a great consummation. Elsewhere (Mt 17:20; Lk
17:6) Jesus speaks of "faith as a grain of mustard seed,"
obviously meaning "even a tiny bit of faith." The wild mustard
of Palestine, which is said to be abundant beside the Sea of

Galilee, has a minute seed but grows to almost twice the height of a man.

This parable too has suffered from over-interpretation. Birds in the branches of a tree, for example, are used in rabbinic literature as a symbol of Gentiles who in the last days will seek shelter in the shade of Israel. Some scholars have therefore seen in this parable a reference to the conversion of the Gentiles. The birds here, however, are simply a part of the picture, emphasizing the size of the bush.

Other expositors are guilty of under-interpretation. They hold that neither the beginning of the growth nor the process itself is compared with the kingdom, but only the outcome. The contrast between the small seed and the large bush only points up the greatness of the result. But the tiny seed belongs to the comparison also. Not merely the greatness of the end, but the contrast between it and the small beginning, is the point of the parable.

In what sense can God's kingdom be said to have a beginning as small as a mustard seed by comparison with its glorious consummation? If the kingdom can be taken here to mean the community of subjects of the heavenly King, then the contrast may be between the little band of disciples and the vast host expected to share in the final redemption. Possibly Matthew understood the parable in this sense. More in accord, however, with what other evidence indicates as Jesus' conception of the kingdom of God (cf. Mt 12:28; Lk 11:20; 17:21) is the view that the seed represents the power of God already manifesting itself by the casting out of demons, and the bush is its ultimate triumph.

In Matthew and Luke this story is followed by the parable of the leaven (Mt 13:33; Lk 13:20-21), which Mark does not have at all. No explanation of this parable is offered by either evangelist. The kingdom is said to resemble "leaven which a woman took and hid in three measures of flour, till it was all leavened." No significance need be sought in the amount of flour used, though it is more than a woman would ordinarily use for a batch of bread. The verb "hid" is unexpected in this connection. It suggests the invisible, mysterious working of the yeast. Having leavened her dough, the housewife has only to wait until the fermentation is complete.

In the enthusiasm of the early days of the "social gospel" it was natural to take these two parables as referring to a gradual transformation of all social relations and institutions according to the will of God. This was a part of the optimistic idea of natural and inevitable progress, an expectation that was rudely shattered by the world wars of the twentieth century. Like the parables of the sower and the seed growing of itself, the parables of the mustard seed and the leaven were certainly not intended to represent a process of social reform. That interpretation, however, was not entirely mistaken, as is often supposed in the disillusioned mood of our day. Jesus did teach that the royal power of God was already at work and that ultimately it would be manifest to all the world in a final victory of God over Satan. But this was not something that men could build or establish; it was the kingdom of God.

Mark's concluding sentence (4:33-34) has already been noted. Matthew condenses it and characteristically appends a reference to prophecy (13:34-35). In this instance what Matthew says was "spoken by the prophet" is from one of the Psalms (78:2).

Instead of Mark's brief statement that Jesus explained everything privately to his disciples, Matthew says that Jesus "left the crowds and went into the house," and the disciples asked him to explain the parable of the weeds (13:36). He responded with an elaborate interpretation that makes the parable virtually an allegory (vv 37-43). It must be admitted that the story lends itself easily to such treatment. But do the parable and the explanation belong together? If Jesus told this story, did he give this interpretation of it? The parable is concerned with the kingdom of heaven, and in the explanation the good seed is said to represent "the sons of the kingdom," who will shine "in the kingdom of their Father." Yet the owner of the field, who sows the good seed, is the Son of man: and he, not the Father, will send "his angels" to reap the harvest and gather the weeds out of "his kingdom."

The idea of the kingdom of the Son of man occurs elsewhere in Matthew; his glorious throne is mentioned twice, and he is twice called "the King" (Mt 16:28; 19:28; 25:31, 34, 40). Other expressions and ideas that are peculiar to Matthew, or to his special source, appear in the explanation of the parable. This does not prove that they cannot have come from Jesus himself; but the fact that Matthew alone records them, and does so repeatedly, at least raises the question whether they represent the views and interests of some group in the church rather than the words and thinking of Jesus.

The same misgivings are aroused by the parable of the dragnet (Mt 13:47-48), also reported only by Matthew. Here the place of the field is taken by "a net which was thrown into the sea and gathered fish of every kind," both good and bad. When it was full, it was drawn ashore and the bad fish were sorted out and thrown away. This time the interpretation immediately follows the parable (vv 49-50), which again is explained as referring to the separation of the righteous and the wicked at the final judgment. A remarkable implication is that the wicked who are to be weeded out are now in the kingdom. To be sure, it is the kingdom of the Son of man (v 41) that is to be rid of "all causes of sin and all evildoers," but it is the kingdom of heaven that is said to be like the man who sowed good seed and the net that gathered both good and bad fish. One is reminded of the references to persons who are least in the kingdom of heaven (Mt 5:19; 11:11; Lk 7:28).

These explanations of the twin parables understand the kingdom of heaven to mean the Christian church, not as an institution but as the community of those who have accepted the royal authority of God and devoted themselves to doing his will as Jesus has revealed it. In this community there are degrees of greater and less; there are even "causes of sin and evildoers." What to do with such unworthy members of the fellowship must have become a problem very early. That it was a matter of special concern to Matthew is evident in other places also (Mt 22:11-14; 16:17-19; 18:15-18). Eventually a system of church discipline was developed, including excommunication. As interpreted by Matthew, these parables signify that it is safer and wiser to leave the sorting out of good and bad for the angels to accomplish at the last judgment. This surely presupposes a more developed community than existed during Jesus' lifetime.

126

Is there then any way to interpret these parables that fits better the situation during his ministry? No feature of that situation is better attested or more characteristic than the scandal caused by his free association with tax collectors and sinners. Why did he not exclude from his fellowship such unhallowed companions and gather about him a select, exclusive band of pure and dedicated souls, as the Pharisees and the Essenes did? If we may take the parables of the weeds and the dragnet as Jesus' answer to such questions, they mean something like this: That is not the way God governs his world. He lets good and evil men live in it together, and it is not for us to judge and try to separate them. He will attend to that when the time comes. This goes with what I have proposed as the meaning of the parable of the sower. Just as we cannot restrict our sowing to what we judge to be good soil, or expect all that we sow to be productive, so while the crop is growing we must not try to separate the grain and the weeds.

So interpreted, these parables reveal another facet of what Jesus meant by the kingdom of God. It is the divine administration of the universe, the way God rules his creation. As Samuel told the people of Israel (1 Sam 10:25 KJV), "the manner of the kingdom," Jesus shows by the parables of the kingdom how God runs the world, and what a difference it will make when his sovereign authority is fully established. Thus the parables, like the sayings, show how to be acceptable citizens of God's kingdom, both now and in the coming age.

Three times in his explanations of these two parables Matthew uses an expression that occurs two more times in his Gospel and only once anywhere else in the New Testament (Mt 13:39-40, 49; cf. 24:3; 28:20; Heb 9:26). It is the expression translated "the end of the world" in the KJV, "the close of the age" in the RSV. The Greek word translated "age" (KJV "world") and the adjective derived from it (usually translated "eternal") are both used often in the New Testament in various connections. Back of them is a Hebrew word that appears often in the rabbinic literature, especially in the expression "this age," meaning the present, final period of world history, and "the coming age," meaning the new, eternal order that will follow the resurrection of the dead and the end of "this age."

That Jesus used this expression is inherently probable, even if the particular passages in which Matthew uses it were not spoken by Jesus. The conception of history as a succession of eras leading to a final denouement, in which the purpose of creation will be realized, is especially characteristic of the "apocalyptic" point of view represented by the visions of Daniel and Revelation, as in many Jewish compositions just before and during the New Testament period.

Four other distinctively Matthaean expressions appear in the explanations of the parables of the weeds and the dragnet: "the sons of the kingdom"; "the sons of the evil one"; "the furnace of fire"; and "there men will weep and gnash their teeth." The Semitic idiom, "sons of the kingdom," has been encountered already in the story of the centurion's servant (Mt 8:12; cf. Lk 13:28). The term "furnace of fire" recalls the "burning fiery furnace" of Daniel 3 (vv 6-26, 8 times). Whether it comes from Matthew or from Jesus himself, the echo of Daniel is probably intentional. Jesus made use of the book of Daniel elsewhere in his teaching. The statement, "there men will weep and gnash their teeth," occurs at four other points in Matthew (8:12; 22:13; 24:51; 25:30). The first of these has a parallel in Luke (13:28).

Four more parables reported by Matthew alone conclude his third discourse (Mt 13:44-52; cf. 6:33; Lk 12:31). All are brief and given without explanation. The parables of the treasure found in a field and the precious pearl go together and have the same meaning: the kingdom of heaven is worth the sacrifice of everything else a man may have. Efforts to find other meanings in these simple little stories seem to me uncalled for and misleading.

The last parable in Matthew's series (13:52) is a very brief and obscure one comparing "every scribe who has been trained for the kingdom of heaven" to "a householder who brings out of his treasures what is new and what is old." The verb translated "trained" is from the same root as the noun translated "disciple." Being trained or educated for the kingdom of heaven might therefore mean being trained for discipleship; but it is hard to think of any sense in which Jesus' disciples would be called scribes.

Some scholars take the Greek word to mean "made a

128

disciple." It is, in fact, a form of the verb so translated elsewhere. Thus instead of "trained for the kingdom of heaven," the meaning is "made a disciple of the kingdom of heaven" (cf. 28:19). The scribe is then a Jewish scribe who has become one of Jesus' disciples. The new and old treasures are his legal learning and the new teaching of the gospel. There are two other sayings in which a scribe is mentioned favorably (Mt 8:19; cf. Lk 9:57; Mk 12:28-34; Mt 22:35; Lk 10:25). The commendation of a scribe who became a disciple of the kingdom of heaven may therefore well be an authentic expression of Jesus' respect for at least some of the scribes.

CHAPTER VIII

THE FOURTH PART OF THE GALILEAN MINISTRY

The end of Matthew's third discourse (Mt 13:53) is marked by the usual formula: "And when Jesus had finished these parables, he went away from there." Mark's series of parables ends with the parable of the mustard seed and the statement that Jesus always used parables in speaking to the people. Mark's narrative then continues (4:35-36). "On that day, when evening had come, he said to them, 'Let us go across to the other side.' And leaving the crowd, they took him with them in the boat, just as he was."

This introduces a series of miracles beginning with the second nature miracle in the Synoptic Gospels, the stilling of a storm on the Sea of Galilee (Mk 4:37-41; Mt 8:23-27; Lk 8:22-25). The first was the miraculous catch of fish narrated by Luke (Lk 5:1-11). This time all three evangelists report the miracle. Luke makes a new beginning, breaking the connection with the teaching by parables: "One day he got into a boat with his disciples." Matthew puts the stilling of the storm much earlier, first inserting, as already noted, two brief items given by Luke considerably later (Mt 8:18-22; Lk 9:57-60), and continuing as though there had been no interruption, "And when he got into the boat, the disciples followed him" (Mt 8:23).

From here on the account proceeds in the three Gospels with only minor differences. The storm rose suddenly, as storms do on hill-encircled lakes. Jesus was asleep when it struck the boat. The frightened disciples woke him and complained of his apparent indifference; but he chided them for their lack of faith and rebuked the sea, "and there was a great calm." Matthew condenses Mark's account slightly, and Luke a little more; yet each also adds details and emphases of his own.

From a modern point of view we can only regard such a story as a devout legend, possibly but not necessarily having some basis in events about which it is futile to speculate. If a violent storm came up when Jesus and the disciples were on the lake and ceased as suddenly as it began, there would be nothing extraordinary in that.

There would also be no particular reason for telling the story. Its point is expressed in the wondering words of the disciples, "Who then is this, that even wind and sea obey him?"

The second miracle in Mark's series (Mk 5:1-20; Mt 8:28-34; Lk 8:26-39) occurred when Jesus and the disciples reached the eastern shore, just where is not clear. The Greek manuscripts vary so widely in the names they give for the place that it is impossible to establish even what was the original reading in any of the Gospels. The evangelists agree that the place was on the eastern side of the Sea of Galilee and not far from the shore. For convenience we may speak of the Gadarene demonaic without implying a conclusion concerning the name.

The healing of the demoniac could almost be classified as a nature miracle, because other creatures than man are involved. What can we make of the transfer of demons from a man into a herd of swine, which thereupon rushed down the bank into the sea and perished? Again it is easy to rationalize and spoil the story. It has been suggested, for example, that the animals, feeding nearby, were stampeded by the wild cries of the lunatic. If so, the marvel of the healing would still remain.

Mark's narrative is again more full and detailed than those of Matthew and Luke, with many vivid touches. Especially graphic is Mark's description of the man's uncontrollable violence. The picture of him after he was healed, "sitting there, clothed and in his right mind," is so effective that the expression has become proverbial. The urgent request of the people that Jesus leave their neighborhood is true to human nature. They did not mind his healing the afflicted, but his presence endangered their livestock. A curious feature of Matthew's story is that there are two demoniacs, just as later he twice has two blind men (cf. Mt 9:27; 20:30). Mark's statement that the man was possessed by not one but many demons, who gave their name as Legion, is omitted by Matthew.

The three accounts agree that the demons addressed Jesus as the Son of God (Mark and Luke say "Son of the Most High God"). This time the healed demoniac was not charged to tell no one of his cure, but was sent home with instructions to tell his friends what God had done for him. "And he went away and began to proclaim in the Decapolis how much Jesus had done for him; and all men marveled'' (Mk 5:18-20; Lk 8:38-39).

Returning to the western side of the lake, Jesus found a great crowd waiting for him. The event now related, the raising of Jairus' daughter (Mk 5:21-24, 35-43; Mt 9:18-19, 23-26; Lk 8:40-42, 49-50), is one of only two instances in the Synoptic Gospels of bringing a dead person back to life. The other is the story of the widow's son at Nain (Lk 7:11-17).

Jairus is said by Mark and Luke to have been a ruler of the synagogue, that is, the official head of a congregation. Matthew calls him only a ruler. Falling at Jesus' feet, Jairus begged him to come and heal his little daughter, who was at the point of death. (In Matthew the father says, ''My daughter has just died''; but according to Mark and Luke it was only when they were on the way that people came from the ruler's house and told him the child was dead.) Telling Jairus not to be afraid, and taking with him only Peter, James, and John, Jesus went on to the house and entered it with the child's parents.

They found the house filled with mourners, but Jesus silenced them all and declared that the child was sleeping. Possibly she had fallen into a coma, and Jesus detected signs of life that the parents and friends had not perceived. Or is this only an example of the rationalizing I have condemned? As the story is told, Jesus pronounced the child alive before going into the room where she lay. His statement was received with scornful laughter; but he ''put them all outside,'' went in, took the child's hand, and said to her, ''Little girl, I say to you, arise.'' Mark preserves the Aramaic words spoken by Jesus, with their Greek translation, as he does on several occasions (Mk 5:41; cf. 3:17; 7:11, 34; 14:36; 15:34). ''And immediately the girl got up and walked.'' Mark adds that she was twelve years old. Jesus strictly charged the parents not to tell what he had done, but Matthew says that the report ''went through all that district.'' Mark ends his account on a human note: Jesus ''told them to give her something to eat.''

Within the framework of this miracle the story of a woman who had suffered a hemorrhage for twelve years is told (Mk 5:25-34; Mt 9:20-22; Lk 8:43-48). Again the vividness of Mark's account is notable. It is crushed into a few sentences by Matthew; Luke changes it only slightly, omitting very little. Many long-suffering invalids can appreciate Mark's statement that the poor woman "had suffered much under many physicians, and had spent all that she had, and was no better but rather grew worse." Believing that if she could even touch Jesus' clothing she would be healed, she made her way through the crowd, touched his robe, and at once knew that she was cured. Jesus asked who had touched him, and the grateful woman confessed that it was she. Addressing her in Semitic fashion as "Daughter," Jesus assured her that her faith had healed her.

After the raising of Jairus' daughter, Matthew has a miracle reported only by him (Mt 9:27-31). Two blind men, he says, followed Jesus even into a house, crying, "Have mercy on us, Son of David." Asked if they believed that he could heal them, they said they did. He then touched their eyes and said, "According to your faith be it done to you." Like the leper and others, instead of obeying Jesus' command to keep the miracle secret, these men too "spread his fame through all that district." This is one of Matthew's "doublets," duplicating a similar incident that comes later (cf. 20:29-34; Mk 10:46-52; Lk 18:35-43).

In Mark the story of Jairus' daughter is followed by Jesus' rejection by his former neighbors at Nazareth (Mk 6:1-6; Mt 13:53-58). Matthew gives substantially the same account after his third discourse. Nazareth is not actually named here, but "his own country" undoubtedly refers to it. Jesus went to the synagogue, and, like the people of Capernaum, the people of Nazareth were astonished at his teaching. They had known him as a boy and a young man, and his family was still living among them. "And they took offense at him," with the result that Jesus "could do no mighty work there, except that he laid his hands upon a few sick people and healed them. And he marveled because of their unbelief." Once more the close connection between faith and healing is brought out.

Luke's very different report of the rejection at Nazareth (Lk 4:16-30) immediately follows Jesus' temptation in the wilderness, when he first returned to Galilee. Coming to Nazareth, Luke says, Jesus went to the synagogue on the Sabbath and "stood up to read''; and, being given a scroll of the book of Isaiah, he opened it at the beginning of chapter 61 and read the first verse and part of the second. A comparison of these verses as Luke quotes them with the Hebrew text of Isaiah and the Septuagint is instructive. Evidently Luke neither copied from the Septuagint nor made a fresh translation of his own. He probably quoted from memory a passage very familiar to him in the Greek. In the second verse, by intention or accident, he inserted a line from Isaiah 58:6.

Luke presents a vivid picture of Jesus rolling up the scroll, handing it to the attendant, and sitting down to speak, with the eyes of the congregation fixed on him. He began by saying, "Today this scripture has been fulfilled in your hearing." The portion he had read begins, "The Spirit of the Lord is upon me, because he has anointed me. . . ." This and other passages in Isaiah are echoed in Jesus' reply to the disciples of John the Baptist (Mt 11:2-6; Lk 7:18-23), who asked, "Are you he who is to come?" There the reference is presumably to the Messiah, whose coming John had foretold. Here what follows shows that the word "anointed" refers to a prophet.

Such references afford a clue to Jesus' conception of his mission. It was not that of a conqueror or monarch, but the prophetic and healing ministry of the servant of the Lord. Whatever historical value Luke's narrative may have, if Jesus thought of himself as Messiah in any sense it was probably as an anointed prophet rather than a king, though there are references to his future kingdom that we shall have to examine.

Up to this point, Luke says, "all spoke well of him, and wondered at the gracious words which proceeded out of his mouth." Then Jesus said, "Doubtless you will quote to me this proverb, 'Physician, heal yourself; what we have heard you did at Capernaum, do here also in your own country.'" (We have seen that Luke here betrays the fact that he has moved the incident forward.) Jesus added, "Truly, I say to you, no prophet is acceptable in his own country." Mark and Matthew also quote this in connection with the visit to Nazareth (cf. Mk 6:4; Mt 13:57). In Luke "his own country" is assumed to mean Israel, and examples from the stories of Elijah and Elisha are cited to show that Gentiles may receive greater favor than the chosen

134

people. At this the mood of the congregation changed. Forcibly ejecting Jesus from the synagogue, they took him "to the brow of the hill on which their city was built," intending to throw him down into the valley. "But passing through the midst of them he went away" (4:29-30).

How much of this is authentic history, how much legend, and how much the creation of Luke's own imagination it is impossible to tell. Jesus may have referred to the Phoenician widow and the Syrian leper on this or some other occasion, but the evangelization of the Gentiles was one of Luke's major interests. The inappropriate reference to Capernaum (Lk 4:23) indicates that he did not compose the account for this place. Probably he found it in his source or received it by tradition and merely transferred it to its present position, touching it up a little for his purpose.

Mark proceeds with a brief account of continued teaching in the villages and the mission of the twelve disciples (6:7-13), which Matthew uses as the occasion of his second discourse (10:1-42). Giving them authority over unclean spirits, Jesus instructed the twelve to travel without provisions or equipment, to lodge in the same house throughout their stay in each village, and to shake the dust from their feet as a testimony when they left any place that would not receive them or listen to them. As they went, Mark says, they "preached that men should repent."

According to both Mark and Luke, the cures accomplished by his emissaries so enhanced the fame of Jesus that a rumor that John the Baptist had risen from the dead spread abroad and came to the ears of King Herod Antipas (Mk 6:14-16; Lk 9:7-9). Matthew puts this directly after Jesus' rejection at Nazareth (14:1-2), having already told of the mission of the twelve. Luke has previously reported John's imprisonment (3:19) and only alludes to his death. Mark and Matthew record both to explain the rumor that John had risen (Mk 6:17-29; Mt 14:3-12). For Mark the recital of these events fills the interval between the departure of the twelve and their return.

Mark and Luke now proceed to what happened after the disciples came back (Mk 6:30-34; Lk 9:10-11; Mt 14:13-14). Matthew connects this with the death of John. To the statement that John's disciples buried his body he adds, "and they went and told Jesus," and continues, "Now when Jesus heard this, he withdrew from there in a boat to a lonely place apart." Mark says when the twelve returned and told Jesus what they had done, he took them "in the boat to a lonely place by themselves." Luke identifies the place to which Jesus took them as "a city called Bethsaida."

As on other occasions, it proved impossible to escape the crowds. Again Mark tells the story more fully and vividly than Matthew or Luke. Apparently Jesus and the disciples crossed a corner or bay of the lake to reach their destination. For the people on the shore, the distance was therefore greater; but they could move more rapidly and could see where the boat was going. Thus they arrived ahead of Jesus and the disciples; but although his attempt to find solitude had failed, "he had compassion on them, because they were like sheep without a shepherd; and he began to teach them many things" (Mk 6:34; Mt 14:14; cf. 9:36; Lk 9:11). Matthew and Luke mention also healing.

This leads to another "nature miracle," the feeding of the five thousand (Mk 6:35-44; Mt 14:15-21; Lk 9:12-17; Jn 6:1-13). This miracle and the one that follows it are the only ones reported both in the Synoptic Gospels and in John. When evening came, the disciples reminded Jesus that it was a "lonely place," with no shops or farms where the people might get food. Instead of sending the crowd away, however, Jesus told the disciples to feed them. They protested that even if they went into town and bought food for such a throng, it would cost two hundred denarii, nearly a year's wages then, though its equivalent now would buy very little. Jesus asked how much food they had with them. They said five loaves of bread and two fish. (The loaves would be something like the round flat loaves still used in Palestine.) With them, we are told, Jesus fed the multitude, and twelve basketfuls of pieces were left over.

In Mark and Matthew, and also in John, the feeding of the five thousand is followed by another nature miracle, Jesus' walking on the water (Mk 6:45-52; Mt 14:22-33; Jn 6:15-21). John says that Jesus did not set out in the boat with the disciples but withdrew to the hills because the people wanted to make him their king. According to Mark and Matthew, he sent the disciples ahead of him by boat while he dismissed the people and then retired to the hills to pray. Mark says that the disciples were sent "to the other side, to Bethsaida," according to Luke the place where the five thousand were fed (Mk 6:45; cf Lk 9:10). The walking on the sea is omitted entirely by Luke; in fact everything in Mark from 6:45 to 8:26 is passed over. This is commonly called Luke's "great omission."

The feeding of the multitude had taken place in the evening; therefore the crossing of the lake was made by night. Rowing against the wind, the disciples were making little headway, when in the fourth watch (*i.e.,* 3:00–6:00 A.M.) they saw what they thought was a ghost walking on the water. They cried out in terror, but it was Jesus himself. He reassured them and told them not to be afraid. Matthew alone tells here of Peter's impetuous attempt to go to Jesus on the water (14:28-31). Frightened by the wind, he began to sink and cried out, "Lord, save me." but Jesus took him by the hand and said, "O man of little faith, why did you doubt?"

It is a lovely little story, whatever we may think of its historical basis, and it lends itself readily to spiritual applications. Perhaps with the feeding of the multitude and the walking on the sea the spiritual lesson came first, and the story grew out of it as a parable or allegory.

Mark and Matthew end the story quite differently. Mark says, "And they were utterly astounded, for they did not understand about the loaves, but their hearts were hardened." The hardness of the disciples' hearts, or, as it may seem to us, their incredible stupidity, appears also in other places, especially in Mark. A strong case has been made recently for a theory that sees it as an essential element in the occasion and purpose of Mark's Gospel. The disciples, it is argued, were used by the evangelist to represent a popular doctrine that ignored the inevitability and necessity of suffering. Matthew's report of the disciples' reaction is more favorable: "And those in the boat worshiped him, saying, 'Truly you are the Son of God.'" If Mark has overstressed the obtuseness of the disciples, one gets the impression that Matthew exaggerates their piety and orthodoxy.

In addition to the two nature miracles, Mark and Matthew tell

137

of many cures after Jesus and the disciples reached the other side of the lake (Mk 6:53-56; Mt 14:34-36). Although Mark has said that the disciples set out for Bethsaida, both he and Matthew now say that they landed at Gennesaret. Once in Luke (5:1) the Sea of Galilee is called the Lake of Gennesaret. The name designates properly a plain on the northwest shore of the lake. This must be what is meant here.

Again people brought their sick to Jesus, and many were healed by touching the fringe of his mantle. All was not well, however. Mark and Matthew tell next of a discussion with Pharisees and scribes from Jerusalem (Mk 7:1-23; Mt 15:1-20). They had observed that some of the disciples were not washing their hands before eating.

As in previous incidents, it is evident that the disciples were not observing the oral law (Mk 2:18-22 and parallels; vv 23-28 and parallels). The Pharisees asked Jesus why this was so. His reply goes to the very heart of his teaching about moral and ritual requirements. The tradition in question here was a matter of the distinction between clean and unclean, which is prominent both in the Old Testament and in the oral law. It was a matter not of hygiene but of ritual purity. Jesus, at least by implication, abolished at one stroke this part of the law.

First (as Mark tells it) he charged his questioners with hypocrisy (7:7), quoting a verse from Isaiah (29:13) that speaks of people who honor God with their lips but not with their hearts, "teaching as doctrines the precepts of men." The word "doctrines" is unfortunate here, because it suggests beliefs rather than regulations for conduct or worship (TEV, God's rules). The point of the text is that the piety of the hypocrites is merely the performance of what they have been taught, a set of man-made rules.

The basic question at issue between the Pharisees and Jesus was how to know what was the will of God. Both he and they accepted the law as revealing God's will, but they had very different ways of interpreting what was revealed. The Pharisees' traditions were attempts to work out in detail what the written law implied. Jesus declared that the result defeated its own purpose. The misuse of the "Corban" is cited as an instance. The word "corban" (*qorbān*) means simply "offering." By declaring any of his property to be an offering, dedicated to God, a man might evade his responsibility to honor his parents. Thus a formally religious act might be an act of disobedience to God.

Now Jesus calls the people to him and makes a radical statement: nothing that goes into a man can defile him; it is what comes out of his mouth that defiles him (Mk 7:15; Mt 15:11). According to Matthew (15:12-14), the disciples came and told Jesus that what he said had offended the Pharisees. He replied that any plant not planted by his heavenly Father would be rooted up; the Pharisees were blind guides (cf. Lk 6:39). "And if a blind man leads a blind man, both will fall into a pit."

When the disciples were alone with Jesus in the house, Mark says (7:17-18), they "asked him about the parable," evidently meaning what he had said about the things that defile a man. Again Jesus expressed surprise at their lack of understanding. What he had said was not a parable; it was meant quite literally. Bodily food does not defile a man; what does defile him is what comes from his heart and finds expression through his mouth. Mark inserts here a parenthetical observation: "Thus he declared all foods clean." Modern scholars have seriously questioned whether Jesus himself would have gone quite that far. When Peter heard in a vision at Joppa "What God has cleansed, you must not call common," he evidently was not yet emancipated from the old dietary restrictions (Acts 10:9-16). After converting the household of Cornelius, he still had to convince the brethren at Jerusalem that he was right (11:1-18). Even then, according to Paul (Gal 2:11-13), he did not quite have the full courage of his convictions, for after eating with Gentiles at Antioch he separated himself from them when some conservative brethren came from Jerusalem.

It is a mistake to assume that Jesus could not have departed more radically from current thought and practice than his followers did. A bothersome question, however, emerges here. The distinction of clean and unclean was not only traditional, it was an integral part of the law itself. The commandment that Jesus pronounced second only to the commandment to love God, "You shall love your neighbor as yourself" (Lev 19:18), is from a chapter that deals with the subject of clean and unclean. That

139

Jesus abandoned entirely such a prominent part of the law is not impossible. If he did not consider the whole concept of ritual cleanness null and void, he clearly considered it relatively unimportant.

The laws of clean and unclean were intended to set Israel apart as the holy people of God (Lev 20:26). Jesus' attitude to them is thus tied up with his conception of the place of the Gentiles in God's plan. We have seen in the story of the centurion's servant (Mt 8:5-13; Lk 7:1-10) evidence that Jesus could appreciate genuine faith in a Gentile. Another instance of this now follows.

According to Mark and Matthew, Jesus left Galilee and went to the region of Tyre and Sidon, ancient Phoenician cities on the Mediterranean coast north of Palestine (Mk 7:24-30; Mt 15:21-28). Here he was approached by ''a woman whose little daughter was possessed by an unclean spirit.'' Mark says that she was ''a Greek, a Syrophoenician by birth,'' that is, a person of Greek descent, born and living in what is now the Republic of Lebanon. Matthew calls her a Canaanite, the Canaanites and Phoenicians being the same people. This need not imply that she was not Greek by descent. Many Greeks had settled in this area, which had close commercial ties with Greece.

Why Jesus had gone outside of his own country we are not told, though there is a suggestion that he was seeking seclusion in Mark's statement, ''And he entered a house, and would not have anyone know it.'' Whether he wished to get away from his adversaries or from the eager crowds that followed him in Galilee, his fame had evidently spread beyond the bounds of Palestine; ''he could not be hid.'' Mark says that the mother of the afflicted girl heard of him ''immediately'' and came to him, begging him to heal her daughter.

According to Matthew she cried, ''Have mercy on me, O Lord, Son of David.'' ''Son of David'' was a current Jewish designation of the Messiah. Others appealed to Jesus in the same way, according to Matthew. Was this pagan woman trying to pose as a Jewess? We can only guess what Matthew had in mind.

Jesus did not answer the poor woman, Matthew continues, and the disciples urged him to send her away. He replied with an expression that he had used, again according to Matthew (cf. Mt

140

10:6), when instructing the twelve for their mission: "I was sent only to the lost sheep of the house of Israel." The frantic mother then knelt before Jesus, saying simply, "Lord, help me," or, as we should probably translate with the NEB, "Help me, sir." This evoked the reply that, in Mark's account, Jesus made to the woman's first appeal: "Let the children first be fed, for it is not right to take the children's bread and throw it to the dogs" (Mk 7:27; Mt 15:26). This seems unfeeling and arrogant; but perhaps it meant, "Do you mean to tell me that you, a Gentile, expect me, a Jew, to heal your daughter? Amazing!" Undeterred the woman answered, "Yes, Lord; yet even the dogs under the table eat the children's crumbs." This drew from Jesus an immediate and positive response. "Just for that," he said in effect, "you shall have what you want; your daughter is healed."

At several points this incident resembles the healing of the centurion's servant (Mt 8:5-13; Lk 7:1-10). Again we have a cure performed at a distance in response to a Gentile's entreaty. In each instance Jesus expresses wonder at finding such faith in a Gentile. I have suggested that personal contacts with persons of other faiths and nationalities may have affected Jesus' attitudes and views. If he ever considered himself and his disciples to be sent only to Israel, the possibility of a change is intriguing.

It is difficult to decide how far we are justified in drawing conclusions about Jesus from the miracle stories. The question whether they contain any historical facts, and if so what, is complicated and delicate. "Blind unbelief is sure to err." A legend may tell more about a person than a precise factual record.

From the region of Tyre, Mark says (7:31), Jesus "went through Sidon to the Sea of Galilee, through the region of the Decapolis." (The KJV follows a different reading, found in late manuscripts.) Tyre is about thirty miles northwest of the Sea of Galilee, and Sidon is about twenty miles farther north on the shore of the Mediterranean. The region of the Decapolis is east and southeast of the Sea of Galilee. To get there from Sidon Jesus could either go back to Tyre and thence southeast or cross the mountain range of Lebanon, proceed eastward to the vicinity of Caesarea Philippi, and then go south. Either route would be a very roundabout way to reach the Sea of Galilee. The advantage of

141

such a detour might have been to avoid the territory of Herod Antipas, west of the Jordan River and the Sea of Galilee. Yet very soon afterward, Jesus is apparently at work again on that side of the lake. Matthew ignores the difficulty: after the healing in the district of Tyre and Sidon he says, "And Jesus went on from there and passed along the Sea of Galilee" (Mt 15:21, 29).

Back again beside the lake, according to Mark (7:32-37), Jesus healed "a man who was deaf and had an impediment in his speech." Matthew (15:29-31) substitutes for this paragraph a brief, general statement that Jesus healed many people afflicted with various ills. In Mark's account Jesus uses a quasi-magical technique, putting his fingers in the man's ears, spitting, and touching the man's tongue. Again the Aramaic word he uttered is quoted and translated (cf. Mk 5:41). A similar procedure is described in John in the healing of a man born blind (9:6).

Familiarity with stories of cures by similar methods in Jewish and pagan literature may have influenced the tradition of this miracle, so different from Jesus' usual practice in the Synoptic narratives. The Aramaic word suggests that the story goes back to an early phase of the tradition. Using mysterious foreign words was a part of magical procedure in the Hellenistic world, but for Jesus this would not be a foreign word.

The next event in Mark and Matthew (Mk 8:1-10; Mt 15:32-39) is almost a duplicate of the feeding of the five thousand. This time four thousand were fed with seven loaves and "a few small fish." Jesus told the disciples that the crowd had no food and would faint on the way if he sent them off hungry. At the end Mark says that Jesus "got into the boat with his disciples, and went to the district of Dalmanutha"; according to Matthew he went to the region of Magadan. Neither region nor district has been identified; there are variant readings in the manuscripts of both Gospels.

It seems obvious that the two accounts of feeding multitudes must reflect two traditions of the same event. If such a miracle could happen once it could happen twice, but as nature miracles these pose a special problem of credibility. Probably Mark, having two forms of the tradition, conscientiously included both in his record. Matthew then simply followed Mark.

A demand of the Pharisees for a sign from heaven is reported

142

next (Mk 8:11-13; Mt 16:1). Jesus declared that no sign would be given to that generation. Matthew inserts here the saying about "the signs of the times," which appears later in Luke (Mt 16:2-3; Lk 12:54-56); then he notes the refusal of a sign, repeating, "except the sign of Jonah" (Mt 16:4; cf. 12:39). What was meant by the signs of the times is not clear, beyond the general implication that any person who observed and understood what was going on about him would not need any other sign from heaven to attest the divine mission and authority of Jesus.

After this, Mark continues, Jesus again crossed the lake; but the disciples forgot to bring any bread, "and had only one loaf with them in the boat" (Mk 8:13-21; Mt 16:5-12). This seems strange almost immediately after the feeding of the four thousand. Had the ease with which Jesus could feed multitudes made the disciples careless? The statement and the paragraph it introduces look like a traditional expansion or *midrash* of the saying that now follows. Luke has this in his special section (Lk 12:1), but omits the discussion that follows it in Mark and Matthew. In Mark it reads, "Take heed, beware of the leaven of the Pharisees and the leaven of Herod" (some good manuscripts read "the Herodians"; cf. Mk 3:6; Mt 22:16). Matthew has the Sadducees; Luke has only "the leaven of the Pharisees," but adds, "which is hyprocrisy" (unless this is a marginal note by an early reader).

Aware that the disciples thought he referred to their failure to bring bread, Jesus rebuked them for their lack of perception. In Matthew Jesus calls them "men of little faith," one of Matthew's favorite expressions (cf. Mt 6:30; 8:26; 14:31; 16:8; also 17:20; Lk 12:28). Lack of faith seems less appropriate than lack of insight. This is what they are charged with in Mark and in the rest of the passage in Matthew. Mark calls it hardness of heart, which means not cruelty but a closed mind. In that time the heart was supposed to be the organ of thought, emotions being located in the bowels.

Mark has another sentence, which Matthew omits (8:18): "Having eyes do you not see, and having ears do you not hear?" The disciples would no doubt recognize the echo of passages in Jeremiah and Ezekiel referring to Israel (Jer 5:21; Ezek 12:2). In the Psalms the same expressions are applied to idols and those who use them (Ps 115:4-8; 135:15-18).

143

Mark and Matthew say that Jesus reproved the disciples also for not remembering the miracles of feeding the crowds. Matthew adds an interpretation different from Luke's: "Then they understood that he did not tell them to beware of the leaven of bread, but of the teaching of the Pharisees and Sadducees."

The fact that Jesus' questions and the disciples' answers presuppose the miracles of feeding the multitudes is significant. The tradition of this conversation, at least in its final form, must have arisen after the two stories had come to be accepted as representing two different miracles. Perhaps the evangelist himself so understood them and edited or composed the account of the conversation accordingly. This would not affect the authenticity of the warning about leaven. A saying originally handed down by itself sometimes gave rise to a story about the circumstances under which it was spoken. Whether Matthew's or Luke's interpretation is correct is another question. Possibly both are wrong. The saying implies some kind of insidious influence to which the disciples are exposed. Beyond that we are limited to conjecture.

Mark now tells of the healing of a blind man at Bethsaida (8:22-26), one of the cities denounced by Jesus for failing to repent in spite of the mighty works done in them (Mt 11:21; Lk 10:13). It has been mentioned in connection with the feeding of the five thousand and the walking on the water. Apparently it was on the north shore of the Sea of Galilee, just to the east of the point where the Jordan River flows into the lake. This incident and the parable of the seed growing of itself (Mk 4:26-29) are the only complete units in Mark that have no parallels at all in the other Gospels.

At several points this miracle resembles the healing of the deaf mute. There people brought a deaf and dumb man and asked Jesus to lay his hands upon him; here they bring a blind man and ask Jesus to touch him. There Jesus took the man aside from the multitude; here he takes the man by the hand and leads him out of the village. In both cases he used physical means, including spitting and laying his hands on the patient. There are differences, however. Here there is no Aramaic word of command. There is also a unique element, the achievement of a cure in two stages.

CHAPTER IX

PETER'S CONFESSION AND THE END
OF THE GALILEAN MINISTRY

From this point Matthew proceeds in Mark's company, and here Luke's "great omission" ends (Mk 8:27-33; Mt 16:13-23; Lk 9:18-22). According to Mark and Matthew, Jesus went to the villages or district of Caesarea Philippi. Luke gives no indication that the event that follows occurred anywhere but at Bethsaida, where he located the feeding of the five thousand. Caesarea was about twenty-five miles north of the Sea of Galilee at one of the sources of the Jordan. It was in the territory of Philip, a son of Herod the Great, and was called "Philip's Caesarea" to distinguish it from Caesarea on the shore of the Mediterranean, the headquarters of the Roman governors of Judea.

Here occurred what may fairly be called the watershed of the gospel record. For the first and perhaps the only time in the Synoptic Gospels, Jesus shows an interest in what people think about him. He asks the disciples, and they report current opinions. Jesus then asks, "But who do you say that I am?" The impetuous Peter, speaking for all the disciples, replies, "You are the Christ" (that is, the Messiah).

Matthew puts Jesus' first question in the form, "Who do men say that the Son of man is?" This would be puzzling unless the disciples understood that the Son of man meant Jesus himself. (The reading of the KJV and previous English translations, "that I the Son of man am," is not supported by the manuscripts or versions.) If the term was commonly understood as a Messianic designation, one possible answer to the question, "Who do men say that I am?" would be, "The Son of man." In the second question Matthew has "I"; Mark and Luke have it in both questions.

Incidentally, KJV's solecism, "Whom do men say that I the Son of man am?" and "But whom say ye that I am?" runs through all the previous English versions from Tyndale on, except that in Luke, Tyndale and the Great Bible have "who." Not until the Revised Version of 1881 was the error corrected.

145

When the disciples said that some people thought Jesus was John the Baptist, some Elijah, ''and others one of the prophets,'' they meant that these men were believed to have risen from the dead in the person of Jesus, or in the case of Elijah that he had come back from heaven. Herod Antipas had thought that Jesus was John the Baptist, whom he had beheaded (Mk 6:14-16 and parallels). On that occasion too some believed Jesus was Elijah; and others, according to Luke (9:8), thought ''that one of the old prophets had risen.'' According to Mark (6:15), however, they said, ''It is a prophet, like one of the prophets of old.'' The manner in which Jesus proclaimed the kingdom of God might well lead people to think of him as a prophet, and they evidently did (Lk 7:16, 39; Mt 21:11, 46).

There are indications that Jesus so thought of himself (Mk 6:4; Mt 13:57; Lk 4:24). At Nazareth he said, ''A prophet is not without honor, except in his own country.'' Later in Luke (13:33), Jesus says, ''It cannot be that a prophet should perish away from Jerusalem.''

In response to Jesus' second question Peter said, ''You are the Christ,'' adding in Matthew, ''the Son of the living God'' (Mk 8:29; Mt 16:16; Lk 9:20). According to Matthew, Jesus enthusiastically welcomed this declaration (16:17). If we did not have the Gospel of Matthew, however, and if it did not come first in the New Testament, Jesus' reaction to Peter's statement would seem very different: ''And he charged them to tell no one about him. And he began to teach them that the Son of man must suffer'' (Mk 8:30-31; Lk 9:21-22).

This need not imply that Jesus denied that he was the Messiah. He clearly did not wish to be so called in public, but that might mean that he felt the time was not ripe to declare himself. Yet Peter's confession was made in the close circle of the disciples. Possibly Jesus was not sure whether he was the Messiah or not. His emphatic, almost violent, reaction to Peter's declaration might even suggest that the idea of Messiahship was a temptation he found it hard to resist. This could explain why Peter's protest against the prediction of rejection and suffering was repudiated as Satanic (Mk 8:33; Mt 16:23). It is possible also, however, that even thinking of himself as Messiah seemed to imply a mistaken conception of his mission. That may be why he proceeded at once to predict the rejection and suffering of the Son of man. If this is correct, it is one of the ironies of history that the title by which Jesus was unwilling to be known became very soon the one most commonly applied to him, even ceasing to be recognized as a title and being used practically as a surname.

In Matthew, Jesus' approval of Peter's declaration (16:17) leads to the passage on which the claims of the Roman papacy are founded (vv 18-19), beginning, "And I tell you, you are Peter, and on this rock I will build my church." The play on words in the name Peter and "on this rock" cannot be reproduced in English, but it is clear in the Greek and would be even more so in Aramaic. Peter's name was Simon. The name Peter is a translation of the Aramaic nickname Kepha, meaning "rock," which according to Matthew was bestowed on Simon by Jesus on this occasion. The Gospel of John tells of Jesus' giving the name in the form Cephas (*i.e.*, Kepha) when Simon was brought to Jesus at the Jordan by Andrew (1:42). Paul also preserves the form Cephas (1 Cor 1:12 and often).

The figure of building on rock as a symbol of solidity and permanence is of course familiar (Mt 7:24; Lk 6:48). Jesus himself used it in the parable of the two builders. In one of the Thanksgiving Psalms from Qumran (1 QH vii. 8) the poet says, "Thou has established my building on a rock," and (vi. 26) "Thou dost establish counsel on a rock," and goes on to say that the powers of evil cannot break into God's fortress. Another Qumran document (1 QS viii. 8) refers to the council of the community as a house with firm foundations.

The word "church" appears in the Gospels only in Matthew, and only three times there (once here and twice in 18:17). The Greek noun *ekklesia* means an assembly of any kind. In Acts (19:39) it refers to the town meeting of Ephesus. The Septuagint uses it for the congregation of Israel, and it occurs twice in that sense in the New Testament (Acts 7:38; Heb 2:12).

At the time of Peter's confession of faith there was no Christian church. If Jesus said, "on this rock I will build my church," he must have referred to a community that he intended to establish later. More probably, however, this statement was first uttered by

147

an early Christian prophet, speaking in the name and (he believed) by the spirit of the risen Jesus. Such prophets are mentioned in the New Testament (*e.g.*, Acts 11:27-30; 21:10-11), and Paul considered the gift of prophecy superior to speaking with tongues (1 Cor 14).

Jesus adds that "the powers of death" (KJV, "the gates of hell") cannot prevail against the church (Mt 16:18). Neither "death" nor "hell" is a good translation of the Greek "Hades" (cf. 5:29). Equally unfortunate is the rendering "powers" for "gates." What is meant by prevailing against the church is not clear. The Greek verb occurs elsewhere in the New Testament only in Luke 23:23, which says of those who demanded that Jesus be crucified, "and their voices prevailed." Gates not only keep captives in, they keep enemies out. The figure of gates prevailing against a person or persons suggests stopping an invasion. The JB reads, "the gates of the underworld can never hold out against it." This means that the church will attack Hades, break down its gates, and take it by storm.

Jesus now (v 19) confers upon Peter the keys of the kingdom of heaven, declaring that what he binds on earth will be bound in heaven and what he looses on earth will be loosed in heaven. The group for which Matthew wrote was evidently troubled by the presence of unworthy members and perplexed about what to do with them. The saying about the keys and the power of binding and loosing suggests that some effort was made to keep such people out of the church. In a later passage (18:18) Jesus grants this power to the disciples in general.

In Matthew, as in Mark and Luke, Jesus now commands the disciples to tell no one about him and says that the Son of man must suffer, be rejected and killed, and rise again. This is the first of three predictions of Jesus' death and resurrection (Mk 8:31; 9:31; 10:33-34 and parallels). They are so specific that the tradition of Jesus' words seems obviously influenced by what had occurred in the meantime. The story of his crucifixion and resurrection was the core of the gospel proclaimed by the church, and a preacher or teacher repeating Jesus' warning of what he saw before him would almost inevitably fill it in with the familiar details.

148

In all three of the predictions in Mark and Luke, and all but the first in Matthew, the one who is to suffer is called the Son of man. The abrupt shift from Peter's "the Christ" to Jesus' "the Son of man" is striking. Whether Jesus meant, "I am not the Messiah, I am the Son of man," or whether he merely used "Son of man" as a substitute for the pronoun "I," we cannot tell.

In Luke, after the Resurrection, Jesus tells the two disciples on the way to Emmaus that the Christ had to suffer (24:26), that is, the same thing is said there about the Messiah that is said here about the Son of man. For the evangelists both terms meant Jesus. On the question whether that was true for Jesus himself we must suspend judgment for the present.

For his disciples as well as himself (Mk 8:34–9:1; Mt 16:24-28; Lk 9:23-27), Jesus foresaw suffering and perhaps death. The saying about taking up one's cross and finding life by losing it has already been used by Matthew in his second discourse (Mt 10:38-39; Lk 17:33). We have considered what it means in that connection.

Mark and Luke read here, "For whoever is ashamed of me and of my words [Mark adds, "in this adulterous and sinful generation"], of him will the Son of man also be ashamed, when he comes in the glory of his Father with the holy angels" (Mk 8:38; Lk 9:26). The shift from "ashamed of me" to "the Son of man also be ashamed" suggests a distinction between Jesus and the Son of man. Matthew reads here (16:27) simply, "For the Son of man is to come with his angels in the glory of his Father, and then he will repay every man for what he has done." The saying is quoted earlier in Matthew and repeated later in Luke (Mt 10:32-33; Lk 12:8-9), but with variations that make it uncertain whether Jesus refers to himself or to a heavenly being other than himself.

The evangelists now report another important saying with perplexing differences (Mk 9:1; Mt 16:28; Lk 9:27). They agree in the first part of it: "Truly, I say to you, there are some standing here who will not taste death"; but the final clause appears in three different forms. In Mark it reads, "before they see that the kingdom of God has come with power"; in Luke, "before they see the kingdom of God''; in Matthew, ''before they see the Son of man coming in his kingdom.''

The idea of the kingdom of the Son of man is peculiar to Matthew. The other Gospels speak of the Son of man as coming in power and glory or as seated at the right hand of God, but they do not refer to his kingdom or throne. Kingship is implied, of course, in the title ''Christ'' (*e.g.,* Mk 11:10); and there are verses that refer to the kingdom that Jesus will receive (*e.g.,* Lk 22: 29-30; cf. Mt 19:28) but without using the term ''Son of man.''

Since the saying is otherwise the same as in Mark, and occurs in a Markan context, we cannot say that Matthew has taken it from some other source. It seems that for Matthew the coming of the Son of man as king has almost taken the place of the coming of God's kingdom, though Matthew preserves many sayings about the kingdom of heaven with no reference to the Son of man. By introducing the kingdom of the Son of man here, Matthew at least avoids the abrupt shift in Mark and Luke from the coming of the Son of man to the kingdom of God.

By itself, Luke's expression, ''see the kingdom of God,'' may mean ''perceive the royal power of God.'' In the Gospel of John, Jesus tells Nicodemus (3:3, cf. v 5) that without a new birth a man ''cannot see the kingdom of God.'' The Wisdom of Solomon says that Wisdom guided Jacob in his flight from Esau and ''showed him the kingdom of God'' (10:10). A Jewish prayer, referring to the crossing of the Red Sea, says, ''and they saw thy kingdom''; in other words, they witnessed a demonstration of God's royal power. Perhaps Luke used this expression instead of Mark's because, when he wrote, the kingdom had not yet come with power.

It did not so come before the generation to which Jesus spoke had passed away. Has the time ever come when Christians could stop praying ''Thy kingdom come''? If this saying is an authentic utterance of Jesus', I can see no honest way to escape the unwelcome conclusion that he expected the full, final, indubitable establishment of God's sovereign power within the lifetime of his contemporaries; and it did not happen.

The only alternative is that Mark 9:1 was not an authentic saying of Jesus. This is ably argued by very competent and

150

conscientious scholars, but I must confess that I do not find their reasoning convincing. It is conceivable that a prophet later delivered this prediction, meaning by "some standing here" his own audience; but a prediction that had not been fulfilled would be less and less likely to be ascribed to Jesus as time went on. That Mark himself composed the saying is to me quite incredible.

Not only this saying is involved, of course. There is "The kingdom of God is at hand" (Mk 1:14-15 and parallels), also "the kingdom of God has come upon you" (Mt 12:28; Lk 11:20), and later "the kingdom of God is in the midst of you" (or "within you") (Lk 17:21). But whatever the coming of the kingdom may mean in any or all of these places, Mark 9:1 speaks unmistakably of a coming with power not many years away.

We cannot reduce Jesus' conception of the kingdom of God to a neat formula. It was not an idea but a complex of ideas. Grounded in the assurance of God's eternal and universal sovereignty, it included his rule over an individual's life, the fellowship of those dedicated to the will of God, the relief of mankind's afflictions by the power of God's Spirit, and the final consummation of the ages in a new world.

Jesus saw that God's sovereignty was not universally acknowledged. There was much in the world that was contrary to his will. The present age seemed to be under the domination of Satan. In spite of this, Jesus was convinced that God's power would prevail; and the success of his own healing mission confirmed his faith that this would happen soon. What has been called "prophetic foreshortening" is not uncommon. The very intensity of a prophet's vision and his overpowering sense of its reality cause the interval before its fulfillment to be telescoped in his mind. It was probably so with Jesus' proclamation that the kingdom of God was near.

Probably he also expected the kingdom to come in something like the way envisaged by the Synoptic evangelists and other New Testament writers. As a real person, speaking a human language in a particular historical situation, he could only speak and think in the intellectual and cultural molds of his time and country. To uncover the significance of his proclamation and teaching for us requires interpretation and reformulation.

151

The kingdom of God did not come as soon as or in the way that he expected. We are therefore thrown back on the core of his faith, his conviction that the heavenly Father was in control and had the power to accomplish his loving purpose. If he was right about that, questions of time and manner are relatively unimportant.

Still proceeding together, the three evangelists relate next the "transfiguration" of Jesus (Mk 9:2-8; Mt 17:1-8; Lk 9:28-36). Mark and Matthew say that it occurred "after six days"; Luke says, "about eight days after these sayings." Taking with him Peter, James, and John, Jesus "led them up a high mountain apart." If they were still near Caesarea Philippi, the mountain might have been Mt. Hermon, which rises to a height of more than nine thousand feet about fifteen miles northeast of that city. Christian tradition has more commonly identified the mount of transfiguration with Mt. Tabor, not far from Nazareth, though it is not a high mountain. There is actually nothing to indicate that the evangelists had any particular mountain in mind.

It is not certain, in fact, that the incident is historical at all, except as it reflects the historic faith of the early church. Quite possibly, however, it preserves an authentic memory of a great spiritual experience of the three disciples who were closest to Jesus. The evangelists' language suggests a vision and has often been so understood. Matthew calls the experience a vision (Mt 17:9). Jesus was "transfigured" or "transformed," say Mark and Matthew; and Matthew adds, "and his face shone like the sun." Luke says, "the appearance of his countenance was altered." A sensation of brightness and light is a common element in the visions of mystics. A vision shared by three men at once, however, would be unusual. More probably the story represents a new insight, a new appreciation of Jesus' goodness, dedication, and authority.

But there is more to the story. They saw Moses and Elijah talking with Jesus. These two outstanding persons of the Old Covenant represent law and prophecy. Jesus' communion with them symbolizes his relation to the old covenant, both fulfilling the law and the prophets and bringing a new and better covenant (Heb. 7:22; 8:6; 9:15).

152

Some New Testament scholars hold that the transfiguration was a post-Resurrection appearance of Jesus, only later supposed to have occurred during his ministry. To me this seems less probable than either of two other possibilities. If there is a historical nucleus in the story, the symbolism of its present form may have been added by Mark or by one of his predecessors. Possibly the whole story is a symbolic legend.

Neither Mark nor Matthew tells what Jesus talked about with Moses and Elijah. Luke says (9:31) they "spoke of his departure, which he was to accomplish at Jerusalem." Luke often refers to Moses and the prophets, especially as foretelling the Messiah's suffering (Lk 16:29, 31; 24:27, 44; Acts 26:22-23; 28:23). Perhaps here too he has in mind the fulfillment of prophecy by Jesus' death.

Luke adds (9:32) that Peter, James, and John "were heavy with sleep." The same thing is said later concerning the same three disciples in Gethsemane (Mk 14:40; Mt 26:43). There, however, they fell asleep; here they "wakened" and "they saw his glory and the two men who stood with him." The expression "saw his glory" recalls John 1:14. It also fits the references to dazzling brightness, for glory is associated with light in the Bible (*e.g.*, 2 Cor 3:7-11, RSV, NEB, JB). The same Greek word is sometimes translated "splendor."

Apparently these touches are Luke's own contribution. He now returns to Mark's narrative, reporting Peter's officious but well meant offer to set up three booths for Jesus and his heavenly visitors (Mk 9:5, RSV footnote, NEB, JB; Mt 17:4; Lk 9:33). In Mark, Peter addresses Jesus as Rabbi, in Matthew as the Lord, in Luke as Master. Luke's word is one used six times by him, never by the other evangelists.

Now a cloud overshadowed the awestruck disciples, and a voice spoke almost the same words that were spoken by the heavenly voice at Jesus' baptism. This time the voice concluded, "Listen to him." Matthew says that the disciples fell on their faces, but Jesus touched them and told them not to be afraid. All three evangelists report that when the disciples looked up they saw Jesus alone. Luke says that they told no one of their experience at the time.

Whatever may have been the origin of this story, its meaning for his followers is clear: their Lord was God's elect and beloved Son, the fulfillment of his promises under the old covenant. Something like this was undoubtedly the experience of the first disciples, whether or not it came in this way and at a definite time to these three.

The paragraph that follows in Mark and Matthew (Mk 9:9-13; Mt 17:9-13) records a conversation between Jesus and the three disciples on the way down from the mountain. Jesus charges them not to tell what they have seen until the Son of man has risen from the dead. They obey but discuss what the resurrection of the Son of man means. Then they ask Jesus why the scribes say that Elijah must come before the Messiah (cf. Mt 11:14). He replies that Elijah has already come "and they did to him whatever they pleased." In Mark Jesus adds, "as it is written of him," but what this alludes to is unknown.

In the midst of this reply, in Mark (9:12), Jesus asks, "And how is it written of the Son of man that he should suffer many things and be treated with contempt?" Instead of this Matthew adds at the end, "So also the Son of man will suffer at their hands." Apparently Mark's text has suffered at the hands of a careless copyist. To make sure that no reader will miss the point of the reference to Elijah, Matthew concludes, "Then the disciples understood that he was speaking to them of John the Baptist."

"And when they came to the disciples," Mark continues, "they saw a great crowd about them, and scribes arguing with them" (Mk 9:14-27; Mt 17:14-18; Lk 9:37-43). The people, seeing Jesus, "were greatly amazed, and ran up to him and greeted him." Jesus asked, "What are you discussing with them?" A man in the crowd replied that he had brought his epileptic son and the disciples could not heal him. Matthew calls the boy an epileptic; Mark and Luke say that he was possessed by a spirit. The seizures suffered by the poor lad are vividly described by Mark.

Hearing the father's statement that the disciples could not heal his son, Jesus exclaimed, "O faithless generation, how long am I to be with you? How long am I to bear with you?" (The rendering

154

"faithless" is unfortunate; what is meant is not "unfaithful" but "lacking in faith.") The father said, "If you can do anything, have pity on us and help us." Jesus replied, "If you can! All things are possible to him who believes." At this the father cried, "I believe; help my unbelief!" And this half-faith, this hope struggling with unbelief to become belief, was accepted and rewarded.

The account of the miracle is again much fuller and more dramatic in Mark than in Matthew and Luke. Jesus, Mark says, rebuked the unclean spirit when he saw a crowd assembling. At his command, the demon came out of the boy, "after crying out and convulsing him terribly." So exhausted was the child that the spectators thought he was dead. "But Jesus took him by the hand and lifted him up, and he arose." Luke adds that Jesus gave him back to his father, and "all were astonished at the majesty of God."

Mark and Matthew have more (Mk 9:28-29; Mt 17:19-20). Back in the house, alone with Jesus, the disciples asked why they could not cast out the evil spirit. In Mark, Jesus replies, "This kind cannot be driven out by anything but prayer," to which many manuscripts and ancient versions add, "and fasting." In Matthew he says, "Because of your little faith," and adds that with even a little faith, small as a mustard seed, one could order a mountain to move and be obeyed (cf. Mk 11:23; Mt 21:20). In a different connection Luke has a similar saying, but instead of moving a mountain he has making a sycamine tree uproot itself and be planted in the sea (17:5-6).

Mark proceeds (Mk 9:30-31; Mt 17:22; Lk 9:43), "They went on from there and passed through Galilee." Matthew says cryptically, "As they were gathering in Galilee . . ." Luke implies that they stayed where they were, "But while they were all marveling at everything he did . . ." Mark adds that Jesus did not want his presence known, because he was teaching his disciples. Apparently after Peter's confession at Caesarea Philippi and the transfiguration, Jesus withdrew from public preaching and endeavored to prepare his disciples for what lay ahead, somewhat as Isaiah did at a critical moment in his life (Is 8:16-17). There is at least a suggestion here that rising official opposition dictated this procedure.

All three Gospels give here the second of Jesus' three recorded predictions of his death and resurrection, the first having been spoken at Caesarea Philippi (Mk 9:31-32; Mt 17:22-23; Lk 9:44-45; cf. Mk 8:31 and parallels). This one is simpler than the other two. It is simpler in Matthew than in Mark, and still more so in Luke. It is by no means improbable that Jesus foretold his rejection by the authorities at Jerusalem and even his death. In Matthew and Luke the prediction is a single statement on a particular occasion; in Mark it is the substance of what Jesus was teaching the disciples at this time. Both Mark and Luke say that the disciples did not understand what Jesus said, but were afraid to ask him about it. Matthew says only, "And they were greatly distressed."

Here Matthew inserts another item concerning Peter (17:24-27). It has to do with the payment of the annual half-shekel tax for the upkeep and ritual of the temple (Ex 30:11-16). It also involves the least convincing and least edifying of the miracle stories. When the collectors of the tax asked Peter whether his teacher did not pay the half-shekel, and he went to tell Jesus, before he could say anything Jesus asked him, "What do you think, Simon? From whom do kings of the earth take toll or tribute? From their sons or from others?" Peter of course replied, "From others"; and Jesus said, "Then the sons are free," implying that he and the disciples as sons of God were exempt from such exactions. Nevertheless, "not to give offense to them" (cf. Mt 3:15), Peter was instructed to cast a hook and take the first fish he could catch, and when he did so he found a coin in its mouth.

Regardless of the origin of this tale, its implication for Jesus' attitude toward the tax is plain. It is hardly the attitude of an uncompromising rebel. Whether it was actually the position taken by Jesus himself, or only that of the Jewish-Christian church in Matthew's day, is uncertain. The whole story may be a creation of second-generation Christians to support their own attitude.

The three Gospels now continue together to the next episode (Mk 9:33-37; Mt 18:1-5; Lk 9:46-48). As Mark tells it, when Jesus and the disciples reached Capernaum, he asked them what

156

they had been discussing on the way. Matthew, having brought them to Capernaum with the incident of the temple tax, picks up Mark's narrative with the phrase "At that time." Luke, still with no indication that they had left the place where the epileptic boy was healed, says, "And an argument arose among them."

The question they had been debating was which of them was the greatest. Matthew says they put this in an impersonal form, "Who is greatest in the kingdom of heaven?" According to Mark "they were silent," and Jesus answered their question without being told what it was (9:35). "And he sat down," says Mark, "and called the twelve; and he said to them, 'If any one would be first, he must be last of all and servant of all.'" Matthew and Luke omit this here, but at the end of the paragraph Luke sums up Jesus' answer to the question (Lk 9:48; cf. Mk 10:43-44 and parallels).

Jesus then "took a child, and put him in the midst of them" (Mk 9:36; Mt 18:2; Lk 9:47). Mark adds one of those graphic touches that Matthew and Luke omit: "and taking him in his arms." What Jesus then said (Mk 9:37) has no bearing on who is greatest: "Whoever receives one such child in my name receives me; and whoever receives me, receives not me but him who sent me." Two independent incidents involving a child seem to be combined here.

Matthew provides a more natural connection with two sentences. The first reads, "Truly, I say to you, unless you turn and become like children, you will never enter the kingdom of heaven" (Mt 18:3; cf. Mk 10:15; Lk 18:17). The second (18:4) reads, "Whoever humbles himself like this child, he is the greatest in the kingdom of heaven." We have already encountered the idea of greater and less in the kingdom (Mt 5:19; 11:11; Lk 7:28).

According to Mark and Luke, what Jesus said about those who received him led John, the son of Zebedee, to tell of a man the disciples had found exorcising demons in the name of Jesus (Mk 9:38-40; Lk 9:49-50). They had forbidden him to do this because he was not one of them, but Jesus said, as Mark reports, "Do not forbid him; for no one who does a mighty work in my name will be able soon after to speak evil of me. For he that is not against us

157

is for us." Luke has only, "Do not forbid him; for he that is not against you is for you" (cf. Mt 12:30; Lk 11:23).

In Mark, Jesus concludes, "For truly, I say to you, whoever gives you a cup of water to drink because you bear the name of Christ, will by no means lose his reward." The use of the word "Christ" without a definite article is characteristic of a later stage of development in Christianity and occurs nowhere else in words attributed to Jesus. So consistently did Jesus discourage any reference to himself as the Messiah that he can hardly be believed to have used the title as reported here. A somewhat different form of the saying in Matthew's second discourse (10:42) reads, "because he is a disciple."

Matthew omits the story of the unauthorized exorcist. In Luke it marks the end of the Galilean ministry. In Mark it is followed by a series of sayings (Mk 9:42-48; Mt 18:6-9) so loosely connected that they seem to have been brought together here for want of a better place to put them. First in the group is the stern warning, "Whoever causes one of these little ones who believe in me to sin, it would be better for him if a great millstone were hung round his neck and he were thrown into the sea."

The disciples' question and the incident of the child introduce Matthew's fourth major discourse (Mt 18). The saying about causing a little one to sin follows naturally, making the "little ones" appear to be children. If Jesus referred here to children, what the clause "who believe in me" meant is not clear. To this Matthew adds another saying: "Woe to the world for temptations to sin! For it is necessary that temptations come, but woe to the man by whom the temptation comes!" Luke has both of these sayings in a different place with some variation (17:1-2).

Next in Matthew as in Mark comes a paragraph about cutting off a hand or foot and plucking out an eye that causes one to sin (Mk 9:43-48; Mt 18:8-9; cf. Mt 5:29-30). Matthew has this also in the Sermon on the Mount but repeats it somewhat more fully here. With the sacrifice of both hand and eye Matthew has the expression "enter life"; Mark speaks of hand, foot, and eye, reading "enter life" twice but the third time "enter the kingdom of God" (Mt 18:9; Mk 9:47, cf. vv 43, 45). Evidently as Mark understands it the kingdom of God and "life" are closely related.

This is not the only place where the two expressions appear as synonymous, as we shall see presently (cf. Mk 10:17, 23-24; Lk 18:18, 24-25). Here the contrast between entering life or the kingdom of God and being thrown into the eternal fire of Gehenna clearly connects the kingdom of God with the coming age.

Another saying in the Sermon on the Mount follows now in Mark in a condensed form (Mk 9:49-50; cf. Mt 5:13; Lk 14:34-35). This is the saying about salt that has lost its saltness. Matthew omits it here. It is preceded and followed in Mark by sentences not found in Matthew or Luke. They have been examined together with the saying where it occurs in Matthew.

At this point Matthew (18:10) introduces another saying about the "little ones." They are not to be despised, for "in heaven their angels always behold the face of my Father who is in heaven." Neither Mark nor Luke records this. Its meaning is by no means obvious. Luke says in Acts 23:8, "For the Sadducees say there is no resurrection, nor angel, nor spirit." If what they rejected had any connection with the resurrection of the dead, the "angel or spirit" may be related to the future life of the individual.

When Peter was released from prison by an angel and appeared at the house of Mark (Acts 12:15), the disciples exclaimed, "It is his angel!" This may mean that they thought Peter had died in prison, and what they saw was his spirit; or it may mean that they believed a person had a spirit-double that might appear visibly, though it is doubtful that this was believed by Jews at that time. Whether either idea has any bearing on "their angels" in Matthew is uncertain. In any case, the conception expressed in old-fashioned gravestone inscriptions, "Gone to be an angel," is not involved here. It is not biblical at all.

Jesus speaks here of little ones who are still living. In Jewish sources as in the Gospels there are references to angels being sent to guard or guide individuals. Whether each person was believed to have his own guardian angel is uncertain. The words "behold the face of my Father" recall the conception of angels as interceding for men. Probably this saying is a warning that the humblest or weakest of men have such intercessors in heaven.

The remainder of Matthew's fourth discourse is not found in

Mark. Some passages have parallels or partial parallels in Luke; others appear only in Matthew. First comes the parable of the shepherd who leaves ninety-nine sheep on the hills to search for one that has gone astray (Mt 18:12-14). This is connected with the preceding saying by the conclusion, "So it is not the will of my Father who is in heaven that one of these little ones should perish." Luke reports this parable later with the parables of the lost coin and the prodigal son (15:3-7). It is a moving expression of Jesus' concern for those who have lost their way in life, and his assurance that God is concerned for them. Current evangelical Christianity often uses the term "lost" as though it meant doomed to eternal punishment. For Jesus it meant having gone astray, being unable to find the way home.

Next in Matthew come sayings about agreements and differences among the disciples (18:15-20). The first deals with the proper treatment of an offending brother. A short, simple form of this appears later in Luke (17:3-4): "Take heed to yourselves; if your brother sins, rebuke him, and if he repents, forgive him." In Matthew it is more formal, a matter of established procedure in three steps, the last of which is to report the offense to the church.

As previously observed, this is one of only two places in the Gospels where the word "church" appears, the other being the declaration that Jesus will build his church on Peter, the Rock (Mt 16:18). There we concluded that the statement is not an authentic utterance of Jesus. Here too that conclusion can hardly be avoided. Jesus could have used the Aramaic word for a local synagogue or assembly. The final clause, however, implies an attitude to Gentiles and tax collectors very different from that of Jesus. The presupposed existence of the church as a body with disciplinary powers also makes it difficult to attribute these elaborate directions to Jesus.

Matthew appends to these rules a statement resembling what he has reported as spoken to Peter at Caesarea Philippi (18:18, cf. 16:19). Here the words are addressed to the disciples or the church: "Truly, I say to you, whatever you bind on earth shall be bound in heaven, and whatever you loose on earth shall be loosed in heaven." Conceivably this might be an earlier form of the promise, but even so it is hard to fit it into the ministry of Jesus and his relationship with his disciples. They appear here either as the disciples of a rabbi who empowers them to make authoritative decisions on legal questions, or as priests authorized to give or withhold absolution of sins. The Gospel of John says that after his resurrection Jesus gave the disciples authority to forgive or retain sins (20:23). Here again Matthew's saying must have been a result of developing situations in the church, perhaps not originally supposed to have come from Jesus at all. Only later, as it was handed down in the church, would it come to be thought of as a saying of Jesus and so be included in the tradition received by Matthew.

The promise that comes next in Matthew (18:19) resembles other Matthean sayings: "Again I say to you, if two of you agree on earth about anything they ask, it will be done for them by my Father in heaven." Where two or three gather in his name, Jesus adds (v 20), he will be with them. Of the two major emphases in the early church with regard to the relation between the risen and exalted Lord and his people, one, far more prominent in the Synoptic record, is the hope of his return in glory to judge the world and inaugurate the new age. The other, expressed here, is the sense of communion with him in worship. In general, concentration on the anticipated coming of Christ is characteristic of the early, predominantly Jewish generation of Christians, while stress on his presence in Christian worship is increasingly prominent in the later Hellenistic church. There is, to be sure, a remarkably similar statement in the rabbinic literature (Pirke Abot 3:3): "Two who sit together occupied with the law have the Shekinah in their midst." The divine Presence takes the place here of the presence of Jesus in the saying recorded by Matthew. Whether either of these two sayings was influenced by the other can only be a matter of speculation. The dates of both are uncertain. Whatever its origin, Matthew's saying has reassured and inspired Christians of all generations.

At this point (Mt 18:21-22) Peter interrupts with a question, "Lord, how often shall my brother sin against me, and I forgive him? As many as seven times?" Jesus replies, "I do not say to you seven times, but seventy times seven" (or perhaps "seventy-seven"). Luke has some variations in detail (cf. Lk

17:4), but what Jesus means is clear. Self-centered resentment and refusal to be reconciled have no place in the life of a Christian.

The last item in the discourse is a parable (Mt 18:23-35). It begins, "Therefore the kingdom of heaven may be compared to a king who wished to settle accounts with his servants." The essence of the story is that a servant for whom the master had cancelled a very large debt threw into prison a fellow servant who could not pay him a much smaller debt, whereupon the master delivered the merciless servant to be tortured until he should pay his own debt, "So also," says Jesus, "my heavenly Father will do to every one of you, if you do not forgive your brother from your heart" (cf. Mt 6:14; Mk 11:25). The fantastic difference between the amounts of the two debts suggests the incomparable vastness of man's debt to God.

The conclusion of the fourth discourse is indicated by the usual formula (Mt 19:1), which in this case marks also the end of the Galilean ministry.

CHAPTER X

THE JOURNEY TO JERUSALEM: LUKE'S SPECIAL SECTION

Now, Matthew says, Jesus "went away from Galilee and entered the region of Judea beyond the Jordan." Mark reads "the region of Judea and beyond the Jordan" (Mk 10:1; Mt 19:1). There was no region of Judea east of the Jordan at this time; the omission of "and" in Matthew is probably a copyist's error. Mark's statement, however, has its own difficulty. It seems to imply that Jesus entered Judea before going to Perea, the territory east of the Jordan. He could have done this by going down into Judea on the west side of the Jordan and then crossing to Perea, but the narrative as a whole gives the impression that he went down on the east side of the river and crossed back farther south, near Jericho. But when and where did he cross over to Perea?

Since there is no clearly marked progress from place to place in this part of Mark's narrative, some scholars think that he had in mind only a change in the area of Jesus' activity from Galilee to Jerusalem. Certainly his account of the journey, which occupies only one chapter, does not suggest an extensive ministry in Perea. There is no reason, however, to doubt that the reference to "beyond the Jordan" is historical.

The instruction of the disciples in seclusion was finished. As in Galilee, "crowds gathered to him again; and again, as his custom was, he taught them" (Mk 10:1; Mt 19:2). A discussion with some Pharisees about divorce is reported at this point by Mark and Matthew (Mk 10:2-12; Mt 19:3-12). Both evangelists say that the Pharisees questioned Jesus only to test him. They may have sincerely wanted to find whether he was teaching sound doctrine. According to Matthew they asked, "Is it lawful to divorce one's wife for any cause?" The great sages Hillel and Shammai differed concerning the acceptable grounds for divorce. In Mark, however, the question is whether divorce is ever permissible at all.

Jesus answered, according to Mark, by asking, "What did Moses command you?" They replied, "Moses allowed a man to write a certificate of divorce, and to put her away" (Deut 24:1). Then Jesus said, "For your hardness of heart he wrote you this commandment. But from the beginning . . .": in other words, human selfishness and weakness necessitated an accommodation that did not embody what God intended for mankind. The rabbis, especially the school of Hillel, recognized that changing circumstances required new ways of applying the law; but, so far as I am aware, they did not pronounce any law contrary to God's original purpose. Many Christians are unwilling to go as far as Jesus does here, or to apply the same principle to his own pronouncements.

Less radical and more common is the interpretation of Scripture by Scripture. Against the Deuteronomic law of divorce, Jesus next adduces two verses from Genesis. He uses them not to explain the commandment, but to demonstrate that it is a concession to human weakness, not what God always wanted and still wants. God created man male and female (Gen 1:27); therefore a man leaves his parents and is joined to his wife, making them one flesh (2:24). "What therefore God has joined together," Jesus concludes, "let not man put asunder." (In Matthew the story proceeds differently but, with an exception to be noted presently, to the same purpose.)

As if this were not sufficiently plain, it is made even more explicit by a statement that Matthew has already quoted in the Sermon on the Mount (cf. Mt 5:31-32): divorce and remarriage constitute adultery. Now Matthew repeats this as the conclusion of what Jesus says to the Pharisees; in Mark it is his answer to the disciples, who (with their usual lack of comprehension) ask him about the matter when they are alone with him in the house (Mt 19:9; Mk 10:10). Mark applies it to the wife as well as the husband. Luke, who omits this whole episode, has the saying later in a miscellaneous group of sayings (Lk 16:18). Evidently it was quoted often, with or without a setting, and was felt to be a difficult but inescapable utterance of Jesus.

Matthew, both here and in the Sermon on the Mount, has a qualifying clause not recorded by the others: "except for unchastity." It seems clear that this was added in the Christian community when the unqualified saying came to be regarded as a fixed rule, a law that could even serve as a basis for civil legislation and be enforced by the state.

Even for the disciples it was still a hard saying. According to Matthew (19:10) they said, to paraphrase slightly, "If that's the way it is, it would be better not to get married." Jesus replied that only those to whom it was given could accept his high standard (vv 11-12). He added a puzzling statement: "For there are eunuchs who have been so from birth, and there are eunuchs who have been made eunuchs by men, and there are eunuchs who have made themselves eunuchs for the sake of the kingdom of heaven." No wonder he concluded, "He who is able to receive this, let him receive it."

There have been Christians who took literally the expression "made themselves eunuchs." Undoubtedly what Jesus meant was foregoing marriage and family life to devote oneself wholly to the service of the kingdom of God (cf. 1 Cor 9:5).

Quite possibly Jesus spoke here out of his own experience. There is no evidence that he was ever married. He apparently suffered some estrangement from his own mother and brothers and sisters (Mk 3:31-35 and parallels). To renounce marriage, he now says, is not given all men. For the majority, "from the beginning of creation," what God requires is marriage.

Luke's whole account of the journey to Jerusalem is quite different from those of Mark and Matthew. His "great insertion" or "special section" (9:51–18:14) begins with the sentence, "When the days drew near for him to be received up, he set his face to go to Jerusalem." Eight chapters follow before Luke returns to Mark's outline. For Luke, therefore, the journey from Galilee to Jerusalem is a major division of Jesus' ministry, even though the selection and arrangement of the material may be governed by considerations other than chronology or geography. The geographical data, in fact, are conspicuously casual and vague.

The route contemplated by Jesus, as Luke represents it, was apparently south through Samaria, in spite of the well-known hostility between Samaritans and Jews. Perhaps as a precaution, he sent some disciples ahead to a Samaritan village to make ready for him; but the people of the village "would not receive him, because his face was set toward Jerusalem'' (9:51-53). James and John, whom Jesus had named "sons of thunder," wanted to call down lightning on the inhospitable villagers after the manner of Elijah (2 Kings 1:10, 12); but Jesus rebuked their vindictive spirit. The KJV, following several manuscripts and versions, adds, "Ye know not what manner of spirit ye are of. For the Son of man is not come to destroy men's lives, but to save them" (cf. Lk 19:10).

Leaving vengeance to God, therefore, "they went on to another village." This need not have been in Samaria. Jesus might have changed his plan after being repelled at the first village. On the whole, the section reads more naturally if understood as being laid mainly in Perea.

Luke tells next (9:57-62) of two men who wanted to follow Jesus after first attending to their own domestic interests. We have compared Matthew's presentation of this material (8:19-22) with Luke's where Matthew has it, just before the stilling of the storm on the Sea of Galilee. According to Luke the two incidents occurred "as they were going along the road" after their unfriendly reception by the Samaritan villagers.

Luke now says that Jesus sent out seventy disciples other than the twelve to go before him to the places he intended to visit (Lk 10:1-16). Much of what is given as Jesus' instructions to the seventy was included by Matthew in the instructions to the twelve (cf. Mt 10). The sending out of the seventy probably prefigures the wider mission of the church to the world (cf. Acts 1:8). A Jewish tradition, represented by the text of Genesis 10 in the Septuagint, regarded the number of Gentile nations as seventy-two. Some manuscripts and versions of Luke read seventy-two here.

When the seventy returned, they reported that the demons had been subject to them in Jesus' name (Lk 10:17-20). He replied, as already noted, "I saw Satan fall like lightning from heaven." The Greek word order favors taking "from heaven" with "lightning" rather than "fall"; *i.e.,* it does not mean "fall from heaven" but "fall like lightning," suddenly. Jesus therefore does not, as often supposed, refer to Satan as a fallen angel, expelled from heaven for rebellion against God. There is no implication that he was ever

166

in heaven. An allusion to "Day Star, son of Dawn" in Isaiah (14:12-20) is excluded also.

In spite of the doubtful historical basis of the mission of the seventy, this saying may well be authentic, and if so it is important. As in the narratives of Jesus' baptism (Mk 1:10-11 and parallels), his words here may refer to a mystical experience, or they may express symbolically his certainty of Satan's downfall. What is meant is in all probability that the subjection of the demons has made the fall of Satan so certain that Jesus sees it as an accomplished fact. Contemplating the fallen prince of demons, he rejoices at the demonstration of God's sovereignty. That this is Luke's understanding is indicated by the Greek verb and the form of it which he uses.

After this brief but significant statement, Jesus tells the disciples (Lk 10:19) that he has given them authority to tread upon serpents and scorpions, "and over all the power of the enemy." The mention of serpents and scorpions recalls the promise of the risen Christ in the longer ending of Mark (16:18).

Jesus continues (Lk 10:20), "Nevertheless do not rejoice in this, that the spirits are subject to you; but rejoice that your names are written in heaven." But is not Jesus himself rejoicing that the demons are subject to the disciples? Surely he does not mean that one's own salvation should be valued above service to others. Perhaps he detected in the disciples a tendency to congratulate themselves on their achievement instead of giving God the glory and being thankful for what he had done through them.

The idea of having one's name written in heaven is familiar from the Old Testament, beginning with Moses' petition to be blotted out of God's book if the sin of the people is not forgiven (Ex 32:32; cf. Is 4:3; Dan 12:1; Rev 3:5). It at least suggests a belief in predestination. Did Jesus accept and teach that doctrine? This verse is the closest approach to a definite statement to that effect. He spoke of things prepared for those whom God chose (Mt 25:34; cf. Rev 13:8; 17:8); and the fulfillment of prophecy implies that the future is at least in part determined. All we can say is that he stressed both personal responsibility and grateful recognition of what we owe to God.

After the story of the seventy, recorded by Luke alone, he

presents three items found also in Matthew but not in Mark: Jesus' thanksgiving to God for his revelation to "babes" (Lk 10:21; Mt 11:25-26), the "Johannine saying" about the Son's unique knowledge of the Father (Lk 10:22; Mt 11:27), and Jesus' reminder that the disciples are seeing what many before them have desired to see but could not (Lk 10:23-24; Mt 13:16-17). These have been discussed where they occur in Matthew.

Next Luke tells of a lawyer who asked Jesus a question (Lk 10:25-28; cf. Mk 12:28-31; Mt 22:34-40). This is the first item in Luke's special section that is found in Mark. Both Mark and Matthew put it later, when Jesus had reached Jerusalem. In Mark a scribe asks Jesus which of the commandments is "the first of all." Matthew calls the man one of the Pharisees, a lawyer. Luke says that a lawyer asked Jesus the question asked by the rich man, "Teacher, what shall I do to inherit eternal life?" (cf. Mk 10:17 and parallels).

In Mark, followed in part by Matthew, Jesus quotes in reply the "Shema" ("Hear, O Israel," and so on) from Deuteronomy (6:4-5), and adds a commandment from Leviticus (19:18) that he says "is like it." The first demands wholehearted love for God, the second loving one's neighbor as oneself. In Luke, Jesus turns the question back to the lawyer, saying "What is written in the law? How do you read?" The lawyer then quotes the verses, not as two commandments but as one; and Jesus says, "You have answered right; do this, and you will live."

Luke's form of the story reflects the fact that the problem of defining the essence of the law was already being discussed in Judaism in the time of Jesus. Hillel's use of the Golden Rule to summarize the law has been noted. The second-century rabbi Akiba pointed to Leviticus 19:18, Jesus' second commandment, as the sum and substance of the law. The two commandments are cited together three times in the pseudepigraphic work called the Testaments of the Twelve Patriarchs (Test Iss 5:2; 7:5; Test Dan 5:3), but whether these references are Jewish or early Christian is disputed.

At the end of Luke's account of the conversation, the lawyer, "desiring to justify himself," asks, "And who is my neighbor?" It has been said that the whole history of man's moral development consists of ever broader answers to that question. Jesus answers it with a typically simple but graphic story (Lk 10:29-37) about a man who was waylaid, robbed, and beaten while "going down" from Jerusalem to Jericho, a steep descent through a rugged, desolate area. The kernel of the story is that the wounded man was left lying helpless beside the road by a passing priest and a Levite, and was given compassionate and effective help by a Samaritan.

Commentators have felt uneasy about the connection between the parable and the lawyer's question. Jesus asks at the end of the story (v 36) not "Who was the Samaritan's neighbor?" but "Which of these three proved neighbor to the man who fell among the robbers?" The parable turns the lawyer's question around, but therein lies the very point of Jesus' reply. Your neighbor, he implies, is anyone to whom you can be a neighbor.

Negatively, the neighbor is not to be defined in terms of belonging to one's own nation, religion, or social group, though undoubtedly in Leviticus "neighbor" meant precisely "fellow Israelite." (Race does not enter into the question here, because Jews and Samaritans did not belong to different races.) The priest and the Levite felt no neighborly obligation to the injured man, though he was presumably a Jew as they were. The Samaritan ignored the barrier of national and religious hostility in the face of human need. And the lawyer, to his credit, recognized that the real neighbor was the person who showed mercy.

Throughout this part of Luke's narrative the geographical designations are very vague. The incident that now follows (10:38-42) is said to have taken place "as they went on their way," in "a village" where two sisters, Martha and Mary, lived. If this was Bethany, as the Fourth Gospel says (Jn 11:1, 18), Jesus was already in Judea and close to Jerusalem. If its traditional identification is correct, Bethany was on the road from Jerusalem to Jericho, so that the story of the Good Samaritan may have been told on the very road where it is supposed to have happened. Later (Lk 13:22), however, we find Jesus still "on his way through towns and villages, teaching, and journeying toward Jerusalem." Still later he arrives at Jericho (19:1). It must be that Luke was not thinking of Bethany, unless he meant the "Bethany beyond the

Jordan'' mentioned (if that reading of the text is correct) in John (1:28). This may be a case of John's having better geographical knowledge than Luke, who probably was not thinking of any particular place.

Regardless of geography, the story of Martha and Mary is one of the richest in the Gospels in human interest. Many a good Christian woman sympathizes with Martha rather than Mary. The friendship of Jesus and these two sisters must have been close to make possible Martha's uninhibited complaint. Tired, hot, and nervous in her effort to serve their great guest, she blurted out her vexation at Mary for neglecting her share of the work, and at Jesus for letting her do it.

"Martha, Martha," said Jesus, and the gentle tone of his reproof is manifest in the repetition of her name; "you are anxious and troubled about many things." Any housewife knows that to get a good meal you must keep your mind on many things at once. Trying too hard to please, however, one may only embarrass a guest. Martha failed to see what Jesus really wanted. Mary, with a truer instinct, was willing to let the dinner wait and give Jesus the quiet attention and understanding he needed.

Certainly Martha and Mary are not mere types or symbols. The story may have been used, to be sure, to inculcate spiritual lessons; its usefulness for that purpose may explain its presence in Luke's source. Originally, however, it was probably preserved just because it was lovingly remembered. Incidentally it illustrates Luke's interest in the part played by women in Jesus' life and in the life of the church.

Luke introduces here the Lord's Prayer, included by Matthew in the Sermon on the Mount (Lk 11:1-4; Mt 6:9-13). In Luke it has a setting in the form of a request by one of the disciples that Jesus would teach them to pray as John the Baptist had taught his disciples. The prayer itself and the differences between Matthew's and Luke's versions of it have been considered where Matthew reports it.

Another of Luke's unique parables comes next (11:5-8), commonly known as the parable of the importunate neighbor, or the friend at midnight. It is told not as a story but as a question addressed to the disciples concerning what they would do in a hypothetical situation. Without waiting for them to reply, Jesus gives his own answer. Suppose one of you has an unexpected guest during the night, he says, and you have nothing in the house to give him to eat. If you go to one of your neighbors and ask him for food for your guest, he will not tell you that he has already gone to bed and cannot help you. Even if he will not do it for friendship's sake, he will get up and give you what you need to get rid of you.

The connection with prayer makes it appear that God is compared to a man who helps his neighbor only in order to get back to sleep. Such apparently unsuitable comparisons, however, are found in several of Jesus' parables and sayings. They were evidently characteristic of his teaching, following the "how much more" principle of the saying a few verses later in Luke: "If you then, who are evil, . . . how much more will the heavenly Father . . ." (Lk 11:13; cf. Mt 7:11).

The word translated "importunity" (KJV, RSV) means more literally "shamelessness" (NEB). The man who has been awakened regards his friend's request as outrageous, but responds, though grudgingly. How much more will the heavenly Father freely answer your prayers.

The parable is followed by a group of sayings (Lk 11:9-13) beginning, "Ask, and it will be given you," and ending with the "how much more" saying just quoted. Matthew has these sayings in the Sermon on the Mount, where we have discussed them (Mt 7:7-11).

Now Luke proceeds to the exorcism of a demon from a dumb man, corresponding to Matthew's healing of a blind and dumb demoniac (Lk 11:14; Mt 12:22-23). Mark does not have this miracle. In Matthew and Luke it leads to the "Beelzebul controversy" (cf. Mk 3:22-26), which is the second piece of Markan material in Luke's special section. Luke agrees here more closely with Matthew than with Mark, apparently combining two versions and adding a few touches of his own.

A saying shared only with Matthew is reported next by Luke (Lk 11:24-26; Mt 12:43-45). It is the one about an unclean spirit that comes back to a man it has abandoned. Then comes an incident reported by Luke alone (11:27-28). A woman in the

171

crowd cries out, expressing in the unsophisticated language of the common people of that time and country a feeling natural to a woman of any land or time, as much as to say, "How happy your mother must be to have such a son!" Jesus, however, replies, "Blessed rather are those who hear the word of God and keep it!" Perhaps the harsh words were spoken sadly. They recall Jesus' response when told that his mother and brothers wished to see him (Mk 3:33-35 and parallels): "Whoever does the will of God is my brother, and sister, and mother." Again some tension between Jesus and his own family is suggested.

The next paragraphs in Luke are strung together loosely with a few references to setting or occasion but no definite indications of time or place (Lk 11:29-32; Mt 12:38-42). First comes the passage about the sign of Jonah already discussed where Matthew gives it as Jesus' response to the demand for a sign (Lk 11:29-32; Mt 12:38-42). Then, as though continuing the same discourse, Luke quotes the saying about putting a lamp under a bushel and the one about the eye as the lamp of the body, which Matthew has used in the Sermon on the Mount (Lk 11:33-36; Mt 5:15; 6:22-23).

Luke continues (11:37–12:1; cf. Mt 23), "While he was speaking, a Pharisee asked him to dine with him; so he went in and sat at table. The Pharisee was astonished to see that he did not first wash before dinner." Earlier in Mark and Matthew some Pharisees criticized the disciples for eating with unwashed hands (Mk 7:1-23; Mt 15:1-20). Here the Pharisees at the dinner are shocked to see Jesus himself commit the same offense; and he delivers the denunciation of the Pharisees, which Matthew gives as the climax of a series of controversies in Jerusalem. We shall consider it in that connection, noting here only that the arrangement of the material in the two Gospels is quite different. In Luke the dinner supplies a setting for Jesus' charge that the Pharisees cleaned only "the outside of the cup and of the dish."

Luke's report of the whole discourse (11:39-52) conveys an impression of inconsiderate boorishness that it is hard to associate with Jesus. Perhaps Jesus actually ignored the niceties of polite behavior on such occasions and preferred to act like the tax collectors and sinners with whom he usually consorted. Conceivably the Pharisees had been treating him with supercilious condescension as a representative of "that class," regarding the dinner as a bit of slumming. Jesus might then have been answering the fool according to his folly (Prov 26:4-5). More probably Luke's setting for the denunciation is partly or wholly imaginary. We shall consider the contents of the indictment with Matthew's more elaborate version of it.

"As he went away from there," says Luke (11:53-54; 12:1), "the scribes and the Pharisees began to press him hard, and to provoke him to speak of many things, lying in wait for him, to catch at something he might say. In the meantime, when so many thousands of the multitude had gathered together that they trod upon one another, he began to say to his disciples first, 'Beware of the leaven of the Pharisees, which is hypocrisy.'"

We have noted the fact that in Mark and Matthew (Mk 8:15; Mt 16:6, 12) the leaven of the Pharisees is not said to be hypocrisy. The clause in Luke could be an insertion by some early reader, or it could be Luke's own interpretation. Either possibility appears more likely than that Jesus explained the expression immediately after using it. It was a natural interpretation in any case, and quite probably what Jesus intended. He did accuse the Pharisees of hypocrisy. Jewish historians have protested, and informed Christian scholars agree, that most of the Pharisees and scribes were not playing a part, pretending to be something that they were not.

A few sayings addressed to the disciples now follow in Luke. They consist of assurances included by Matthew in his second discourse (Lk 12:2-7; Mt 10:26-33), sayings about blasphemy against the Holy Spirit that Mark and Matthew have given in connection with the Beelzebul controversy (Lk 12:10; Mk 3:28-29; Mt 12:32), and the promise of the Spirit's aid in hearings before religious and civil authorities, which is quoted in Matthew's second discourse and later in Mark's apocalyptic discourse (Lk 12:11-12; Mt 10:19-20; Mk 13:11).

Then, to a man who says, "Teacher, bid my brother divide the inheritance with me," Jesus replies, "Man, who made me judge or divider over you?" (Lk 12:13-21). This refusal to act as a magistrate illustrates both Jesus' scorn for preoccupation with material possessions and his insistence on the individual's responsibility for his own decisions and conduct. The former emphasis is reinforced by a remark to the crowd (v 15): "Take heed, and beware of all covetousness; for a man's life does not consist in the abundance of his possessions." A parable presses the point home. God says to a rich man who thinks his large crops have brought him security, "Fool! This night your soul is required of you; and the things you have prepared, whose will they be?"

Sayings about anxiety used by Matthew in the Sermon on the Mount are presented next by Luke (Lk 12:22-32; Mt 6:25-33), coupled with one which combines the images of God as Shepherd, Father, and King. With this Luke gives (Lk 12:33-34; Mt 6:19-21) another saying in the Sermon on the Mount, the exhortation to lay up treasure in heaven.

The warnings that come next in Luke are used in Matthew's fifth discourse (Lk 12:35-46; Mt 24:42-51; 25:1-13). There they appear in an apocalyptic context, where it will be more convenient than here to discuss them. Here, however, at the end of the passage, there are three sentences that Matthew does not have (Lk 12:47-48). A servant who has not acted according to his absent master's will or prepared for his return will be beaten; one who did not know what the master wanted will receive a lighter beating. What is required of a man is in proportion to what has been given to him.

Here Luke records a difficult saying about casting fire on the earth and having a baptism to be baptized with (Lk 12:49-50). Neither Mark nor Matthew has this. The baptism with which Jesus expects to be baptized is mentioned a little later in Mark (10:38), where Jesus asks the ambitious sons of Zebedee whether they can undergo it. In that context it evidently means the suffering that Jesus and any who would share authority with him in his kingdom must endure. Luke attaches the saying to the ones about bringing division instead of peace; Matthew has these in his second discourse (Lk 12:51-53; Mt 10:34-36).

Luke adds here also the passage about interpreting the present time, quoted by Matthew as Jesus' answer to the demand for a sign (Lk 12:54-56; Mt 16:1-3). A saying preserved by Luke alone follows (12:57): "And why do you not judge for yourselves what is right?'' This leads to the saying about reconciliation with an accuser given by Matthew in the Sermon on the Mount (Lk 12:58-59; Mt 5:25).

Some distinctive and very important material found only in Luke is presented next. First comes a paragraph (13:1-5) that is almost unique in the Gospels in that it refers to contemporary events. Luke says that ''some present at that very time'' told Jesus of a massacre of Galileans ''whose blood Pilate had mingled with their sacrifices.'' If we could identify and date this event, and could be sure that it was reported to Jesus immediately, we should have one definite chronological point in his ministry. Unfortunately it is not recorded anywhere else. It would be only one of many cruel acts that eventually brought about Pilate's downfall.

In response to the news, Jesus mentioned another tragedy otherwise unknown. A tower in Siloam, a suburb of Jerusalem, had fallen and killed eighteen people. Those who lost their lives in these disasters, Jesus said, were not therefore to be considered greater sinners than other people. With reference to each event he added ''unless you repent you will all likewise perish.'' Nothing is more certain in Jesus' teaching than that sin without repentance will be punished. There is no softness in his assurance of God's love. God's forbearance is not unconditional or inexhaustible.

A parable brings this out (vv 6-9). The owner of an unfruitful fig tree ordered it cut down; but the gardener asked permission to cultivate and fertilize it one more year, and then destroy it if it bore no fruit. The view that Jesus was referring here to Israel as a whole rather than to individuals does not seem to me well founded.

After this comes a miracle of healing not related by the other evangelists (Lk 13:10-17). Like some other miracles, it was performed in a synagogue on the Sabbath and was denounced as a desecration of the holy day. The afflicted person this time was a woman who had suffered for eighteen years from a ''spirit of infirmity.'' Apparently her trouble was rheumatism or arthritis, for it is said that she was bent over and unable to straighten up, and when Jesus healed her ''she was made straight.'' Satan had bound her, Jesus said, but the cure is not reported as an exorcism. He called her, told her she was cured, and laid his hands upon her.

The ruler of the synagogue condemned this work of mercy, saying that sick people should come to be healed during the week. Jesus, however, called him a hypocrite. Any man, he said, would untie his ox or ass and lead it to water on the Sabbath. It was right to untie the bond of Satan that had held this "daughter of Abraham." The same argument has appeared in Matthew concerning the healing of a man with a withered hand (12:11-12). It will appear again in Luke with reference to a man who had dropsy (14:5).

Luke continues, "He said therefore," and quotes the parables of the mustard seed and the leaven, included by Mark and Matthew in their collection of parables (Lk 13:18-21; Mk 4:30-32; Mt 13:31-33). The narrative then proceeds (Lk 13:22), "He went on his way through towns and villages, teaching, and journeying toward Jerusalem." Luke crowds a good deal of material into the framework of the journey to Jerusalem, but none of it suggests that Jesus was working his way south gradually or indirectly.

When "some one" along the way asked, "Lord, will those who are saved be few?" Jesus responded with an exhortation to enter by the narrow door (Lk 13:22-27), adding a reference to knocking and not being admitted that resembles the conclusion of Matthew's parable of the bridesmaids (Mt 25:10-12) and is more intelligible there than here. Then comes the saying about many from east and west used earlier in Matthew (Lk 13:28-29; Mt 8:11-12). The passage ends with a cryptic statement quoted once in Mark and twice in Matthew: "And behold, some are last who will be first, and some are first who will be last" (Lk 13:30; Mk 10:31; Mt 19:30; 20:16).

CHAPTER XI

LUKE'S SPECIAL SECTION CONTINUED

Next we come to an incident related only by Luke (13:31-33). Some Pharisees said to Jesus, "Get away from here, for Herod wants to kill you." He replied, "Go and tell that fox, 'Behold, I cast out demons and perform cures today and tomorrow, and the third day I finish my course. Nevertheless I must go on my way today and tomorrow and the day following; for it cannot be that a prophet should perish away from Jerusalem.'"

When this was spoken, Jesus must have been in the territory of Herod Antipas, which included Galilee and Perea, but not Samaria. We have nowhere been told that he left Samaria, if he was ever there (cf. 9:51-52); but unless he was still in Galilee he must have crossed the Jordan somewhere. Most of the material in Luke's special section thus far appears in Mark and Matthew, if at all, in the Galilean portion of their narratives. This puzzle will require further attention presently.

The designation of Herod as "that fox" shows that Jesus neither admired nor feared him. The words "today, tomorrow, and the third day" are idiomatic (cf. Hos 6:2). Jesus' declaration means simply, "I have not finished my work yet; and until I do, Herod cannot hurt me." In the last clause Jesus indirectly refers to himself as a prophet (v 33). He also clearly implies that he expects to meet his death in Jerusalem (cf. Mk 8:31; 9:31; 10:33-34 and parallels).

Very appropriately Luke (13:34-35) connects this with Jesus' lament over Jerusalem, which Matthew (23:37-39), also appropriately, reports as spoken in the temple after the saying about "all the righteous blood shed on earth." Jesus condemns Jerusalem for killing the prophets and stoning those sent to her, but cries, "How often would I have gathered your children together as a hen gathers her brood under her wings, and you would not!"

When had Jesus tried to gather the people of Jerusalem? So far as anything in Luke's Gospel indicates, he had not been in Jerusalem since he was twelve years old. According to Matthew, when he uttered this lament he had been in Jerusalem about two days, and had not been there before that since he was a child. Yet the lament implies repeated efforts to appeal to the wayward city.

The saying about the righteous blood shed on earth is quoted by Luke (11:49) as spoken by "the Wisdom of God." Perhaps the reference here to having tried often to gather Jerusalem's children was originally conceived as spoken by the Wisdom of God or by God himself. That Jesus felt such a tender yearning and grief for Jerusalem is entirely probable, whether or not he spoke these particular words.

Now we have another dinner at the house of a Pharisee, this time on the Sabbath (Lk 14:1-6, cf. 11:37). Again only Luke reports the incident. The host was "a ruler who belonged to the Pharisees" (RSV), or more literally, "one of the rulers of the Pharisees." As often, Jesus was in hostile company. The other guests, Luke says, "were watching him." An occasion for controversy was afforded by the presence of a man afflicted with dropsy. This time Jesus himself raised the question, "Is it lawful to heal on the Sabbath, or not?" He then proceeded to heal the man, referring again to merciful treatment of an ass or an ox on the Sabbath (Lk 14:5; cf. 13:15). To this, Luke says, "they could not reply."

Jesus went on to tell his fellow guests how to behave (Lk 14:7-11). Seeing them pick places of honor for themselves at the table, he said that one who took the highest place at a marriage feast risked being asked to move down to make room for a more eminent guest, whereas one who took the lowest place would be conspicuously honored by being told to come higher. Luke calls this a parable, meaning an example for comparison. The point is stated as a general principle: "For every one who exalts himself will be humbled, and he who humbles himself will be exalted." (v 11; cf. 18:14; Mt 23:12). We shall find this repeated later.

Jesus then gave the host also some good advice (Lk 14:12-14). When you have a dinner, he said, you should invite not those who will return the favor but those who cannot do so, the poor and afflicted. Thus you will be truly blessed, and you will be rewarded at the resurrection of the righteous. One suspects that Luke is

178

using the dinner as a suitable setting for various sayings about such occasions.

What follows confirms this suspicion (Lk 14:15-24; cf. Mt 22:1-10). The mention of the resurrection evokes from one of the guests a devout ejaculation, "Blessed is he who shall eat bread in the kingdom of God!" The allusion to the Messianic banquet introduces a parable reported by Matthew as a part of Jesus' teaching in the temple.

A comparison of the two forms of this story provides an instructive example of the way Jesus' teaching was sometimes expanded and given new applications to meet the needs of the growing church and the interests of the evangelists. With some variations we have first a story that fits the situation confronted by Jesus in his ministry, reflects the social customs of Palestine in his day, and illustrates a point characteristic of his teaching. The invited guests represent the respectable portion of the Jewish nation who did not accept the invitation of the gospel. The outcasts brought in from the streets are the "sinners" who joyfully received the good news and entered the kingdom.

This much the two forms of the story have in common, but each Gospel has an addition of its own. In Matthew (22:10-14) the servants filled the wedding hall with "all whom they found, both bad and good." As a result, the king perceived in the throng a man without a wedding garment. Unable to explain his presence so improperly attired, the scoundrel was bound and thrown out. Here the point of the original parable is lost. What is stressed is Matthew's characteristic concern for the purity of the church.

For Luke it is not enough that the places of those who declined the invitation were filled by the poor and afflicted of the city. Having brought these in, the servant reported that there was still room, and he was sent out into the country to bring in others from the highways and hedges (Lk 14:22-23). This implies that not only the most despised members of the Jewish people may be admitted to the kingdom of God, there is room also for many from the east and the west (cf. Lk 13:29-30; Mt 8:11-12).

From here on Luke tacitly abandons the setting of the dinner at the Pharisee's house. Apparently assuming that Jesus was walking from one place to another, he says, "Now great multitudes

179

accompanied him; and he turned and said to them'' (14:25); then follows the saying about hating father and mother, which we have discussed with its parallel in Matthew (vv 26-27; Mt 10:37-38).

After this Luke has a twofold parable (14:28-33; cf. 11:5-8), in the form of two questions and the answers to them. A man wanting to build a tower, Jesus says, will "first sit down and count the cost, whether he has enough to complete it." Likewise a king thinking of going out to oppose an invasion will first consider whether his army can successfully resist the enemy. "So therefore," the parable ends, "whoever of you does not renounce all that he has cannot be my disciple." Jesus demands a complete sacrifice of personal possessions and attachments. We have encountered this theme and shall come back to it later.

Here Luke quotes the saying about salt that Matthew has in the Sermon on the Mount, and concludes with the familiar formula, "He who has ears to hear, let him hear" (Lk 14:34-35; Mt 5:13; Mk 9:50).

A notable trilogy of parables is next introduced by the statement, "Now the tax collectors and sinners were all drawing near to hear him. And the Pharisees and the scribes murmured, saying, 'This man receives sinners and eats with them'" (Lk 15:12; cf. Mk 2:15-16 and parallels). The complaint is answered first by the parable of the lost sheep, which has appeared earlier in Matthew (Lk 15:3-7; cf. Mt 18:12-14). Luke adds some details and states the meaning of the story: "There will be more joy in heaven over one sinner who repents than over ninety-nine righteous persons who need no repentance."

Luke alone reports the next parable (15:8-10). A woman who has a meager hoard of ten small silver coins, and loses one of them, Jesus says, will call her friends and neighbors together to share her joy when she finds it; and the conclusion follows: "Just so, I tell you, there is joy before the angels of God over one sinner who repents."

These two parables are not stories but generalizations in the form of questions, like the parable of the friend at midnight (cf. 11:5-8). The climax of the series, however, is a story (15:11-32). This time no moral is attached at the end; it is not needed, though the full impact of the parable is often missed through failure to read it against the background of the situation described at the beginning of the chapter.

Commonly called the parable of the prodigal son, the story has three equally important characters. They are all very real. We know people like them: the self-indulgent, confused younger son, who almost too late comes to himself; the father, who lets the boy make his own decisions but never stops loving him; the virtuous but hardhearted older son, reluctant to share the reward of his fidelity with a spendthrift brother. (One wonders whether the Pharisees and scribes recognized themselves in that picture.) The first two parables say, "Your Father loves his wandering children and welcomes them when they come home." The third says, "And so should you."

Next comes a parable (16:1-9), also reported only by Luke, which has probably caused more confusion than anything else in Jesus' teaching. This is the parable of the dishonest steward. An inefficient and corrupt estate manager, about to be thrown out of his job, arranges a soft landing place for himself by inducing his employer's debtors to falsify the amounts of their debts; and Jesus says, "The master commended the dishonest steward for his shrewdness." All kinds of rationalizations have been dreamed up to clear Jesus of any suspicion of praising such a scoundrel.

This is another "how much more" parable. In the statement that the master commended the dishonest steward, readers sometimes take the word "master" or "lord" to mean Jesus. The sentence is a part of the parable; it means that the employer said something like this: "You rascal, I must admit that you are clever, and I admire your resourcefulness." The Greek says literally, "because he acted shrewdly"; that is, he used his wits in the emergency.

Any interpretation that tries to make the steward anything other than a clever scoundrel misses the point. The significance of the master's commendation is expressed by the clause, "for the sons of this world are more shrewd in dealing with their own generation than the sons of light." The contrast of the sons of light and the sons of darkness marks the distinction between the worldly and those who seek the kingdom of God and his righteousness. To paraphrase Jesus' comment, people who are

181

concerned only with the affairs of this world often show more ingenuity in seeking their ends than religious people do in trying to accomplish God's will. In short, being good does not require being stupid.

The next sentence (16:9) reads, "And I tell you, make friends for yourselves by means of unrighteous mammon, so that when it fails they may receive you into the eternal habitations." The word "mammon" means wealth, and should be translated instead of being merely carried over into English. The clause, "when it fails," and the contrasting "eternal habitations," imply that you cannot take money with you, but you can use it to make friends, and friendship is eternal.

Providing for his own security by making friends is precisely what the steward did. Whether this verse was a part of the original parable, however, is another question. It is hard to reconcile with what Jesus says elsewhere about wealth. Perhaps it represents a generation that had relaxed the radical renunciation of wealth he demanded, and felt that after all you must be realistic and practical; wealth is all right if you make the right use of it. This gives the parable a meaning different from the quite adequate one stated in the previous verse, the need of intelligence in spiritual matters. For that reason verse 9 is probably a later addition to the parable. If it was spoken by Jesus at all, it was surely in some other connection.

If this parable has received a disproportionate amount of attention here, it is because it is so widely misunderstood. Our difficulties in interpreting the parables did not exist for those who heard Jesus tell them.

The sayings that now follow in Luke (16:10-13) were apparently placed here because they contain the word "mammon," which thus serves as a catchword to bind them together. The first one even repeats the expression, "unrighteous mammon." There is no good reason to doubt that they were spoken by Jesus, though not necessarily at the same time.

The statement, "He who is faithful in a very little is faithful also in much," is made more specific by the question, "If then you have not been faithful in the unrighteous mammon, who will entrust to you the true riches?" What is meant by the true riches is not indicated. It might be the knowledge of spiritual truth called in Mark "the secret of the kingdom of God" (Mk 4:11), but this is only one guess among many.

The next verse (Lk 16:12) is even more obscure: "And if you have not been faithful in that which is another's, who will give you that which is your own?" The steward in the parable had been unfaithful in what belonged to another, but what the application intended here may have been is not apparent. Perhaps the original context or circumstances made the reference clearer than it is now.

To these sayings Luke appends the one about serving God and mammon found also in the Sermon on the Mount (v 13; cf. Mt 6:24). Luke continues (16:14), "The Pharisees, who were lovers of money, heard all this, and they scoffed at him." Like the charge of hypocrisy, the description of the Pharisees as money lovers was not true of them as a group. Why they are singled out here is a mystery. Luke's remark seems to betray a personal animosity toward them.

To the scoffing of the Pharisees, Luke reports, Jesus replied (v 15), "You are those who justify yourselves before men, but God knows your hearts; for what is exalted among men is an abomination in the sight of God." Justifying themselves before men seems to mean expressing popular views and living the kind of life men admire. God knows the heart, and what wins the admiration of men has no value for him.

Now Luke records three sayings (16:16-18) given by Matthew in different places. First is the saying about the work of the prophets until John the Baptist and the proclamation of the kingdom of God since then, which we have already discussed (v 16; cf. Mt 11:12-13). Next is Jesus' statement that not a dot of the law will become void, reported by Matthew in the Sermon on the Mount (v 17; cf. Mt 5:18). Then comes the saying equating divorce and remarriage with adultery, also used in the Sermon on the Mount and repeated later by Matthew where Mark has it (v 18; cf. Mt 5:32; Mk 10:11-12; Mt 19:9).

The parable of the rich man and the beggar now follows (Lk 16:19-31). The beggar, named Lazarus, who received only "evil things" during his life, is taken at his death to Abraham's bosom

183

and comforted. The rich man, who received his "good things" on earth, goes to Hades, where he suffers torment and anguish in the flame, and begs Abraham to send Lazarus to warn his brothers, so that they may not "come into this place of torment." Abraham replies, "They have Moses and the prophets; let them hear them." It is evidently assumed that the rich man's life of ease and sumptuous feastings was evil, presumably because he was indifferent to the suffering of the beggar at his gate.

The picture of life after death in this parable is more detailed than any other in the Gospels. It is significant also because it deals with the intermediate state before the resurrection of the dead. Jesus was not imparting new information about the future life; his hearers understood the expressions used and accepted their presuppositions. The Gospels nowhere suggest that Jesus rejected or criticized the current beliefs. How literally the language and imagery were understood is of course another matter. It is interesting that the righteous and the wicked are separated at death (cf. 23:43). The dead are not simply asleep until the resurrection, or in a place of waiting or probation.

When Abraham said that the living had Moses and the prophets, the tormented man persisted: "No, father Abraham; but if someone goes to them from the dead, they will repent." Abraham denied that they would be convinced even "if some one should rise from the dead." Inevitably this strikes Christian readers as an allusion to the resurrection of Jesus. No doubt it was so intended; indeed the man's second plea and Abraham's reply were probably added later to the parable to make it a prophecy of the resurrection.

Luke introduces here the saying about one who caused a little one to sin, previously reported by both Mark and Matthew (Lk 17:1-2; cf. Mk 9:42; Mt 18:6-7). As in Matthew, this is coupled with the saying about a person through whom temptations come. Then comes the passage concerning a brother who sins and repents, followed by the saying about forgiving an offender seven times or more (Lk 17:3-4; cf. Mt 18:15, 21-22).

For the next saying, concerning faith like a grain of mustard seed (Lk 17:5-6; Mt 17:20), Luke provides an occasion: "The apostles said to the Lord, 'Increase our faith!'" The reference to the twelve as "the apostles" and the designation of Jesus as "the Lord" are both characteristic of Luke.

Then follows a saying, found only in Luke, which is clear in its religious meaning but somewhat disturbing in its apparent social implications (17:7-10). It is another "which of you?" parable; that is, not a story but a hypothetical case involving the hearers (cf. 11:5-8). To paraphrase, Jesus says: "When your servant comes in from a day's work in the field, you expect him to prepare and serve your supper before he eats or drinks anything himself. You don't thank him for doing what he was told, do you?" What a far cry from Jesus' characteristic compassion for those who labored! Essentially, though not formally, we may consider this a "how much more" parable. Jesus takes the farmers before him for what they are, and tells them not to expect God to give them any more credit for doing their duty than they give their servants. Man has no claim upon God. Having done his best, he is still an unprofitable servant. No room is left here for any doctrine of merit.

Next comes a healing miracle (Lk 17:11-19). Ten lepers, meeting Jesus as he was entering a village, stood at a distance and cried, "Jesus, Master, have mercy on us." Jesus told them to go and show themselves to the priests, and "as they went they were cleansed." One of them, a Samaritan, turned back to thank Jesus, who again, as in the case of the centurion's servant, expressed his wonder that only a foreigner praised God. "Rise and go your way," he said; "your faith has made you well."

The story is introduced with a very perplexing statement; "On the way to Jerusalem he was passing along between Samaria and Galilee." (KJV's "through the midst of Samaria and Galilee" appears at first sight to be a literal translation, but it is not what the Greek means, and creates an even greater geographical difficulty.) The last previous indication of the place Jesus had reached was the warning by the Pharisees that Herod wanted to kill him (13:31), implying that he was then either in Galilee or in Perea.

The only meaning that "passing along between Samaria and Galilee" can have is proceeding along their common boundary, which ran for about twenty miles in a generally southeast direction, along the edge of the plain of Esdraelon until it reached the head of the valley of Jezreel. There it turned south, dividing Samaria from the Decapolis instead of Galilee. If Jesus first crossed from Galilee to a Samaritan village somewhere along this border, and then proceeded southeast, possibly crossing back and forth once or twice along the way, that might explain Luke's cryptic expression. In that case Jesus had not yet crossed into Perea when he healed the ten lepers. The fact that Jesus called the Samaritan "this foreigner" suggests that they were on Jewish soil. The frequent mention of Pharisees in this part of the narrative also points to that conclusion.

No doubt Luke had little interest in geographical details, but it does not follow that he was utterly ignorant of the geography of Palestine. The general framework of his narrative must have had at least some basis in tradition, though Luke exercised complete freedom in fitting the units of the tradition into that framework. Possibly, therefore, he moved the story of the lepers, including the geographical note, to a later place than it had occupied in his source, though why he should do this is not apparent.

For Luke the incident affords one more demonstration that the Jews had no monopoly on the grace of God or on the qualities that God approved. Again a member of the community with which they had no dealings had shown himself better than representatives of the chosen people. "Where are the nine?" Jesus asked sadly.

Now the Pharisees come into the picture again, asking when the kingdom of God would come, and so evoking what must be the most debated of all Jesus' sayings about the kingdom (Lk 17:21). Even the correct translation of the Greek is a matter of disagreement among scholars. The rendering of the KJV, "within you," is literal and may be correct. Why then do so many modern versions change it to "among you" or "in your midst"? Not because the translators themselves do not believe in the presence of God's kingdom in the soul. The question is not whether what the KJV says is true, but whether it is what Jesus meant by this particular saying. A footnote on "among you" in the NEB shows how uncertain this is. It reads, "*Or* for in fact the kingdom of God is within you, *or* for in fact the kingdom of God is within your grasp, *or* for suddenly the kingdom of God will be among you."

The Greek preposition is ambiguous, and the two or three Aramaic prepositions that it might represent are equally so.

When God's kingship is accepted by an individual, it has in a sense come for him. In the context of the saying in Luke this interpretation seems unlikely, but that context may not be historical. Jesus might have said ''among you'' in the sense that he said ''has come upon you'' (cf. Mt 12:28; Lk 11:20). Or the saying may refer to the future. Jesus may have meant, ''While you are wondering when the kingdom will come, suddenly there it is in your midst.'' Such a prophetic use of the present tense for the future is not unusual. The conclusion of many, which I accept, that this is probably what Jesus meant, is based not on this verse by itself but on the combined evidence of all that he said about the kingdom of God.

Turning from the Pharisees to the disciples, Jesus continues (Lk 17:22-37; cf. Mt 24:26-27): ''The days are coming when you will desire to see one of the days of the Son of man, and you will not see it. And they will say to you, 'Lo, there! or 'Lo, here!' Do not go, do not follow them. For as the lightning flashes and lights up the sky from one side to the other, so will the Son of man be in his day.''

Matthew's version of this saying occurs in the apocalyptic discourse (Mt 24:23-25; Mk 13:21-23), combined with a warning against false Messiahs and false prophets. Instead of ''the days of the Son of man,'' Matthew says, ''the coming of the Son of man.'' Other differences between Matthew and Luke here do not affect the essential meaning of the passage. When the Son of man comes there will be no uncertainty about the fact; it will be unmistakably manifest everywhere.

The collocation of ideas in these sayings raises two questions: what is the relation between the coming of the Son of man and the coming of the kingdom of God, and what is the relation of the Son of man to the Messiah? For the evangelists, and probably for Jesus, the Son of man was the Messiah, both terms referring to Jesus himself, and the coming of the Son of man was a phase or aspect of the coming of the kingdom of God.

Luke explicitly identifies the Son of man with Jesus by adding here (v 25), ''But first he must suffer many things and be rejected

187

by this generation." Thus to the three predictions of the cross found in all three Synoptic Gospels (Mk 8:31; 9:31; 10:33-34 and parallels), and one explicit in Matthew but not in Mark (Mk 9:12; Mt 17:22), Luke gives here another mentioning only suffering and rejection. The expression "suffer many things" occurs also in two of Mark's predictions (Mk 8:31; 9:12).

Next Luke picks up another passage used by Matthew in the apocalyptic discourse (Lk 17:26-27; Mt 24:37-39), comparing the days of the Son of man with the days of Noah (cf. 2 Pet 3:1-9). (Again where Luke has "days" Matthew has "coming.") Luke adds a similar reference to the time of Lot, when Sodom was destroyed by fire and sulfur from heaven (Lk 17:28-30).

A saying included by both Mark and Matthew in the apocalyptic discourse follows, urging anyone who is on the housetop at that time not to come down into the house for his goods, and anyone who is in the field not to turn back (Lk 17:31; Mk 13:15-16; Mt 24:17-18; cf. Lk 21:21). Luke has the passage in that context also with some alteration. Here he omits fleeing to the mountains but adds (17:32) "Remember Lot's wife."

Then a saying reported earlier in all the Synoptic Gospels, and also included by Matthew in the instructions to the twelve, is repeated by Luke: "Whoever seeks to gain his life will lose it, but whoever loses his life will preserve it" (Lk 17:33; cf. Mk 8:35; Mt 16:25; Lk 9:24; Mt 10:39).

Now comes a series of three sayings corresponding to three given by Matthew in the apocalyptic discourse (Lk 17:34-37; Mt 24:40-41). Two deal with the sudden separation of the saved from the lost. The time is indicated as "that night." In Luke's form of the first saying, one of two men in the same bed will be "taken and the other left." Matthew speaks of two men in the field. The second saying declares that one of two women grinding grain together will be taken. Whatever is meant here by being taken or left, these sayings do not justify the lurid ideas of the "rapture" sometimes inferred from them and from what Paul says in 1 Thessalonians 4:17.

In Luke the passage ends with still another saying used by Matthew in the apocalyptic discourse (Lk 17:37; Mt 24:28). Characteristically Luke introduces it with a question by the disciples, "Where, Lord?" This can only mean "Where will one be taken and the other left?" Jesus replies, "Where the body is, there the eagles will be gathered together." In Matthew this saying follows the one about a flash of lightning, so that it plainly refers to the coming of the Son of man, which will not have to be sought here or there but will be clearly manifest.

Two more of Luke's unique parables follow. The first is another "how much more" parable (18:1-8). If a corrupt magistrate, indifferent alike to human need and divine law, would grant an importunate widow her rights merely to get rid of her, surely God, the altogether righteous judge, will speedily vindicate his elect when they cry to him. At the end of the parable there is a question: "Nevertheless, when the Son of man comes, will he find faith on earth?" This may have been a sad reflection by Jesus on the general lack of faith when he spoke. It reads, however, very much like a comment of the evangelist, or even of some reader or scribe.

"He also," Luke continues, "told this parable to some who trusted in themselves that they were righteous and despised others." Who they were is made plain by the parable, the story of a Pharisee and a tax collector who went to the temple to pray (18:9-14). The former thanked God that he was better than other men; the latter acknowledged that he was a sinner and begged God to forgive him. It was the tax collector, Jesus said, who went home "justified." Of course Jesus did not mean that the Pharisees were alone in being self-righteous, or that all tax collectors were humbly repentant. The point was that any person, regardless of appearances or status, who acknowledged his unworthiness was more acceptable to God than one who was proud of his righteousness. This was not only a general principle but an observed fact, as when he said to the chief priests and the scribes and elders, "The tax collectors and the harlots go into the kingdom of God before you" (Mt 21:31). Luke appends a maxim he has quoted before (v 14; cf. 14:11; Mt 23:12): "for everyone who exalts himself will be humbled, but he who humbles himself will be exalted."

CHAPTER XII

THE CONCLUSION OF THE JOURNEY TO JERUSALEM

Now Luke comes back to Mark's order of presentation with the story of Jesus' blessing children (Mk 10:13-16; Mt 19:13-15; Lk 18:15-17). This incident recalls the earlier one of the child "in the midst of them" (Mk 9:36; Mt 18:2-4; Lk 9:47); in fact, the saying about receiving the kingdom of God like a child, which Matthew has in that place, appears here in Mark and Luke. This time, however, the children are brought to Jesus that he may touch them, and the disciples rebuke the parents for doing this.

Jesus, says Mark, was indignant at the attempt to keep the children from him. "Let the children come to me," he said; "do not hinder them, for to such belongs the kingdom of God," that is, to children and to those who are like them (Mk 10:14, cf. Mt 5:3, 10; Lk 6:20). No doubt the reference is to the trusting dependence of children, their susceptibility to influence, readiness to imitate, and ability to learn.

All three Gospels relate now the story of the "rich young ruler," commonly so called because Matthew says he was young, Luke calls him a ruler, and all say that he was rich (Mk 10:17-27; Mt 19:16-26; Lk 18:18-27). This encounter is important for Jesus' attitude toward material wealth; yet it is generally accepted and passed over with surprising complacency.

In Mark and Luke the man asks, "Good Teacher, what must I do to inherit eternal life?" Jesus says "Why do you call me good? No one is good but God alone." In Matthew the man asks, "What good deed must I do to have eternal life?" and Jesus answers, "Why do you ask me about what is good? One there is who is good." The question and answer fit each other so much better in Mark and Luke than in Matthew that we can be sure it was Matthew who made the change, perhaps to avoid implying that Jesus was not good. The statement that only God is good need not imply that Jesus considers himself a sinner. He does distinguish between God and himself, but that should not be disturbing. Even in the Gospel of John, with its notably "high" Christology, Jesus constantly makes this distinction (*e.g.*, Jn 5:19; 14:20; 16:28; cf. 10:30; 17:21).

In both forms of the rich man's question it is assumed that salvation is to be gained by doing something. For Judaism the law is the revelation of God's will, by obedience to which eternal life is attained. This is presupposed by Jesus' reply, "You know the commandments," or as Matthew explicitly puts it, "If you would enter life, keep the commandments."

The rich man's purpose is "to inherit eternal life." The rendering "inherit" it not really appropriate. That is not the Greek verb's only meaning. It corresponds to a Hebrew and Aramic verb commonly used in the general sense of getting possession. Some such word as "obtain" or "gain" would be a better translation here.

The expression "eternal life" also requires explanation. It means much more than endless existence. The same expression appears again in this chapter (Lk 8:29-30; Mk 10:30; Mt 19:29) where Jesus assures Peter that those who have left everything to follow him will "receive . . . in the age to come eternal life." Once in the Old Testament (Dan 12:2) the two words are combined as in the Gospels: "And many of those who sleep in the dust of the earth shall awake, some to everlasting life, and some to shame and everlasting contempt." (The use of "everlasting" instead of "eternal" here merely retains the rendering of the KJV.)

The Jewish literature of the centuries after the completion of the Old Testament often contrasts "this age" and "the coming age." Being saved is called having a share in the coming age. The word for "age," however, came to mean also something like "world," and the idea of a new age shaded into the idea of a heavenly world already existing and "coming" only for those still alive on earth. (Hence KJV's "world to come" where the RSV has "age to come.") The word we translate "eternal" is derived from the word for "age" or "world." It refers not to the duration of the future life but to its quality: eternal life is the life of the coming age, the life of the kingdom of God.

Jesus' answer to the rich man's question mentioned some of the commandments. All three Gospels cite the prohibition of killing,

191

adultery, stealing, and false witness, and the command to honor parents. Mark adds another, "Do not defraud." This is not one of the ten commandments, but at the beginning of Deuteronomy 24:14 one major manuscript of the Septuagint reads, "Do not defraud" instead of "Do not wrong." Matthew adds another commandment not in the Decalogue (Lev 19:18), "You shall love your neighbor as yourself," given later by Jesus as the second greatest commandment in the law (Mk 12:31 and parallels).

The rich man protested that he had kept the commandments from his youth. "And Jesus looking upon him loved him," says Mark. Once more the appealing human note is passed over by Matthew and Luke. But had the man really kept the commandments? The third-century theologian Origen quotes an expanded version of this incident from the lost "Gospel According to the Hebrews," in which Jesus says to the rich man, "How can you say, 'I have fulfilled the law and the prophets,' when it is written in the law 'You shall love your neighbor as yourself'; and lo, many of your brothers, sons of Abraham, are clothed in filth, dying of hunger, and your house is full of many good things, none of which goes out to them?"

Jesus may have intended something like this when he went on to say, "You lack one thing." Perhaps he did not mean "Something more than keeping the commandments is needed," but rather "No, you have not fully kept the commandments." In Matthew the man asks what he still lacks, and Jesus' reply begins, "If you would be perfect," using the word found once before in Matthew, where, however, perfection is not optional: "You, therefore, must be perfect," Jesus says (Mt 5:48). Matthew's "If" here suggests that obeying the commandments will gain eternal life, but there is a higher stage attainable only by a few. Probably this reflects a time when the sharing of goods, as practiced at first in the church at Jerusalem, was coming to be regarded as requisite only for a limited inner circle of disciples.

What Jesus said the rich man still needed—"sell what you have, and give to the poor"—was too hard for him to accept, and "he went away sorrowful." He wanted to win eternal life, but not at the price of giving up what this age offered, "for he had great possessions." The sacrifice was harder for him than for one who

192

had nothing to lose. Jesus recognized this and said "How hard it will be for those who have riches to enter the kingdom of God!"

Again Jesus' effective use of hyperbole is manifest. "It is easier for a camel to go through the eye of a needle than for a rich man to enter the kingdom of God." The fact that there is a word for "rope" which is almost the same as the word for "camel" has tempted interpreters to suppose that Jesus spoke here of a rope, but to thread a needle with a rope is still impossible.

The astonishment of the disciples is amusing. If the recognized pillars of society cannot enter the kingdom, they thought, what hope can there be for poor people like us? Even now wealth is not commonly considered a barrier to influence or position in the church. Jesus said that anything is possible with God. It is worth noting that the rich man asks what to do to inherit eternal life, Jesus speaks of entering the kingdom of God, and the disciples ask who can be saved.

Impetuous Peter hastens to say, "Lo, we have left everything and followed you." Jesus assures him that the twelve and all who do as they have done will have ample recompense, both now and in the coming age (Mk 10:28-31; Mt 19:27-30; Lk 18:28-30). Mark specifies what the blessings of the present age are: "houses and brothers and sisters and mothers and children and lands, with persecutions." Certainly this does not mean that Jesus' followers will have new and larger families and new and richer estates, as Job did (Job 42:12-13). The new fellowship, new friendships, and mutual sharing of what little material goods any of them may have will more than make up for what they have lost. All this will come "with persecutions." Possibly this phrase was added later, when persecution had become a major factor in Christian experience (cf. Mt 10:17-25). Jesus himself, however, had enough experience of persecution to be aware of what his followers would have to expect.

Matthew reports here a promise (Mt. 19:28; cf. Lk 22:28-30) that when the Son of man sits on his glorious throne the disciples will "sit on twelve thrones, judging the twelve tribes of Israel." In Luke this is spoken at the last supper. The thrones correspond to the twelve tribes and to the twelve disciples, but what twelve? Was Judas included? The twelve tribes of Israel are surely not to

193

be taken in a literal, exclusive, or preferential sense, any more than the thrones are to be taken literally. It must mean the whole people of God, first Jews but also Gentiles.

The story of the rich man and what follows it raise searching questions for Christian life in our world today. Did Jesus issue a challenge that we do not and cannot meet? Did Jesus mean that any person who would enter the kingdom of God must divest himself of possessions and sever all family ties? His call for repentance and faith was directed at least to the whole house of Israel. The promises were unmistakably intended for all who were humble and merciful and pure in heart, all who accepted the kingdom like little children. Jesus condemned rich men who were indifferent to the plight of those less fortunate (*e.g.*, Lk 16:19-31), but he accepted the hospitality of others. Martha and Mary (Lk 10:38-42) had not left all to follow him, and the women who ministered to him out of their own means (Lk 8:2-3; cf. Mk 15:40-41 and parallels) had not given all they had to the poor. Later Zacchaeus is declared saved after giving half of his goods to the poor and restoring fourfold what he had gained by fraud (Lk 19:8-9). Joseph of Arimathea is called both a rich man and a disciple by Matthew (27:57; cf. Mk 15:43; Lk 23:51).

Jesus asked of the rich man not only "sell and give" but also "come, follow." Disposing of his property was required not so much to help the poor as to enable the man to follow Jesus. The verb "follow" does not necessarily involve becoming a disciple, but it often implies going about with Jesus and eventually going with him to Jerusalem. Nowhere is "follow" used in a figurative sense of accepting Jesus and his gospel and being guided by his teaching.

Did Jesus then limit the hope of eternal life to the group of those who so followed him? Not unless there was a change in his thinking during his ministry. To suppose so is precarious; it is also precarious to assume that there was no change. There was a change in the situation he faced, from the enthusiasm in Galilee, through the growing opposition of the authoritites, and the falling off of his following as it became clear that he was not what many expected. Possibly therefore his own hope of general acceptance was chilled, and his estimate of the number that would prove ready for the kingdom of God reduced. The poor and humble, to whom the kingdom belonged, might then have been almost identified with his immediate followers. Yet Mary and Martha probably, Zacchaeus and Joseph certainly, come near the end of the story.

The evangelists distinguished between the many who heard gladly and believed and the relatively few who accompanied Jesus. This is shown not only by Matthew's use of the word "perfect" (Mt 5:48; 19:21). Mark has the idea of the secret of the kingdom of God, which is hidden from "those outside" (Mk 4:11 and parallels). This appears in connection with a mistaken conception of Jesus' reason for using parables but to assume that the whole idea of an inner circle reflects later developments is unjustified.

Were there then different conditions of entrance to the kingdom for those inside and those outside? Jesus made extra demands of those who literally followed him. The historical situation and the circumstances of his ministry made this inevitable, but those who sincerely endeavored to do God's will within their normal social relations were the people to whom he said the kingdom belonged. It is quite incredible that he would have changed his mind about that.

Sayings demanding radical renunciation exist along with others that resemble the directions for everyday life in the wisdom literature. There are also sayings that make no reference to a change in the existing order of the world and others that indicate that the end of the present age is near. The sayings that presuppose that things will continue unchanged are, on the whole, those which give instructions appropriate to such a situation. The sayings that demand radical renunciation, however, are not those which stress the imminent end of the age. In what Jesus says to the disciples after the rich man departs, for instance, the distinction between the two ages is clear, but there is no suggestion that the change is coming soon. The sayings that do stress the nearness of the change say nothing about leaving home and possessions, but emphasize the same everyday virtues exalted by the beatitudes and similar sayings (Mt 24:45-51; 25:31-46; Lk 12:42-48; 21:34).

What does loom on the horizon in the "leave all and follow"

195

sayings is the crisis of rejection, suffering, and death at Jerusalem. If Jesus hoped that the kingdom of God would come then, there is nothing to suggest this in the sayings themselves. It is because of this impending crisis, at least after Caesarea Philippi (Mk 8:31, 34 and parallels), that the call to follow Jesus involves renunciation of possessions and human ties. Before that, the exigencies of constant travel entailed more or less similar sacrifices, but after Jesus "set his face to go to Jerusalem" (Lk 9:51) it became clear that to follow him one must repudiate all other involvements. What Jesus said about the inevitability of such sacrifice was not so much a demand as a warning of what they must expect.

This means that the two sets of requirements—those which apply to life in this world and those which amount to a denial of the world—were prescribed for different people. For much the larger group, being a disciple of Jesus meant adopting his faith and the way of life he taught. For the small group, it meant giving up all ambition or hope in this age and relying on the blessings of the age to come. Both groups would inherit the kingdom.

Jesus' response to Peter's reminder of what the disciples have sacrificed ends with the warning, "But many that are first will be last, and the last first" (Mk 10:31; Mt 19:30). Luke has used this earlier (13:30), referring to those who hear the word but do not practice it. Here it suggests that the first disciples cannot expect precedence or superiority in the kingdom of God. Matthew evidently understands it so, for he gives here (20:1-16) the parable about the laborers who were hired at different hours of the day to work in a vineyard, but were all paid the same wages for their day's work; and at the end of the parable he says, "So the last will be first, and the first last."

As in other parables, the conduct of the owner of the vineyard in this story is not only peculiar but questionable, both economically and morally. The men who worked all day seem justified in feeling that they should be paid more than those who have worked only an hour. The owner, however, dismisses their complaint, saying that they have received what they bargained for, and he has a right to be generous to the others with his own money. The parable has been cited in support of minimum wage

196

laws and unemployment compensation. The fallacy of using it in this way lies in attaching significance to details that were intended only to make an interesting story. Such items, however, show at least that Jesus observed with sympathy the plight of hired labor in the economic and political situation of Palestine. He was talking, however, about the kingdom of God, which is not governed by the economics of secular society.

As a rebuke to any who might expect a superior place in the kingdom because they had been the first to follow Jesus (cf. Mk 10:35-41 and parallels), the parable makes the assurances in the preceding paragraph appear to be only preliminary. "You may be sure," Jesus says in effect, "that you and all who have given up so much to follow me will have abundant compensations, but don't suppose that because you were the first to do so you are better than others. The blessings of the kingdom of God are not measured by length of service. They are not earned but granted by God's grace."

With Mark and Luke, Matthew now records Jesus' third prediction of his death (Mk 10:32-34; Mt 20:17-19; Lk 18:31-34). "And they were on the road, going up to Jerusalem," says Mark, "and Jesus was walking ahead of them; and they were amazed, and those who followed were afraid." When he took the twelve aside, what he said showed that there was reason for their fear. It was the same as the first two predictions (Mk 8:31; 9:31 and parallels) but even more specific. Luke adds two items; "everything that is written of the Son of man by the prophets will be accomplished" (18:31); and, "But they understood none of these things; this saying was hid from them, and they did not grasp what was said" (v 34).

The Old Testament nowhere says that the Son of man will be rejected, betrayed, and killed. There must have been some prophecy to which these reiterated statements refer, but it would have to be one in which the term Son of man was not used. In Luke's account of the appearance at Emmaus (Lk 24:25-27, 44-47) similar expressions are applied to the Messiah, but there are no such prophecies about the Messiah either. In another place (Lk 22:37) Jesus says, "This scripture must be fulfilled in me," and "what is written about me has its fulfillment." That is obviously the meaning in all these passages.

If we ask what prophecy or prophecies may be referred to regardless of particular designations, the only chapter in the Old Testament that tells of one who innocently suffered and "bore the sin of many" is the fifty-third chapter of Isaiah (53:12). It is often denied that Jesus himself understood his suffering and death in terms of Isaiah 53. That interpretation, it is maintained, arose among his followers after the crucifixion and resurrection. The evangelists believed that Jesus found in this prophecy the meaning of his own rejection and suffering. The reasons given for considering this erroneous do not seem to me conclusive. Whatever the prophet meant by his description of the suffering servant of the Lord, what seemed obvious to Jesus' disciples may very well have been equally so for him.

The caution against expecting special privilege in the kingdom of God seems not to have been taken to heart by all the disciples. Next in Mark and Matthew but omitted by Luke is the request of James and John (or their mother, as Matthew has it) that they might sit at Jesus' right and left in his glory (Mk 10:35-40; Mt 20:20-23). "You do not know what you are asking," Jesus replied, and asked whether they could drink his cup and be baptized with his baptism. Whether two different trials are symbolized is not clear. Matthew mentions only the cup.

Evidently the sons of Zebedee still had very little understanding of Jesus' mission. They expected him to set up an earthly kingdom and distribute high offices in it among his followers. The other ten expressed self-righteous indignation, but perhaps it was the effort to get ahead of them that aroused their ire.

The disciples' inability to comprehend what Jesus tried to tell them is a recurrent theme in all the Gospels (Mk 6:52; 7:18; 8:17-18, 21; Mt 15:16; 16:9, 11; Lk 9:45). A critical reader may suspect that this idea grew out of later reflection and served an apologetic interest; yet it is true to human nature and experience. On this occasion Jesus called them to him and told them, as he had before (cf. Mk 9:35; Lk 9:48), that the greatest among them would be the slave of the rest; they were not to lord it over men, as the rulers of the nations did (cf. Lk 22:24-26). To this is added

(Mk 10:45; Mt 20:28), "For the Son of man came not to be served but to serve, and to give his life as a ransom for many." The word "many" in this connection recalls Isaiah 53:11-12: "By his knowledge shall the righteous one, my servant, make many to be accounted righteous; and he shall bear their iniquities," and "he bore the sin of many." Here, as in Daniel (12:2, 4, 10), "many" is meant to suggest a contrast not between many and all but between few or none and many.

In this saying the Son of man is unmistakably Jesus, but the statement may not be a part of what Jesus said. It may be a comment by the evangelist or some teacher or preacher before him (cf. Mk 2:28). If so, this use of "Son of man" may have to be ascribed to a predilection for this title in some part of the early church, which gave these sayings their present form. In that case the conception of Jesus' death as a ransom may also have originated in the church. That would not make this interpretation of the cross less true, but it would substantially reduce our evidence for what Jesus taught about himself and his work.

There is a saying in Luke that is similar to this one but lacks the term "Son of man," the reference to Jesus' death, and the allusion to Isaiah 53. Luke reports it after the last supper (22:27). In the Gospel of John, Jesus acts out this idea, rising from the table, girding himself with a towel, and washing the disciples' feet (13:3-17). One wonders whether the story grew out of Luke's saying.

After the rebuke of the sons of Zebedee, the Synoptic Gospels all report a miracle of healing at or near Jericho (Mk 10:46-52; Mt 20:29-34; Lk 18:35-43). Mark and Matthew say it occurred as Jesus was leaving Jericho; Luke says it was "as he drew near to Jericho." Presumably they had just crossed the Jordan, if they had been moving southward through Perea. Mark calls the man who was healed "Bartimaeus, a blind beggar, the son of Timaeus." Since Bartimaeus means "son of Timaeus," this is an instance of Mark's practice of quoting Aramaic expressions with their meaning in Greek (cf. Mk 3:17; 7:11, 34; 14:36; 15:34). Luke does not mention the name; Matthew again has two blind men. Both here and in Matthew's earlier account (9:27-31) the blind men address Jesus as Son of David, and Jesus touches their eyes.

199

Why Matthew has both stories and has two blind men in each of them is a mystery. It must be more than a coincidence that he also has two demoniacs in his account of the Gadarene swine (Mt 8:28; cf. Mk 5:2; Lk 8:27).

According to Mark, Bartimaeus was told that his faith had cured him; and "immediately he received his sight and followed him on the way." Luke adds, "glorifying God," and concludes characteristically, "and all the people, when they saw it, gave praise to God."

The accounts of this miracle agree that Jesus was addressed as "Son of David." This term appears only here in Mark and Luke in addressing Jesus. Matthew has it in several other places.

Luke alone recounts another incident (19:1-10) as Jesus "entered Jericho and was passing through," the conversion of Zacchaeus. The amusing picture of the rich tax collector who climbed a tree to see Jesus is familiar. It is easy to imagine his suprise when Jesus looked up and said, "I must stay at your house today," as well as the murmuring of the crowd because Jesus had chosen to visit a "sinner." Even more astonishing must have been Zacchaeus' announcement that he would give half of his goods to the poor and restore fourfold any amount by which he had defrauded anyone.

Jesus welcomed the declaration, saying, "Today salvation has come to this house, since he also is a son of Abraham." The last clause apparently means that Zacchaeus had shown himself to be a true Jew after all. It seems strange that Luke, of all the evangelists, most often uses such expressions as "son of Abraham" (1:73; 13:16; 16:24-30). Perhaps the idea, reinterpreted as a matter of faith and life rather than ancestry (cf. Rom 4:13, 16; Gal 3:7, 29), was already popular in the circle from which Luke's unique material was derived.

The account of this incident closes with the statement (Lk 19:10; cf. Mt 18:11), "for the Son of man came to seek and to save the lost" (the Greek word is a neuter singular). Some manuscripts and versions have an almost exact parallel to this in Matthew after the saying about the angels of the little ones. Probably the sentence had circulated separately and was not originally a part of the story of Zacchaeus. More important than the origin of the saying is the conception of Jesus' mission expressed here and elsewhere. That it represents his own conviction is confirmed by his conduct. His attention and concern were not devoted to the respectable, self-satisfied, and no doubt usually sincere "righteous people," but to those whom they despised as outside the pale.

Luke continues (19:11-27), "As they heard these things, he proceeded to tell a parable, because he was near to Jerusalem, and because they supposed that the kingdom of God was to appear immediately." From Jericho to Jerusalem there was still a long, steep climb, but the disciples may have felt that they were nearing the consummation of their hopes. Thus the parable of the pounds, which now follows, is given a definite setting and purpose. At the time when Luke's Gospel was written the delay of the kingdom, thought of in terms of Jesus' coming again, had become an urgent problem. It is quite possible, however, that as Jesus drew near to Jerusalem there were many who expected him to manifest himself as Messiah there and set up again the kingdom of David. Not a few scholars have believed that this was his intention. If, however, he expected rejection and suffering, he might well try to allay such a misapprehension.

Whether that was the original purpose of this parable is another question. Its bearing, if any, on an expected coming of the kingdom could only be that Jesus was about to leave his disciples but would return and require an accounting of what they had done during his absence. For the early church, fervently expecting his coming at any moment, this understanding of the parable would be natural. In either context it implied that there was still time for a diligent use of God's gifts. This applies also to Matthew's parable of the talents (Mt 25:14-30), undoubtedly a variant form of the same story.

The basic meaning of the parable of the pounds or talents as a whole is that God's servants are required to make the best use they can of what he gives them. To this Matthew's story adds the idea that the responsibility of individuals varies in proportion to their gifts. The word "talent," through its use in this parable, has come to mean any special ability or aptitude. The responsibility that

201

such gifts or deposits carry with them is not always remembered by those who speak of talent or of being talented.

One servant merely hid his master's money and returned the exact amount he had received. His share was taken from him and given to the one who had made the largest profit. That seems unfair. It is quite in keeping, however, with the unequal distribution of abilities and advantages in real life. At the end of the parable both Matthew and Luke have the statement that he who has will receive more, and he who has not will lose even what he has. This too is often the case in life. Whether it is in accord with the will of God is another question. Is God hard, like the master in this parable? Jesus probably intended it only to enforce each person's responsibility for his use of what God gave him. This general statement, then, merely notes a common fact, though Matthew and Luke treat it as part of the master's words and add another sentence. The original point of the parable was like that of the parable of the faithful and unfaithful servants (Lk 12:48); "Every one to whom much is given, of him will much be required; and of him to whom men commit much they will demand the more."

After the parable Luke says (19:28), "And when he had said this, he went on ahead, going up to Jerusalem," Here Luke's account of the journey from Galilee ends. Mark and Matthew have already finished this part of their narratives with the healing of Bartimaeus or the two blind men.

CHAPTER XIII

THE FIRST DAYS AT JERUSALEM

Even in the spring, at Passover time, the trip up to Jerusalem from Jericho is a hot one. No doubt when Jesus and his followers reached a village near the foot of the Mount of Olives they were glad to stop there (Mk 11:1-10; Mt 21:1-9; Lk 19:29-38). Mark and Luke say they "drew near to Bethphage and Bethany"; Matthew mentions only Bethphage. There is now at the traditional site of Bethany a little village called El-Azzariyah, the name being derived by a curious corruption from the name Lazarus. Bethphage is located by tradition a little farther up the eastern slope of the Mount of Olives.

On arriving in this vicinity Jesus said to two of his disciples, "Go into the village opposite you, and immediately as you enter it you will find a colt tied, on which no one has ever sat; untie it and bring it." The expression "opposite you" probably means here "ahead of you." Which village is meant is not clear. Jesus' assurance that a colt was there ready for him, and that the disciples would be allowed to take it, seems like supernatural knowledge. It is pleasant to imagine, however, that an inhabitant of the village had seen Jesus and heard him speak somewhere, and had been aroused to such admiration that he said, "Master, I have a fine young donkey at home. He's yours any time you want him."

Matthew has a curious variation here. The disciples find "an ass tied, and a colt with her," with the strange result that Jesus sits on both of them. (The Greek says this plainly.) How this came about is plain. Matthew says that the incident "took place to fulfil what was spoken by the prophet," and quotes from Zechariah:

> Tell the daugher of Zion,
> Behold, your king is coming to you,
> humble and mounted on an ass,
> and on a colt, the foal of an ass.

(Zech 9:9)

203

This is an instance of a characteristic feature of Hebrew poetry known as parallelism, that is, a close relation in meaning between two successive lines (cf. Gen 49:11). The ass and the colt are the same animal; but Matthew supposes that the prophecy refers to two animals, and therefore there must have been two when it was fulfilled.

The narrative continues, "And many spread their garments on the road, and others spread leafy branches which they had cut from the fields." This joyful procession is commemorated by Christians on Palm Sunday, yet neither Mark nor Matthew mentions palm branches, and Luke says nothing of branches at all. Only in the Gospel of John is it said (12:13), "So they took branches of palm trees," and there the people who bring them are pilgrims who come out from the city to meet Jesus (11:55-56; 12:12-13). Palms are uncommon at the altitude of Jerusalem, though a few may be seen there. Mark says the branches were cut from the fields, and Matthew says the people cut them from the trees. Possibly they were olive branches.

The words of acclamation shouted by the crowd are quoted from the 118th Psalm (v 25). The evangelists report them with considerable variation. The word "Hosanna" is the Hebrew verb translated in the Psalm, "Save us, we beseech thee"; but it is used here as a noun like "glory" or "praise." That use of it must have arisen among Greek-speaking Christians.

The second sentence in the acclamation comes from the same Psalm (v 26). Originally it may have been meant for the king of Judah when he entered the temple to celebrate the feast of Tabernacles, or perhaps for citizens or pilgrims who came for the same purpose. That the Jews of Jesus' day believed this verse to be addressed to the Messiah is not likely. In Matthew it becomes a Messianic blessing through the insertion of the phrase "to the Son of David." Mark is only a little less definite: he adds, "Blessed is the kingdom of our father David that is coming." Luke reads, "Blessed is the king who comes in the name of the Lord!" (cf. Jn 12:13).

This event is of crucial importance for the much debated question whether Jesus believed himself to be the Messiah. The triumphal entry, as it is commonly called, is usually regarded as a deliberate demonstration of his Messianic authority. The evangelists clearly so understood it, looking back at it from their later Christian point of view. Probably many of those present at the time so regarded it. Possibly Jesus so intended it. It is equally possible, however, that he rode a donkey for the last part of the journey because it was given to him and he was tired, and that the popular acclaim was not welcome to him. Riding into Jerusalem on a donkey was not unusual. Which interpretation is more probable can be judged only on the basis of all that Jesus said and did, not only at this time but before and after he entered Jerusalem.

In Matthew (21:10-11) "all the city" is stirred and asks, "Who is this?" The crowds answer, "This is the prophet Jesus from Nazareth of Galilee." The crowds who said this could hardly be the same as those who hailed him as the Son of David. No doubt there were other bystanders who knew of his work in Galilee.

Jesus' approach to Jerusalem undoubtedly looked like a march on Washington. He could have been a prophet of revolt, however, without claiming to be the Messiah. Many have argued that he was a revolutionist like the Zealots, or even one of them. Such an interpretation is in some ways tempting. Certainly the vociferous enthusiasm of the throng must have aroused the suspicious attention of the authorities, both religious and civil. Disturbances among the people at the time of a religious festival, when the city is crowded with strangers, have always been feared at Jerusalem. Messianic pretenders were nothing new in first-century Palestine (cf. Acts 5:36-37; 21:38).

According to Luke (19:39-40), "some of the Pharisees in the multitude" urged Jesus to rebuke his disciples; but he replied, "I tell you, if these were silent, the very stones would cry out." Like what he said later about the children in the temple, as reported by Matthew (21:15-16), this sounds as though Jesus approved what his followers were saying. Luke adds here, however, a prediction of Jerusalem's doom (19:41-44), which suggests that Jesus was only saddened by the wild hopes of a restored kingdom of David. "And when he drew near and saw the city"—that is, when he crossed the top of the Mount of Olives and saw Jerusalem before him across the Kidron Valley—"he wept over it, saying, 'Would

205

that even today you knew the things that make for peace! But now they are hid from your eyes. For the days shall come upon you," and a specific prediction of the fall of Jerusalem follows. Only Luke reports this, but there are passages in the other Gospels to compare with it (cf. Mt 23:37-39; Lk 13:34; Mk 13:2; Mt 24:2; Lk 21:6).

Many commentators see here such a clear reflection of the siege of Jerusalem by Titus in A.D. 70 that they feel the prediction must have originated after that event. There is nothing here, however, that goes beyond the normal procedure for reducing a rebellious city in those days. The important point in what Jesus says is that it condemns a political, military type of Messianic hope and repudiates as futile the Zealots' program of revolt against Rome. Jerusalem has failed to recognize the real way to peace.

On reaching the city, according to all the Synoptic Gospels, Jesus went immediately to the temple (Mk 11:11; Mt 21:10-17; Lk 19:45-46). Crossing the narrow valley, he could go directly into the temple area through a gate in the eastern wall of the city. Matthew and Luke indicate that he performed at once what they, or at least Matthew, evidently consider an act of Messianic authority, the cleansing of the temple (Mt 21:10-13; Lk 19:45-46). Mark, however, puts this on the following day and says that on the first day Jesus only "looked round at everything." We can only imagine what thoughts may have stirred in his mind as he stood there. Then, "as it was already late, he went out to Bethany with the twelve" (Mk 11:11).

Matthew says that blind and lame people came to Jesus in the temple that day and were healed (21:14). The chief priests were indignant at some children who cried, "Hosanna to the Son of David" in the temple. "Do you hear what these are saying?" they asked Jesus. He replied with a verse of Scripture that was notably appropriate but must have seemed impertinent to the priests and elders (Ps 8:2): "Yes; have you never read, 'Out of the mouths of babes and sucklings thou hast brought perfect praise'?"

On the way back to the city the next morning Jesus was hungry. According to Mark and Matthew, he went to a fig tree beside the road but found no fruit on it, and said, "May no one ever eat fruit from you again" (Mk 11:12-14; Mt 21:18-19). It is hard to believe that Jesus would have uttered a wish so unworthy of him. He might have expressed impatience at not finding fruit on a tree when he wanted it. But would he have expected it at that time of year? Normally figs are not ripe in the vicinity of Jerusalem until late in the summer. Jesus would know this. Even at a more appropriate season, such a reaction would not be admirable or consistent with what we know of Jesus' character.

Perhaps this explains Luke's omission of the incident. Mark and Matthew, however, are interested in the miraculous aspect of the story. Matthew even says that the tree ''withered at once,'' though according to Mark it was when Jesus and the disciples came back the next day that they found the tree withered.

Both Mark and Matthew treat the incident as a demonstration of the power of faith (Mk 11:20-24; Mt 21:20-22). According to Mark, when Peter called attention to the withering of the tree, Jesus said. ''Have faith in God.'' Both Gospels report here the saying about causing a mountain to be uprooted and cast into the sea by faith. Then follows a general statement that one who prays for anything with faith will receive it (cf. Mt 7:7-11; Lk 11:9-13). In Mark, as in the Sermon on the Mount, this is qualified by the condition that we must forgive others before we can expect God to forgive us (Mk 11:25; cf. Mt 6:14). This is one of only two places where Mark has a parallel to anything in the Sermon on the Mount, and the only place where Mark has the expression ''Father who is in heaven.'' Verse 26 is omitted by some important manuscripts and most recent translations (RSV, NEB, JB, NAB; TEV brackets it).

Some interpreters suppose that Mark and Matthew saw here a symbolic reference to the Jewish nation's failure to accept the gospel (cf. Mt 21:43). There is no hint of this in the narrative or its context. Many scholars believe that in the development of the tradition a parable had come to be misunderstood as a record, and robbed of its real meaning in the process (cf. Lk 13:6-9).

As it stands, this is the last of the nature miracles in the Synoptic Gospels. Three of these, the feeding of the five thousand and the four thousand and the walking on the sea, may have originated as allegories of the power of Christ to preserve his disciples and supply their needs. The miraculous catch of fish and the stilling of the storm are devout legends exalting Christ and encouraging faith. The discovery of a coin in the mouth of a fish and the withering of the fig tree are quite incredible tales, the former probably a legend of the early church and the latter perhaps a denatured parable. All can be explained without assuming any basis in actual, specific acts of Jesus.

Between the cursing of the tree and its withering Mark puts the cleansing of the temple (Mk 11:15-19; Mt 21:12-13; Lk 19:45-46; cf. Jn 2:13-17). The Johannine account of this event says that Jesus made "a whip of cords" and "drove them all, with the sheep and oxen, out of the temple." The words translated "with the sheep and oxen" (RSV) may mean "both the sheep and the oxen" (cf. TEV, NAB), implying that the whip was used only on the animals. There is no such ambiguity in the Synoptic account: "And he entered the temple and began to drive out those who sold and those who bought in the temple." Nothing is said of oxen and sheep, but Mark and Matthew say that Jesus "overturned the tables of the money-changers and the seats of those who sold pigeons." Luke says only that Jesus "began to drive out those who sold."

Mark adds, "and he would not allow any one to carry anything through the temple," and continues, "And he taught." Matthew and Luke omit this but agree with Mark that Jesus said, "It is written, 'My house shall be called a house of prayer', but you make it a den of robbers." The quotation is from Isaiah 56:7; the statement echoes Jeremiah's protest (7:11), "Has this house, which is called by my name, become a den of robbers in your eyes?" The temple cultus, with its sacrifices and offerings and the arrangements for providing sacrificial victims, had become such an elaborate, noisy, and odorous affair that to the earnest young prophet from Galilee the spirit of true worship must have seemed to be lost. His reaction was like that of the Old Testament prophets (*e.g.*, Is 1:12; Amos 5:21; Hos 6:6; Mic 6:6-7).

This event is undoubtedly historical, and it is important. Unfortunately, it is also open to more than one interpretation. If the "triumphal entry" looks like a march on Washington or Rome, the cleansing of the temple looks very much like an occupation of the administration building and a sit-in, such as marked the turbulent sixties. It is so considered by more than one recent writer. Some have even supposed that Jesus and his followers took possession of the temple area and held it by force. This is contrary to all the evidence. There is no indication that Jesus tried to take over the administration of the temple, or that the disciples had any part in the proceedings.

The incident is often cited to justify the use of force. Jesus did not expel the traders by force. One man could not have done that if there had been any resistance. On the other hand, something more than gentle persuasion was involved. Upsetting tables and chairs and scattering the coins on the pavement was, to say the least, direct action. To judge not only by this incident but also by the bitter invective Jesus sometimes uttered, as well as Mark's statement (3:5) that on one occasion he "looked around at them with anger," he was capable of a flaming wrath. The Gospel of John says, "His disciples remembered that it was written, 'Zeal for thy house will consume me'" (Jn 2:17; Ps 69:9).

Like the evangelists, most commentators have understood Jesus' act as a demonstration of Messianic authority. It is possible that he considered himself authorized to purify the Lord's house if he believed that he was the Messiah. If he thought of himself rather as a prophet, that could explain his action. Even as an earnest worshiper and teacher he might have been moved to such indignation that he acted without thought of his right to take matters into his own hands. In short, neither the manner of his entrance into Jerusalem nor the cleansing of the temple proves that he regarded himself as the Messiah. The picture of him as carrying out, step by step, a program derived from prophetic utterances about the Messiah makes him look like an actor following a script instead of a living man of God moved by compassion and indignation.

Mark's narrative proceeds (11:18), "And the chief priests and the scribes heard it and sought a way to destroy him; for they feared him, because all the multitude was astonished at his teaching." Luke mentions the plot but does not connect it so directly with the cleansing of the temple. He says (19:47-48): "And he was teaching daily in the temple. The chief priests and scribes and the principal men of the people sought to destroy him;

209

but they did not find anything they could do, for all the people hung upon his words.'' Matthew does not refer to the matter at all. The statement that the multitude was astonished at Jesus' teaching occurs in several places (cf. Mk 1:22; 6:2; Mt 7:28; 13:54; Lk 4:32).

Apparently the priests and the rest made up their minds overnight to challenge Jesus' authority, which threatened theirs (Mk 11:27-33; Mt 21:23-27; Lk 20:1-8). The next morning they came to him in the temple and bluntly asked by what authority he acted, and who gave it to him. This is the first of a series of five such questions and answers while Jesus was teaching in the temple. Again Mark's arrangement of his material by topics is evident.

Jesus answered the question about his authority with another: ''Was the baptism of John from heaven or from men?'' The august and learned inquisitors were caught in a dilemma. If they had frankly stated their real opinion, they might have said, ''He had no authorization at all from God or men.'' But to admit that John's baptism was from heaven would evoke the question why they had not believed him; and they did not dare to say it was only human, because all the people regarded John as a prophet. They could only say, ''We don't know.'' Jesus said, ''Very well, then I won't tell you by what authority I do these things.''

In Matthew, Jesus' refusal is reinforced by a parable (21:28-32) not recorded in the other Gospels, the story of a man who told his two sons to work in his vineyard. One of them refused but went; the other said he would go but did not. The application is explicitly stated (vv 31-32): ''Truly, I say to you, the tax collectors and the harlots go into the kingdom of God before you. For John came to you in the way of righteousness, and you did not believe him, but the tax collectors and the harlots believed him; and even when you saw it, you did not afterward repent and believe him.''

The three evangelists now proceed together to a parable about the owner of a vineyard and his tenants (Mk 12:1-12; Mt 21:33-46; Lk 20:9-19). This is one of the few parables that are almost, if not quite, allegorical, and so is especially liable to erroneous and fanciful interpretations. It resembles Isaiah's song

210

of the vineyard (5:1-7), the main difference being that in Isaiah the vineyard itself is condemned because it produced wild grapes instead of good grapes, whereas here the sharecroppers are condemned because they will not give the owner his share of the fruit but abuse the agents sent to collect it. Isaiah's poem is directed against the disobedient people of Israel and Judah. The chief priests and Pharisees who challenged Jesus' authority "perceived that he has told the parable against them" (Mk 12:12; Mt 21:45; Lk 20:19). The implication seems to be that these leaders and their predecessors have exploited the privileges of their position instead of rendering to God the obedience and service that he demands. The servants sent to collect the owner's share appear therefore to be the prophets, and perhaps John the Baptist in particular.

So far all is in keeping with what Jesus may reasonably be supposed to have said. When the servants are succeeded by the owner's son, however, and he is killed and thrown out of the vineyard, a reference to Jesus himself is obvious. That he would have said all this is improbable. It would therefore be easy to suppose that the whole story was a product of the later church. More probably Jesus told the story of the landlord and the tenants, but the part about the son was added after the crucifixion.

After the parable, in all three Gospels, Jesus quotes Psalm 118, much as he has quoted Psalm 8 a little earlier (Mk 12:10-11; Mt 21:42; Lk 20:17-18; Ps 118:22-23). In Luke the quotation is followed by a comment, "Every one who falls on that stone will be broken to pieces; but when it falls on any one it will crush him." (Most of the manuscripts and versions have this in Matthew also, but for technical reasons the best critical editions of the text omit it.) Here the reference is not to a cornerstone (or more exactly the keystone of an arch), but to any stone large enough for a man to be injured by falling over it, or heavy enough to crush him if it fell on him.

Matthew adds here (21:43) that Jesus said to the priests and the Pharisees, "Therefore I tell you, the kingdom of God will be taken away from you and given to a nation producing the fruits of it." The noun rendered "nation" would be better translated here "people" (cf. JB, TEV). The new people of God to whom the

kingdom will be given can only be the church. There is no
implication that it will consist of Gentiles rather than Jews. What
is rejected is the official Jewish establishment, controlled by the
priests and scribes. (So also the Essenes denounced the temple
priesthood and considered themselves the true Israel.) This is one
of only four places (cf. 12:28; 19:24; 21:31) where Matthew has
"kingdom of God" instead of "kingdom of heaven." Perhaps he
followed some special source here, or perhaps the sentence is a
later insertion in the text. At the end of the episode another effort
to apprehend Jesus is reported, and again it is frustrated by fear of
the people (Mk 12:12; Mt 21:46; Lk 20:19).

Now Matthew presents his parable of the wedding feast,
already considered in connection with its parallel at an earlier
point in Luke (Mt 22:1-14; cf. Lk 14:16-24). After it Matthew
proceeds with Mark and Luke to the second of the controversies in
the temple (Mk 12:13-17; Mt 22:15-22; Lk 20:20-26), introduced
by a question about paying taxes to the Romans that was asked by
"some of the Pharisees and some of the Herodians." Luke says
they were "spies, who pretended to be sincere, that they might
take hold of what he said, so as to deliver him up to the authority
and jurisdiction of the governor." Mark and Matthew say simply
that the delegation was sent to trap him. According to Matthew, it
was the Pharisees who sent them.

After a flattering statement that they knew Jesus taught God's
way truly and without fear or favor, the questioners asked with an
air of seeking guidance, "Is it lawful to pay taxes to Caesar, or
not?" The Herodians (cf. Mk 3:6 and some manuscripts in 8:15)
were presumably pro-Roman, since Herod the Great and his sons
had been dependent upon the Romans for their power. The
Pharisees regarded the Romans as usurpers and oppressors, but
opposed active rebellion against them. If Jesus said that the taxes
should be paid, the Pharisees could call him a traitor to his own
people; if he said they should not, the Herodians could accuse him
of inciting rebellion against Rome.

His reply was both a neat evasion of the trap and an indication
of his position without a direct yes or no. Asking why they were
putting him on trial, he called for a denarius, the coin used as the
unit in assessing taxes. Taking it and examining it, he again

answered the question with another: "Whose head is this that is stamped on the coin, and whose inscription is this?" They told him, "Caesar's" (that is, the emperor's). "Well then," said Jesus, "pay Caesar what belongs to Caesar, and pay God what belongs to God." This was no clarion call to insurrection; neither was it an explicit counsel of submission. It seems to show no concern for what was a burning issue for Palestinian Jews. But not only was Jesus dealing with an insincere effort to trap him, he never allowed men to transfer to his shoulders the burden of deciding what they should do. No wonder his critics were amazed and silently withdrew.

What all this means for a follower of Jesus today is a difficult question. A valid answer must take into account the fact that Judea was then occupied territory. The coming of the kingdom of God would end the rule of the Romans. There was that much truth in the charge brought against Jesus later that he was preaching sedition. On the question how to deal with the Romans in the meantime, however, Jesus certainly did not agree with the Zealots. On this he was closer to the Pharisees. His attitude may be called passive resistance, but there is no indication that he practiced civil disobedience, which would have been both futile and fatal.

It is true that the evangelists were anxious to avoid any impression that Christianity was a seditious movement. This is especially evident in Luke and Acts. Conceivably they might have toned down any political implications of his acts and words. To recognize this, however, is not to conclude that Jesus' real convictions were disguised or concealed by deliberate fabrication. What the evangelists wanted to bring out was the truth. To prove otherwise would require positive evidence, of which there is none.

Undoubtedly, political conditions and action were not Jesus' primary concern. No doubt his position was influenced not only by the practical impossibility of a successful revolt against Rome, to say nothing of reform by democratic means, but also by the fact that he expected the kingdom of God to come very soon. It is legitimate to wonder whether his attitude on political and social issues might have been different if he had not had this expectation;

213

yet he did not draw the conclusions sometimes drawn by people who think the end of the world is at hand. There was no march into the wilderness, no gathering on the Mount of Olives. He required those who went with him to Jerusalem to forsake possessions and family, but in order to be ready for the kingdom of God what was essential was first of all righteous living according to the law of God.

Our atomic age offers a real parallel to the situation confronted by Jesus. There are those who lose hope and take the line of least resistance. Others ignore the peril of our predicament and indulge in wishful thinking. Those best advised recognize the uncertainty of the future but follow the course of mutual compassion and cooperation, which will be most rewarding whether this world ends today or lasts for millennia.

The third controversy in the series (Mk 12:18-27; Mt 22:23-33; Lk 20:27-40) revolves about a question raised by the Sadducees, who did not believe in the resurrection of the dead. On this subject Jesus was evidently known to agree with the Pharisees, as Paul did later (Acts 23:6-10; 1 Cor 15:12-57). The Sadducees who came to him in the temple tried to refute the belief by an argument based on the law of levirate marriage (Deut 25:5-6), by which, if a man died and left no son, his wife was taken by his brother, and their first son was legally reckoned as the son of the deceased. The Sadducees said that seven brothers died childless, and the first one's wife was taken in turn by all of them. ''In the resurrection,'' they asked, ''whose wife will she be?'' Jesus replied that the life of those raised from the dead would not be like the present life. On the contrary, ''when they rise from the dead, they neither marry nor are given in marriage, but are like angels in heaven.'' In Luke this is considerably expanded. His version is notable for the contrast of ''the sons of this age'' and the ''sons of the resurrection,'' who are also ''sons of God,'' and also for the fact that the coming age is directly connected with the resurrection. These facts suggest that Luke's form of the statement may be closer than that in Mark and Matthew to the original words of Jesus.

The saying has been taken to mean that only those who do not marry in this life are qualified to participate in the resurrection.

214

This is not the meaning of the text. What it says is that those who, literally, "have been accounted worthy," and have been raised, are not married in the other world. This is even clearer in Mark and Matthew.

Not only have the Sadducees an erroneous conception of the resurrection, their question betrays also ignorance of the Scriptures. Here Jesus speaks as a child of his age. His interpretation of the Old Testament is alien to modern historical exegesis, but that is no indication that it was not what he believed. God's declaration to Moses (Ex 3:6), "I am the God of your father, the God of Abraham, the God of Isaac, and the God of Jacob," is cited as proof that the patriarchs are still alive, because God is not God of the dead but of the living. How seriously Jesus himself took this kind of exegesis we do not know. Here and in other places one sometimes suspects that he is playing with his adversaries in the way he uses Scripture; in fact, the same suspicion arises regarding stories told about some of the rabbis. It is possible, however, that Jesus, thoughtfully considering the story in Exodus, might think, "Truly God *is* the God of the fathers; he is still their God, for they are alive and worship him in heaven."

Whatever form of the statement best represents Jesus' own words, his reply to the Sadducees implies a spiritual, perhaps even incorporeal kind of existence, like Paul's conception of the spiritual body (1 Cor 15:35-50).The resurrection of the body is thus transformed into something approaching the immortality of the soul, with the important difference that, at least for Paul, the resurrection is still in the future (vv 51-53; cf. 1 Thess 4:13-18). What being like angels would mean to Jesus' contemporaries is clear enough. The rabbis said that the angels had bodies of fire, which was about as close as the ancient Hebrew mentality could come to the idea of immaterial existence.

Jesus' argument was apparently sufficient to silence the Sadducees. Matthew says that when the crowd heard it they were astonished, and no wonder. Probably few of them could follow such subtle reasoning, but they could see that the Sadducees were embarrassed and had nothing more to say. According to Luke, some of the scribes said, "Teacher, you have spoken well"; but no doubt they were Pharisees, who were glad to see the Sadducees put to confusion. Mark simply proceeds to the next incident, the fourth of his five controversies, which is the conversation about the greatest commandment (Mk 12:28-34; Mt 22:34-40; Lk 10:25-28). We have already discussed this where Luke reports it. Strictly speaking, only Matthew treats it as a controversy.

In the fifth controversy (Mk 12:35-37; Mt 22:41-46; Lk 20:41-44) it is Jesus who asks the question. Having repelled the attacks of both Pharisees and Sadducees, he now carries the war into the enemy's territory. As Matthew tells the story, Jesus asks, "What do you think of the Christ? Whose son is he?" (cf. TEV). They reply, as a matter of course, "The son of David." This question as the KJV gives it, "What think ye of Christ?" has been the text of countless sermons on faith in Christ. In its context, however, it only asks for a theological opinion, about which Jesus then proceeds to raise a further question. (In Mark and Luke there is only one question, "How can the scribes say that Christ is the son of David?")

Quoting Psalm 110:1, "The Lord said to my Lord," Jesus says, "David himself calls him Lord; so how is he his son?" (It is assumed that "my Lord" means "the Messiah.") Does Jesus' question imply that the Messiah will not be a descendant of David? Such an implication would run counter not only to the common Jewish belief but also to the unanimous testimony of the New Testament. Later Christian theology could take the question to mean that the Messiah would be not only a descendant of David but also far more than that, the Son of God. Assuming this interpretation, some scholars consider the whole incident a product of the church. The story itself, however, does not suggest a "not only but also." Its implication is *"not* David's son *but* his Lord."

According to almost all the evidence, the very first Christians, convinced that Jesus was the Messiah, took it for granted that he must therefore be a descendant of David. The only possible indication to the contrary is this incident in the temple. The tradition of Jesus' question may actually be older than the belief in his Davidic ancestry. It is even possible that he was not in fact a descendant of David, and the point of his argument was that this did not disqualify him for the divine choice as Messiah. In that case—and it is no more impossible than many widely accepted theories—this tradition is very old indeed, perhaps going back to Jesus himself. This would mean, of course, that Jesus did after all consider himself the Messiah.

Perhaps the only safe inference is that the Messiah would be greater than David, which none would deny. Again it is even possible that Jesus was playing with the scribes, demonstrating that they were not such clever interpreters of Scripture as they thought. It is extremely unlikely that a story of his raising such a question would originate in the later community. So far as we know, the question was never raised again.

CHAPTER XIV

LAST PUBLIC TEACHING
AND THE APOCALYPTIC DISCOURSE

Mark ends the series of controversies with the statement, "And the great throng heard him gladly." The KJV translates this, "And the common people heard him gladly," converting a reference to a particular occasion into a general assertion about the attitude of the common people toward Jesus. All three evangelists indicate that a large crowd heard what Jesus said and was pleased with it.

And now Jesus turns to them directly (Mk 12:38-40; Mt 23:1-12; Lk 20:45-47). Matthew (vv 2-5) characteristically gathers together and inserts some material that appears at other points in Luke and some things not recorded by Mark or Luke at all. In Mark and Luke, Jesus first warns his hearers against the scribes, whom he accuses of making themselves conspicuous and pretending to be very devout while they "devour widows' houses." Of course this was not true of all the scribes. Jesus recognized humility and sincerity in some of them; but the least worthy members of a group are often most conspicuous, and it was these that Jesus castigated.

In Matthew the Pharisees are included with the scribes as the objects of Jesus' denunciation (23:2), which begins in a moderate vein but becomes extremely bitter. The scribes and Pharisees, Jesus says, "sit on Moses' seat" (that is, the teacher's seat in the synagogue), and what they say is to be followed. Their conduct, however, is not to be emulated, "for they preach, but do not practice." They will not so much as touch with their fingers the heavy burdens they lay on the shoulders of others. Luke gives this as a part of the table talk when Jesus dined with a Pharisee (Lk 11:46). It is the sort of thing that Jesus may have said repeatedly, but the settings provided here by Matthew and Luke are both almost certainly artificial.

The saying that follows in Matthew (23:5) resembles one in Mark and Luke (Mk 12:38; Lk 20:46). Instead of the long robes mentioned there Matthew says, "they make their phylacteries

218

broad and their fringes long.'' The phylacteries were little boxes attached to the forehead or wrist, containing pieces of parchment with texts from Exodus (13:16) and Deuteronomy (6:8). The fringes were no doubt the tassels prescribed by the Law (Num 15:38; Deut 22:12). Jesus himself wore the customary tassels (Mt 9:20; Lk 8:44; cf. Mk 5:27) and probably a phylactery.

In all three Gospels Jesus speaks of the scribes' predilection for public attention and respect. Matthew adds (23:7-10), ''and being called rabbi by men''; and this introduces an important passage. The disciples, Jesus says, are not to be addressed as rabbi, because they have only the one teacher, and they are all brothers. They are not to address any man as father, for they have the one Father in heaven. And they are not to be called masters, for they have one master, the Christ. The Greek noun here translated ''master'' (literally ''guide'' or ''leader'') is used nowhere else in the New Testament.

After this Matthew has a saying that Mark and Luke have already used and all three use again (Mt 23:11; cf. 20:26-27; Mk 9:35; 10:43-44; Lk 9:48; 22:26): ''He who is greatest among you shall be your servant.'' Matthew also gives here another oft-repeated statement (Mt 23:12; cf. 18:4; Lk 14:11; 18:14): ''whoever exalts himself will be humbled, and whoever humbles himself will be exalted.'' Then Matthew proceeds in prophetic style (Mt 23:13-51; cf. Is 3:9, 11; Hab 2:6-19) with a series of seven ''woes'' (eight if 14 belongs to the original text). Variants of six of these appear in Luke's account of a meal at a Pharisee's house (Lk 11:42-52), preceded (vv 39-41; cf. Mt 23:25-26) by an accusation that corresponds to Matthew's fifth woe. Three of Luke's woes are directed against the Pharisees and three against the lawyers. Evidently neither Matthew's nor Luke's collection is a record of an actual discourse. Whether Jesus ever delivered such a prolonged diatribe is an open question.

All but one of Matthew's woes begin, ''Woe to you, scribes and Pharisees, hypocrites.'' We have considered the charge of hypocrisy before. The first woe (Luke's sixth) accuses the scribes and Pharisees of shutting the kingdom of heaven against men (Mt 23:13; Lk 11:52). Luke reads, ''You have taken away the key of knowledge.'' Matthew's second woe (23:15), not recorded by

219

Luke, reflects an intense missionary activity in Judaism in the first century which ceased not long after that. The third woe in Matthew (23:16), also lacking in Luke, imputes to the Pharisees and scribes a faulty sense of proportion, manifested in their rules concerning the validity of oaths. The passage recalls the earlier discussion of what defiles a man (Mk 7:1-23; Mt 15:1-20); it also reflects Jesus' reverence for the temple as God's dwelling (1 Kings 8:27) and for heaven as his throne (Mt 5:34).

The fourth woe, Luke's first (Mt 23:23; Lk 11:42), charges the Pharisees with exacting tithes on spices and herbs but neglecting "the weightier matters of the law, justice and mercy and faith." The three weighty matters recall what Micah says God requires of man (6:8). "Justice" echoes Micah's "to do justice," but "mercy" is not an exact translation of "to love kindness" (literally, "love of steadfast love"). "Faith," though commonly taken here to mean "faithfulness," may reflect "walk humbly with your God." In the next clause, "these you ought to have done, without neglecting the others," the demonstrative "these" refers to what is nearest in the context, the weightier matters of the law; that is, "justice and mercy and faith" should have prior attention, but the minor duties should be done too. The nail is driven home by a typical example of Jesus' trenchant humor (Mt 23:24): "You blind guides, straining out a gnat and swallowing a camel!" We have seen the same kind of ridicule by grotesque exaggeration in other sayings. Perhaps it reduced the tension when Jesus spoke, making the people laugh and deflating the self-importance of the Pharisees.

In the next woe (Mt 23:25-26; Lk 11:39-41), given by Luke as a direct accusation, the piety of the Pharisees is made to appear absurd by another vivid metaphor: they are represented as carefully washing a cup or plate on the outside and leaving it dirty inside. In the two forms of this saying we find one of the clearest instances in the Gospels of different Greek expressions representing the same or similar Aramaic words. The verb translated "cleanse" in Matthew probably stands for an Aramaic verb that was very close, if not identical, to the one translated in Luke "give alms." The expressions translated "those things which are

220

within'' (Luke) and ''the inside'' (Matthew) are probably also different renderings of the same Aramaic.

The same idea is conveyed even more forcefully in Matthew's sixth woe, which is Luke's third (Mt 23:27-28; Lk 11:44). Jesus compares the hypocritical Pharisees and scribes to ''whitewashed tombs'' (KJV ''whited sepulchres''), outwardly beautiful, but within ''full of dead men's bones and all uncleanness.'' (Luke's version is less impressive: ''You are like graves which are not seen, and men walk over them without knowing it.'') Palestine is full of ancient tombs, many of them made during the Roman occupation. They not only contained the bodies of the dead, but in time were occupied by bats and rats or used by wandering shepherds to shelter their flocks. One who explores any of them will retain a vivid memory of the accumulated filth.

Matthew's seventh and last woe, Luke's fifth (Mt 23:29-31; Lk 11:47-48), depicts the hypocrisy of the scribes and Pharisees as building tombs and monuments for the prophets and righteous men killed by their fathers, and claiming that they would have had no part in such deeds. Building tombs for the prophets could be a sincere repudiation of sins of previous generations, but Jesus does not recognize it as such in his contemporaries.

The language of the next two verses in Matthew (32-33) is so violent that Jesus seems to be beside himself with rage. ''Fill up, then, the measure of your fathers,'' he says; ''you serpents, you brood of vipers, how are you to escape being sentenced to hell?'' Luke does not have this outburst. John the Baptist had said to some of those who came to be baptized (Mt 3:7; Lk 3:7): ''You brood of vipers! Who warned you to flee from the wrath to come?'' These words sound more like John than like Jesus, though we must beware of letting our judgment be warped by the traditional ''gentle Jesus, meek and mild.''

In Matthew (23:34) Jesus continues, ''Therefore I send you prophets and wise men and scribes, some of whom you will kill and crucify, and some you will scourge in your synagogues and persecute from town to town.'' Instead of this, Luke reads (11:49), ''Therefore also the Wisdom of God said, 'I will send them prophets and apostles, some of whom they will kill and persecute' ''—a curious anticlimax, probably the result of condensation. What is meant here by the Wisdom of God is uncertain. Some scholars believe that there was a book, now lost, that was entitled "The Wisdom of God," and that Luke here quotes from it. Others hold that "the Wisdom of God said" means simply, "God said in his wisdom"; or that Wisdom is here personified as in the current wisdom literature. Why Luke should do this, however, remains unexplained. To say that he was following a source other than Matthew's only pushes the mystery back one step.

What Matthew's "I said" means is no less obscure. It seems to imply that Jesus himself, before his incarnation, sent the "prophets and wise men and scribes." That might be natural in the post-apostolic church, but it would be quite without parallel in the Synoptic Gospels. Also possible in a later generation would be a conception of the risen Lord of the church speaking thus of the Christian missionaries and teachers. In some way the later situation of the church, during and after the split with Judaism, has colored the tradition of what Jesus said. Matthew's language, however, remains within the circle of Judaism. His version of what will be done to the envoys also indicates the kind of persecution that Jesus elsewhere warns the disciples to expect (cf. Mt 10:17, 23). One is reminded of the treatment of the owner's agents in the parable of the wicked tenants (Mk 12:2-5 and parallels).

These things will happen, Jesus continues in Matthew (23:35-36), "that upon you may come all the righteous blood shed on earth, from the blood of innocent Abel to the blood of Zechariah the son of Barachiah, whom you murdered between the sanctuary and the altar. Truly, I say to you, all this will come upon this generation." Luke's form of the saying (11:50) is somewhat different and omits "the son of Barachiah." If we had only Matthew's record, we might suppose that Jesus' knowledge of Old Testament history was imperfect. The event referred to occurred in the reign of Joash, and the Zechariah who was stoned to death was a son of the priest Jehoiada (2 Chron 24:20-21). Zechariah the son of Barachiah (Berechiah) was the prophet associated with Haggai some three hundred years later (Zech 1:1; Ezra 5:1; 6:14). The confusion need not be attributed to Jesus, however, or to Matthew. It was probably introduced into the text by an early copyist.

More serious misgivings are aroused by the implication that Jesus' contemporaries will be punished for crimes committed in previous centuries. Men's acts often have consequences for innocent persons, which may accumulate until they burst in a flood. In that sense the blood of the prophets might have been said to "come upon" the Jews of Jesus' day. That, however, is obviously not what is meant here. Jesus condemns the scribes and Pharisees, not because of what their fathers did, but because they are no better than their fathers.

These bitter denunciations, like similar statements already examined, are far too sweeping to be fair to the Pharisees or the scribes en masse. It may be that Jesus, frustrated by their opposition, felt that as a group they were guilty of such faults. The evangelists, however, especially Matthew, probably colored their reports too highly, betraying their own resentment toward Jewish leaders of their day who rejected and persecuted Christians.

Matthew now gives Jesus' lament over Jerusalem, which comes at an earlier point in Luke (Mt 23:37-39; Lk 13:34-35). To what has already been said about it we may add that it ends with the same quotation from Psalm 118 that was shouted by the crowd at Jesus' entrance into Jerusalem. Thus Matthew's order of presentation makes Jesus seem to ignore the fact that he has already been hailed in these terms (Mt 21:9). If it was only people from other places who so acclaimed him then, however, the meaning here may be that the citizens of Jerusalem have yet to do so.

When Jesus says, "You will not see me again, until you say, 'Blessed is he . . .'" (Mt 23:39), the word "again" represents a Greek phrase meaning literally "from now" (KJV "hence-forth"). According to the subsequent narratives, Jesus remained in the vicinity of Jerusalem, observed the Passover in the city, and expected to be betrayed and put to death there. Matthew probably understood the statement as a reference to Jesus' death, after which the people of Jerusalem would see him no more until he returned in glory. What Jesus meant by these words, if he used them, is an unsolved problem.

In Mark and Luke the charges against the Pharisees are followed by the story of the widow's mites (Mk 12:41-44; Lk 21:1-4), which Matthew omits. The Greek word rendered "copper coins" (KJV "mites") designates the smallest coin then in circulation, worth only one sixty-fourth of a denarius. If the denarius was a day's wage for a farm laborer (cf. Mt 20:2), the widow's offering was only what a man might earn in about fifteen minutes. It was all she had, however, and Jesus rated it more highly than the "large sums" that the rich "contributed out of their abundance."

It is a strange picture that we are given of Jesus during these first days in the temple: arguing freely with Sadducees, scribes, and Pharisees; parrying more or less subtle attempts to lure him into statements that could be used against him; answering sincere questions and approving good answers to his own questions; pronouncing fiery invectives against influential teachers who opposed him; lamenting the failure of Jerusalem to respond to his challenge; and then calmly pointing out to his disciples the tiny but sacrificial offering of a poor widow. Luke briefly summarizes (21:37-38): "And every day he was teaching in the temple, but at night he went out and lodged on the mount called Olivet. And early in the morning all the people came to him in the temple to hear him." After the excitement of the arrival at Jerusalem and the cleansing of the temple, it all seems very peaceful, relaxed, undramatic. Yet the tension was there under the surface: the leaders' fear of a popular uprising if they tried to silence Jesus by force; their futile efforts to trap him in his speech; the crowd's evident satisfaction when he put his opponents to confusion. What creates the impression of a mild confrontation is his own unruffled calm, his contempt for subterfuge, his fearlessness for himself.

After the things done or said in the temple, the Gospels proceed with what Jesus said one day when he left the holy place to spend the night on the Mount of Olives (Mk 13:1-4; Mt 24:1-3; Lk 21:5-7). As they went out, the disciples called his attention to the great buildings in the sacred area and the huge stones of which they were made. Jesus replied that the time was coming when not one stone would be left on another. This was literally fulfilled about forty years later, though a few parts of the enclosing wall

224

still remain, including the "Wailing Wall" on the western side and a section of the southeastern corner. Other portions have been uncovered recently.

When they reached the top of the Mount of Olives, "Peter and James and John and Andrew" asked Jesus when his prediction would be fulfilled, and what would be the sign that it was about to happen. In Mark and Luke the question refers only to the destruction of the temple; Matthew, however, reads, "Tell us, when will this be, and what will be the sign of your coming and of the close of the age?"

What now follows is commonly known as the apocalyptic discourse (Mk 13:5-37). In Matthew it constitutes the last of the five major discourses (24:4-51; 25:1-46). Luke has already used much of the material that Mark and Matthew have here. His version of Jesus' reply (21:8-36) is consequently shorter than Mark's. In all three Gospels the burden of what Jesus says is the "Messianic woes," meaning the calamities and trials that will precede the appearance of the Messiah. Nowhere in the whole discourse is the destruction of the temple mentioned.

The first paragraph is a warning against premature expectations of the end (Mk 13:5-8; Mt 24:4-8; Lk 21:8-11). False Messiahs will lead many astray. There will be "wars and rumors of wars," but "the end is not yet." There will be earthquakes and famines; Luke adds other catastrophes. In Mark and Matthew the paragraph ends, "this is but the beginning of the birth-pangs."

The second paragraph of the discourse warns the disciples that they will be persecuted (Mk 13:9-13; Mt 24:9-14; Lk 21:12-19, cf. Mt 10:17-21; Lk 12:11-12). The situation contemplated is that which the church was to face later: being delivered to councils, flogged in synagogues, and haled before governors and kings to bear testimony, with the assurance that the Holy Spirit will speak through them.

In Mark the paragraph ends, "But he who endures to the end will be saved" (Mk 13:13; Mt 24:13; Lk 21:19; cf. Rev 2:10, 26). The expression "be saved," used in Acts and the epistles as it is now in evangelical Protestantism, has not yet acquired such a specific meaning in the Gospels but refers to deliverance from any kind of harm or calamity. Twice in Matthew it is used of saving a person from drowning. Frequently with reference to deliverance from a physical or mental affliction it is translated by KJV "heal" or "make whole." In a few places being saved has a theological meaning, but it is never sharply defined.

The noun "salvation" does not occur at all in Mark or Matthew. Luke has a related Greek noun twice (2:30; 3:6; cf. Is 52:10) and a more common word four times (1:69, 71, 77; 19:9), the reference being once to "knowledge of salvation . . . in the forgiveness of their sins." The last appearance of the word (19:9) is in the story of Zacchaeus: "Today salvation has come to this house." This is the only place where "salvation" appears in a saying of Jesus.

Having omitted Mark's previous statement (13:10) about preaching the gospel to all nations, Matthew now adds (24:14), "And this gospel of the kingdom will be preached throughout the whole world, as a testimony to all the nations; and then the end will come." To the troubled church of later generations, wondering why the Son of man had not come, this paragraph says, "Not yet! You still have before you the mission of proclaiming the gospel to the world" (cf. Mt 28:19-20).

Before this, where Mark (13:13) has "And you will be hated by all for my name's sake," Matthew reads (24:9) "by all nations." In his second discourse, where he used part of this passage (10:17-21), the preaching to the nations would have been inappropriate for the mission of the twelve in Galilee or Judea; yet in the verse there about standing before governors and kings "to bear testimony before them" (v 18; cf. Mk 13:9) he added "and the Gentiles." The same Greek word is unfortunately translated "Gentiles" there and "nations" here (Mt 24:9, 14).

The third paragraph of the discourse (Mk 13:14-20; Mt 24:15-22; Lk 21:20-24) continues the description of the Messianic woes. Mark and Matthew begin by referring to the "desolating sacrilege" (KJV "abomination of desolation") which will be "set up where it ought not to be" (Mark), "standing in the holy place" (Matthew). The allusion, as Matthew notes, is to the book of Daniel (11:31; 12:11; cf. 9:27). There the expression refers to the desecration of the temple in 167 B.C. by Antiochus Epiphanes, whose forces "erected a desolating sacrilege upon the altar of burnt offering'' (1 Macc 1:54). The Hebrew term is a barely disguised imitation of the name of a pagan god, Baal Shamayim (Lord of Heaven), who was identified with the Greek Zeus Olympios. Antiochus called the Jerusalem temple ''the temple of Olympian Zeus'' (2 Macc 6:2). The desolating sacrilege on that occasion must have been an image of the god or a small altar for his worship.

In the apocalyptic discourse the expression has a new application. In A.D. 40 the Roman emperor Caligula commanded that an image of himself be set up in the temple at Jerusalem. His death prevented the execution of the order, but meanwhile there was much excitement among both Jews and Christians. The reference to the desolating sacrilege in the Gospels was almost certainly written in this emergency. The first readers would not have needed the admonition, ''let the reader understand,'' but for the disciples who heard Jesus the allusion would have had no meaning. This clause, with much of what precedes and follows it, must come from a later writer. The discourse may include some authentic sayings of Jesus; indeed it may include portions of a pre-Christian Jewish apocalypse. As a whole, however, it is a Christian composition. It had already been erroneously attributed to Jesus before it was incorporated in the Gospel of Mark, where Matthew and Luke found it.

Instead of the allusion to Daniel, Luke has here (21:20), ''But when you see Jerusalem surrounded by armies, then know that its desolation has come near.'' This suggests a later edition of the discourse, changing its application from the crisis of A.D. 40 to the siege and fall of Jerusalem and the destruction of the temple thirty years later. Thus the discourse as a whole would be connected with Jesus' prediction that the temple would be destroyed. There is nothing, however, here or elsewhere in Luke, that cannot be found in woes on wicked cities in the Old Testament. Luke either knew that Jerusalem had fallen or was convinced that it was doomed, but what he wrote does not prove that it had already fallen.

According to Mark and Matthew, when the readers see the desolating sacrilege, ''those who are in Judea'' must flee for safety to the mountains (Mk 13:14-15; Mt 24:15-18). Luke

(17:31) has already used this; now (21:21) he changes the picture from house and field to beleaguered Jerusalem. Before the Roman siege of Jerusalem the Christians in the city fled, not to the mountains but to Pella in the Jordan valley.

In all three Gospels the paragraph proceeds with an expression of pity for pregnant women and those nursing babies in the time of distress (Mk 13:17; Mt 24:19; Lk 21:23). Mark continues (13:18), "Pray that it may not happen in winter." Matthew adds (24:20), "or on a sabbath." Luke omits the sentence.

More about the coming tribulation follows (Mk 13:19-20; Mt 24:21-22; Lk 21:23-24). Mark and Matthew stress the unique severeity of the afflictions. Luke's picture is one of war, with death by the sword and captivity among the nations, and again Jerusalem is at the center of it, trodden under foot by Gentiles "until the times of the Gentiles are fulfilled." The conception of a period of foreign occupation and oppression of the holy city as a part of the divine plan was not new. Perhaps it was the only way to preserve faith in God at a time when all the hopes of his people were dashed to earth by the Romans as they had been by the Babylonians in the sixth century B.C. (cf. Is 63:18; 64:11; Rev 11:2). The "times of the Gentiles" are often compared with the time of Israel's hardening "until the full number of the Gentiles come in," as conceived by Paul (Rom 11:25); but there is no suggestion of the salvation of the Gentiles here in Luke. The idea is rather that the desecration and desolation of the holy city were a part of God's judgment on the wicked and a trial of his saints as by fire (cf. Zech 13:8-9; Mal 3:1-4).

For those who see in Scripture a detailed blueprint of future events, cut up into small bits and scattered throughout the Bible like pieces of a picture puzzle, the times of the Gentiles offer an irresistible challenge to their ingenuity and imagination, stimulated by tempting parallels with events of our own day. The worst thing about this kind of interpretation is that it misses the real point and purpose of prophecy. Jesus rebuked his contemporaries for demanding signs from heaven and failing to discern the signs of the times (Mt 16:1-3; Lk 12:54-56). Like the Old Testament prophets, he predicted the fall of Jerusalem because he saw it as the inevitable result of acts and attitudes already evident.

The next paragraph in Mark and Matthew (Mk 13:21-23; Mt 24:23-25) is omitted by Luke, perhaps because it is similar to what he has previously recorded (cf. Lk 17:20-23). In language and ideas it belongs with its context in the apocalyptic discourse. The disciples must not believe anyone who says, "Look, here is the Christ," or "Look, there he is!" There will be false Christs and false prophets who will show such signs and wonders as might lead even the elect astray.

Matthew inserts here a paragraph that in Luke is a part of the passage about the days of the Son of man, and with it a statement about eagles or vultures, which Luke has later in that passage (Mt 24:26-28; cf. Lk 17:23-24, 37). The point of the paragraph is that the coming of the Son of man will not be a local phenomenon, which one will have to go out to the wilderness or into an inner room to see. It will be universal and unmistakable, "as the lightning comes from the east and shines as far as the west." The statement about eagles or vultures in this connection apparently means that there will be no question where the event occurs; it will be manifested as clearly as the location of a carcass is shown by the vultures wheeling above it. The fact that Matthew and Luke quote this paragraph at different places, and Mark does not have it, suggests that it was not originally a part of the apocalyptic discourse. It may be a genuine utterance of Jesus even though the discourse is a later composition.

Matthew has here (24:27) the noun translated "coming" (*parousia*), which he used in the disciples' question as they left the temple with Jesus (v 3). Its basic meaning is "presence" (literally "being beside"). It is so translated twice in Paul's epistles, both referring to the apostle himself (2 Cor 10:10; Phil 2:12). It also, however, means "arrival" or "coming," and is used by Paul in this sense too (1 Cor 16:17; Phil 1:26). Once he uses it of the coming of the Antichrist (2 Thess 2:9). A papyrus document found in Egypt indicates by this noun an expected visit by the king. In the Epistles the word often refers to Jesus' coming from heaven. Matthew, however, is the only one of the evangelists who uses it at all, and he has it only four times, all in the apocalyptic discourse. Elsewhere in the Gospels "coming" represents a form of the common Greek verb meaning "come."

The next paragraph (Mk 13:24-27; Mt 24:29-31; Lk 21:25-28) tells of the coming of the Son of man, which will be preceded by convulsions of nature and extraordinary celestial phenomena recalling what the prophets said about the "day of the Lord." Luke adds several details to those given by Mark. How literally such portents were meant to be understood we cannot tell; but in Acts (2:16-21), when Peter says on the day of Pentecost, "this is what was spoken by the prophet Joel," he quotes not only the verses about the outpouring of the Spirit but also those about the "wonders in the heaven above and signs on the earth beneath" (Joel 2:28-32), though there is no indication that the sun was actually "turned to darkness, and the moon to blood" on that occasion. Apocalyptic literature is so full of symbolism that the line between what is literal and what is figurative is often indiscernible.

The climax is reached with the appearance of the Son of man (Mk 13:26; Mt 24:30; Lk 21:27), "coming in clouds with great power and glory." The picture is obviously a reflection of Daniel 7, where, after four beasts representing successive world empires have come out of the sea (vv 3-8, 17), a human figure ("one like a son of man"), representing "the saints of the Most High," comes "with the clouds of heaven" and receives universal, everlasting dominion (vv 13-14, 18, 27). Here the vision is avowedly symbolic. In the Gospels the Son of man is an individual person, but how literally his coming in (or on) a cloud (or clouds) is to be understood is another question.

Mark and Matthew say that the Son of man will send out angels (Matthew adds "with a loud trumpet call"), and "gather his elect from the four winds, from the ends of the earth to the ends of heaven" (Mk 13:27; Mt 24:31; cf. 1 Thess 4:16). Instead of this Luke reads (21:28), "Now when these things begin to take place, look up and raise your heads, because your redemption is drawing near."

A brief paragraph now follows (Mk 13:28-29; Mt 24:32-33; Lk 21:29-31) to the effect that as the first new leaves and softening branches of the fig tree show that summer is near, so "these things" show "that he is near, at the very gates." How this is related to what has gone before is not clear. If people have already

230

seen the Son of man coming with power and glory, do they still need to be told that he is near? Perhaps these verses belong somewhere else, though the evangelists agree in reporting them here. Instead of "he is near, at the very gates," Luke says, "the kingdom of God is near."

Mark probably received this discourse as a separate composition, accepted it as a record of what Jesus had said, and fitted it into his narrative at what seemed the most appropriate place. If verses 5-29 are removed, verse 30 appears as the direct answer to the disciples' question in verse 4. To their expression of wonder at the temple buildings and the great stones used in their construction Jesus replied in effect, "Yes, but solid and permanent as they seem, they will all be thrown down." The disciples ask in dismay when this will be, and he says, "Before this generation passes away" (cf. Mk 9:1 and parallels). Many of that generation, including some of his disciples, must have lived to see this come true.

The prediction is followed by a solemn assurance that even when heaven and earth are no more, Jesus' words will endure (Mk 13:31; Mt 24:35; Lk 21:33). The same things are said in the Sermon on the Mount about the law (Mt 5:18; Lk 16:17). Yet even while claiming that what he has said will be fulfilled within a generation, Jesus warns that no man or angel or even the Son knows the exact time, but only the Father (Mk 13:32; Mt 24:36; cf. Acts 1:7). This is the only place in Mark where the expression "the Son" is used (cf. Mt 11:27; Lk 10:22). Instead of trying to calculate the time or looking for signs, the disciples must be attentive and watchful (Mk 13:33).

In Mark the apocalyptic discourse ends with a parable about an absent householder whose servants must be prepared for his return at any moment (Mk 13:34-36). Matthew and Luke omit this, but both have similar material at various other places (cf. Mt 25:14; Lk 19:12). The parable begins like Matthew's parable of the talents, and the closing exhortation resembles several sayings quoted by Matthew and Luke in connection with other parables (Mt 24:42; 25:13; Lk 12:38, 40). Instead of Mark's parable Luke has here an exhortation apparently addressed to the people at large (Lk 21:34-36). This concludes the apocalyptic discourse in Luke.

Matthew is not yet ready to bring his last major discourse to an end. He continues with sayings that Luke has used earlier (Mt 24:37-41; Lk 17:26-27, 34-35). The rest of the discourse emphasizes the element of surprise in the coming of the Son of man (Mt 24:42-44; cf. Mk 13:34; Lk 12:39-40). Picking up the idea of Mark's concluding parable, Matthew proceeds with another passage used earlier in Luke, warning the disciples against being like a householder unprepared for the coming of a thief.

Luke has at this point (12:41) a characteristic editorial transition. Peter asks, "Lord, are you telling this parable for us, or for all?" As in Matthew, the passage continues with a blessing on a faithful and wise servant who will be put in charge of all his master's possessions, and a warning that one who uses his master's absence to abuse his fellow servants will be punished (Mt 24:45-51; Lk 12:42-46).

Matthew gives next (25:1-13) what is commonly known as the parable of the wise and foolish virgins. At some points this resembles an exhortation in Luke to be like servants who are ready for their master's return from a marriage feast (Lk 12:35-38), but the principal characters here are ten girls waiting for the bridegroom to arrive for the feast. In the bridegroom's delay we can hardly fail to see a reference to the delay of Jesus' return from heaven (cf. Mt 24:48; Lk 12:45). Five of the girls will be admitted to the marriage feast, but to the rest, who failed to bring sufficient oil to keep their lamps burning, the bridegroom will say, "I do not know you" (cf. Mt 7:23; Lk 13:27). The most distinctive note in this parable is the suggestion that those who are unprepared cannot count upon the foresight and faithfulness of others to get them into the kingdom.

Another parable about servants whose master is away from home now follows (Mt 25:14-30; Lk 19:12-27). This is the parable of the talents, which we have examined together with Luke's parable of the pounds. Then Matthew's discourse reaches an effective conclusion in the dramatic scene of the final judgment by the Son of man (Mt 25:31-46). Often quoted and highly valued because of the stress on service to "the least of these my brethren," this passage is notable also for the fact that it conveys a social message in an apocalyptic envelope. How far Jesus accepted and how much he used apocalyptic concepts and imagery is still open to argument, but that his gospel was both social and eschatological is certain.

The account begins, "When the Son of man comes in his glory, and all the angels with him, then he will sit on his glorious throne." The Son of man's glory and the angels are mentioned elsewhere (cf. Mk 8:38; 13:26-27 and parallels; Mt 10:32-33; Lk 12:8-9). Another saying refers to his glorious throne (Mt 19:28). The apocalyptic book of Enoch also says that the Son of man will sit on his glorious throne to judge the world (Enoch 62:3, 5).

Only here (Mt 25:34) is the Son of man called "the King," but the idea is implicit in references to his kingdom (Mt 13:41; 16:28; 19:28). Those who are counted as sheep and placed at the King's right hand are summoned to receive a kingdom prepared for them from the foundation of the world. In Daniel 7 "judgment was given for the saints of the Most High, and the time came when the saints received the kingdom" (vv 22, 26-27).

The gathering is by nations, but the dividing is by individuals (the pronoun "them" is masculine); and the judgment is based on individual conduct. The expression "all the nations" may go back more or less directly to the book of Joel (3:2), where God says, "I will gather all the nations"; but there the judgment is to be on the foreign nations that have oppressed Israel. Here the word translated "nations" might better be translated "peoples." Sometimes it means "Gentiles," but certainly in Matthew the meaning is not that only the Gentiles will be judged.

Mercy is the quality by which men will be judged (cf. Mt 6:12, 14-15; Mk 11:25-26; Lk 11:4). Those who have not been merciful will be committed to "the eternal fire prepared for the devil and his angels" (Mt 25:41). It is assumed that men have had their opportunity and made their choice in this world and must now face the eternal consequences. The last of Matthew's five discourses ends (v 46), "And they will go away into eternal punishment, but the righteous into eternal life."

The idea that what is done to one of the least of his brethren is done to Jesus has inspired many devout legends and has been a potent stimulus of mercy to the unfortunate. There is nothing quite like it anywhere else in the Synoptic Gospels or perhaps in the whole New Testament. If Jesus said this, he may have meant only that he aligned himself with the poor and afflicted and felt every wrong done or service rendered to them as though it had been done to him. The statement readily lent itself to a more mystical understanding, however, when the memory of the human Jesus dissolved more and more into the worship of the heavenly Christ, still evoking an extraordinary warmth of personal devotion.

If this judgment scene represents even approximately an actual utterance of Jesus, it leaves no room for doubt that he expected to pronounce judgment at the end of the age—unless, of course, he meant by the Son of man a person other than himself.

By way of transition to the last part of the narrative, Matthew (26:1) uses his regular formula, "When Jesus had finished these sayings . . ." Luke (21:37-38) gives the brief summary that we have already quoted. Mark (14:1) simply continues the story without a break.

CHAPTER XV

THE LAST SUPPER

The shadows deepen as the end draws near. "It was now two days before the Passover and the feast of Unleavened Bread," says Mark (14:1-2; cf. Lk 22:1-2). Matthew (26:1-5) puts this in the form of a statement by Jesus with another prediction of his betrayal and death. Mark continues, "And the chief priests and the scribes were seeking how to arrest him by stealth, and kill him; for they said, ''Not during the feast, lest there be a tumult of the people.''" According to Matthew, the plotting was done at the palace of the high priest Caiaphas.

Mark and Matthew relate here the anointing at Bethany (Mk 14:3-9; Mt 26:6-13). Luke omits it, having recounted an incident like it much earlier (7:36-50). Though the stories are similar, there are noteworthy differences. According to Luke, during Jesus' ministry in Galilee he was invited to eat at the house of a Pharisee. The KJV says that he "sat down to meat," and the RSV "sat at table," but what follows shows that he was reclining in Roman fashion on a couch beside the table, and that is what the Greek verb means. During the meal, "a woman of the city, who was a sinner, . . . brought an alabaster flask of ointment, and standing behind him at his feet, weeping, she began to wet his feet with her tears, and wiped them with the hair of her head, and kissed his feet, and anointed them with the ointment."

The host thought that if Jesus had been a prophet he would have known what the woman was and would have forbidden her. Seeing what he was thinking, Jesus said, "Simon, I have something to say to you," and said it with a parable (vv 41-42): "A certain creditor had two debtors; one owed five hundred denarii, and the other fifty. When they could not pay, he forgave them both. Now which of them will love him more?" The host condemned himself by his answer: "The one, I suppose, to whom he forgave more."

Saying "You have judged rightly," Jesus went on to contrast what the woman had done with Simon's failure to extend to him even the customary courtesies. "Therefore I tell you," he concluded, "her sins, which are many, are forgiven, for she loved much; but he who is forgiven little, loves little." To the woman he said, "Your sins are forgiven"; and while the people at the table were saying to one another, "Who is this, who even forgives sins?" Jesus added, "Your faith has saved you; go in peace." The parable does not exactly fit the situation: the woman does not love much because she is forgiven much, but is forgiven because she loves much. There is a similar difficulty in the parable of the Good Samaritan (cf. Lk 10:29-37). Precise logical consistency, however, is not always to be expected in ancient Oriental literature.

Instead of a Pharisee's house in Galilee, the scene of the incident in Mark and Matthew is the house of a leper at Bethany (Mk 14:3; Mt 26:6). Is it a mere coincidence that the host's name in both instances is Simon? Or do the accounts reflect varying memories of the same event? This is at best a matter of uncertain inference. We still have to account for other differences between the two accounts. As a matter of fact, we have not two but three versions of the story if they are all based on the same event. The Fourth Gospel also tells of an anointing at Bethany (Jn 12:1-8), with echoes of both of the other stories. Lazarus was apparently one of the guests; Martha served them; and it was Mary who anointed Jesus' feet and wiped them with her hair. Of all the details of these accounts, the association with Jesus' friends at Bethany seems most likely to be a legendary development.

Only Luke says that the woman was a sinner and that the host disapproved Jesus' failure to rebuke her. Neither in Mark's and Matthew's story nor in John's is any criticism by or of the host indicated. The only objection expressed is based not on the woman's character but on her extravagance. It is voiced by "some" in Mark, by the disciples in Matthew, and by Judas in John. In John as in Luke the woman anoints Jesus' feet; in Mark and Matthew she pours the ointment on his head, implying that he was seated at the table instead of reclining. Mark alone says that she broke the costly alabaster flask.

In both Mark and John the self-righteous critics say that the ointment could have been sold for three hundred denarii or more to give to the poor. That the criticism was not prompted by genuine concern for the poor is shown by Jesus' reply (Mk 14:7; Mt 26:11; Jn 12:8): "For you always have the poor with you, and whenever you will, you can do good to them; but you will not always have me." Incredible as it may seem, this has been quoted to discourage any effort to abolish poverty. It echoes a verse in Deuteronomy, "For the poor will never cease out of the land" (15:11); but that is stated as a reason for generosity. A little earlier in the same chapter (vv 4-5) Moses says, "But there will be no poor among you . . . if only you will obey the voice of the Lord your God." Jesus' statement is a rebuke of the critics' hypocrisy.

After the episode at Bethany, Mark and Matthew proceed to the betrayal of Jesus, which in Luke comes directly after the plotting of the chief priests and scribes (Mk 14:10-11; Mt 26:14-16; Lk 22:3-6). Only Matthew specifies thirty pieces of silver (cf. Zech 11:12) as the price paid to Judas. Some connection between the anointing and the betrayal is suggested by Mark's statement: "Then Judas Iscariot, who was one of the twelve, went to the chief priests in order to betray him to them," as though Judas, angered by what had happened, went directly to the priests from the house of Simon. Luke says, "Then Satan entered into Judas called Iscariot." Perhaps it is idle to speculate on the motive that prompted Judas. That he was moved only by greed is hard to believe of a man chosen by Jesus to be one of his chief witnesses and to share his glory. Misguided patriotism and disappointment growing out of false expectations may have been involved.

Preparations for observing the Passover now follow (Mk 14:12-16; Mt 26:17-19; Lk 22:7-13). The disciples asked Jesus where they should prepare for the supper, and he sent two of them (Peter and John, according to Luke) into the city with instructions for finding the place. A man carrying a jar of water would meet them. They were to follow him, enter the house after him, and say to the householder, "The Teacher says, 'Where is my guest room, where I am to eat the Passover with my disciples?'" He would then show them "a large upper room furnished and ready." They obeyed and found all as Jesus had said.

Presumably the householder, perhaps a secret disciple, had previously invited Jesus to use his house for the meal and had made the arrangements for him to find the house. As in the case of fetching the colt before the entry into Jerusalem, an unnamed man is given what seems to be a password and provides assistance apparently agreed upon in advance. The hostility of the authorities no doubt made a certain amount of secrecy advisable, in spite of Jesus' bold activity in public during the daytime, or perhaps because of it. Caution was all the more imperative if Judas had already gone to the priests (Mt 26:25) and Jesus knew it.

"And when it was evening, he came with the twelve" (Mk 14:17; Mt 26:20; Lk 22:14). It is impossible to straighten out the sequence of events at the supper. There are not only three but four accounts of it. The Gospel of John (chapter 13) tells of a supper "before the feast of the Passover," but the breaking of bread and the passing of the cup are not even mentioned. In addition to the accounts in the Synoptic Gospels, however, we have the report of Paul (1 Cor 11:23-25), who says that he received his account from the Lord. This sounds like a claim to a special revelation, but more probably it refers to the tradition handed down from Jesus himself through the apostles. Irregular and scandalous ways of celebrating the Lord's supper have developed in the church at Corinth, and Paul feels it necessary to appeal to the tradition to correct them.

Luke differs in important details from the other Gospels and from Paul. In Mark and Matthew the story of the supper begins with the words of Jesus, "Truly, I say to you, one of you will betray me" (Mk 14:18-21; Mt 26:21-24, cf. Ps 41:9). Mark adds, "one who is eating with me." The disciples began to ask, "Is it I?" Jesus answered, "It is one of the twelve, one who is dipping bread into the dish with me." Matthew adds (26:25; cf. v 64 and 27:11) that Judas asked, "Is it I, Master?" and Jesus replied, "You have said so," an idiomatic way of saying "Yes." In Luke all this is placed later (22:21-23) and much condensed.

While they were eating, Mark tells us (14:22-25), Jesus took bread and, after pronouncing the customary blessing, broke it and gave it to the disciples, saying, "Take; this is my body." He also took a cup, gave thanks, and passed it to the disciples. As they drank it, he said, "This is my blood of the covenant, which is poured out for many. Truly, I say to you, I shall not drink again of the fruit of the vine until that day when I drink it new in the kingdom of God" (cf. Mk 10:45; Mt 20:28). Matthew's account (26:26-29) is almost identical.

Luke begins (22:15-18) with Jesus saying to the twelve, "'I have earnestly desired to eat this Passover with you before I suffer; for I tell you I shall not eat it until it is fulfilled in the kingdom of God.' And he took a cup, and when he had given thanks he said, 'Take this, and divide it among yourselves; for I tell you that from now on I shall not drink of the fruit of the vine until the kingdom of God comes.'" Then, Luke says (v 19), Jesus gave thanks and broke and distributed the bread, saying, "This is my body which is given for you. Do this in remembrance of me" (cf. 1 Cor 11:24). In putting the cup before the bread Luke differs from Paul as well as from Mark and Matthew. In what seems to be the best text of this passage, however, the giving of the cup is divided into two acts. The saying about not drinking wine until the kingdom of God comes accompanies the first cup; but after the distribution of the bread Luke continues (22:20), "And likewise the cup after supper, saying, 'This cup which is poured out for you is the new covenant in my blood.'" This agrees closely with Paul's version of the story, except that Paul adds (1 Cor 11:25), "Do this, as often as you drink it, in remembrance of me." What historical basis, if any, Luke had for his variations cannot be determined.

With all these differences it is hardly surprising that ministers in the nonliturgical churches, when conducting communion services, often confuse and combine the different accounts and even insert sentences or phrases not found in any of them. We should not necessarily be any nearer to the real Jesus if we knew exactly what was done and said. Several more or less important questions, however, are raised by the variations in the story.

One is the question whether the supper was a Passover meal. The Synoptic Gospels so regard it. The two disciples were sent into the city (Mk 14:12 and parallels) for the express purpose of preparing to eat the Passover. The meal took place that evening (v 17 and parallels), which by Jewish reckoning was the beginning of the next day. But why is there no mention of the lamb or the bitter herbs? John puts the supper on the night before the Passover

(Jn 13:1; 19:31, 36, 42), so that the crucifixion takes place at the time when the lamb was killed, making Jesus himself the true Passover sacrifice (cf. 1 Cor 5:7).

Several explanations have been offered for the absence of any reference to the lamb, but there is nothing in the records to support them. To be sure, if Jesus broke the bread "as they were eating" (Mk 14:22), they must have had something to eat that is not named. Dipping the bread in the dish implies this (Mk 14:20; cf. Mt 26:23; Lk 22:21). It still seems strange that there is no specific mention of the distinctive elements of the Passover meal. Perhaps the evangelists took them for granted.

Involved with these considerations is the question of the year in which the last supper and the trial and crucifixion of Jesus took place. This is a complicated problem, apparently insoluble at present, not because there is not enough evidence but because there is so much of it and it is not consistent. According to all the Gospels the resurrection took place early Sunday morning, the day after the Sabbath and the third day after the crucifixion according to the ancient custom of counting both the first and the last days. The crucifixion must therefore have been on Friday, and the last supper was eaten Thursday evening. If it was the Passover, this would be the beginning of the fifteenth day of the month of Nisan; if it was the night before the Passover, it would be the beginning of the fourteenth. Unfortunately, since the Jewish calendar was not based on the solar year, we cannot tell in what year the fourteenth or the fifteenth of Nisan began on a Thursday evening.

Nearer to the heart of the matter, but not so unanswerable, is a third question: Did Jesus himself partake of the bread and wine? He had asked for a room where he might eat the Passover with his disciples (Mk 14:14; Mt 26:18; Lk 22:11), but everything in the accounts of the supper itself can be taken to mean that only the disciples ate and Jesus talked to them. According to Luke, who actually says nothing of the meal itself, Jesus said before giving the disciples either wine or bread (22:15-16), "I have earnestly desired to eat this Passover with you before I suffer; for I tell you I shall not eat it until it is fulfilled in the kingdom of God." Many manuscripts and versions read here, "I shall never eat it again until it is fulfilled in the kingdom of God." It is impossible to determine whether this means that this is the last time Jesus will eat the Passover, or that in spite of his wish he will not eat it now.

Even if he ate the meal, however, it is unlikely that he partook of the bread and wine. When he gave the first cup to the disciples, Luke continues (vv 17-18), he said, "Take this, and divide it among yourselves, for I tell you that from now on I shall not drink of the fruit of the vine until the kingdom of God comes." Mark and Matthew do not have the saying about eating the Passover. They put the saying about the wine after the distribution of both bread and wine, reading, "I shall not drink again of the fruit of the vine until the day when I drink it new in the kingdom of God" (Mk 14:25; Mt 26:29). Both Mark's and Matthew's "again" and Luke's "from now on" may mean either that Jesus would drink the wine this time but not again, or that he would not now partake of it. The latter seems more natural in view of the meaning he ascribed to the bread and wine: "This is my body," and "This is my blood" (Mk 14:22, 24 and parallels).

With these and other complications and problems, no wonder some have concluded that the whole story of the supper is not the record of an event that was remembered and celebrated, but the cult myth of a rite that it served to explain. The rites and myths of the contemporary pagan cults afford impressive materials for comparison, and they undoubtedly had an influence on the later development of the Christian sacrament. Their deities, however, were mythical beings shrouded in the mists of antiquity. The Christian story and observance had to do with a real person, who had been personally known and was remembered by people still living when the story was being told and put on record.

The problems remain, but there is a solid core of reliable tradition. That Jesus not only distributed bread and wine to the disciples but also accompanied the acts with words giving them a new, special meaning cannot be reasonably questioned. All the accounts agree on this much at least. The significance of the event, however, as Jesus intended it to be understood, depends on the authenticity and meaning of the words attributed to him.

All the accounts include the idea of the covenant. Its Old Testament background makes clear what it means. The statement

241

"This is my blood of the covenant" echoes the words of Moses at Sinai (Ex 24:8; cf. Zech 9:11), "Behold the blood of the covenant which the Lord has made with you in accordance with all these words." This was said as a part of the ceremony ratifying the covenant between God and the people of Israel, when oxen were sacrificed, and Moses, following the ancient custom of the blood covenant, threw half of the blood against the altar and the other half on the people.

What covenant did Jesus refer to when he said, "This is my blood of the covenant"? Paul and Luke call it "the new covenant" (1 Cor 11:25; Lk 22:20, cf. Mk 14:25; Mt 26:28), and the word "new" has crept into many later manuscripts and versions of Mark and Matthew (cf. KJV, "my blood of the new testament"). The idea of a new covenant comes from the Old Testament. Jeremiah, contemplating the capture of Jerusalem by the Babylonians and the deportation of king and people, promised a new covenant to replace the old one, which Israel had broken by disobeying God's laws (Jer 31:31-34).

The community that produced the Dead Sea Scrolls made much of the covenant idea. To the Christian church the promise of the new covenant seemed to be fulfilled. Jesus, by his death and his intercession in heaven, had become "the surety of a better covenent" (Heb 7:22). Whether or not Jesus himself used the word "new," he was probably thinking of Jeremiah's promise when he spoke of the covenant. He was convinced that only through his death could God's kingdom be established. His own blood would seal the new covenant as the sacrificial "blood of the covenant" had sealed the old one at Sinai.

Was it Jesus' intention to establish a new rite to be observed by his followers, or was he, like the Old Testament prophets, trying to say by symbolic acts what he had been telling the disciples and they had been unable to comprehend? The only suggestion of an observance to be repeated is in the words reported by Paul and Luke, "Do this in remembrance of me" (1 Cor 11:24-25; Lk 22:19). If Jesus said this, however, he need not have meant that what he did was to be repeated as a ritual observance. He may have meant only, "Remember me whenever you eat your bread and drink your wine."

This is apparently what happened in the apostolic church. The breaking of bread mentioned in Acts (2:42, 46) does not seem to have been a formal rite. What evoked Paul's account of the last supper was the fact that the "love feasts" of the church at Corinth were all too informal (1 Cor 11:20-21). Paul's indignant declaration (v 34) that those who were hungry should eat at home before coming to the Lord's table probably influenced the separation of the sacrament from a common meal. That Jesus had any intention of initiating a rite to be repeated is thus improbable. If the church, however, wished to express and nourish its sense of what his life and death meant to them by an act of worship commemorating a particular event, it could not have chosen one more appropriate than the last supper.

At the end of Paul's narrative (v 26), he adds a comment of his own, giving the supper both a backward and a forward look: "For as often as you eat this bread and drink the cup, you proclaim the Lord's death until he comes." In the Gospels the forward look is seen in the references to the fulfillment of the passover and drinking the wine new in the kingdom of God. For Paul, Jesus' coming again had taken the place of the coming of the kingdom.

Luke reports here briefly Jesus' prediction of his betrayal, which Mark and Matthew have given at the beginning of the supper (Lk 22:21-23; cf. Mk 14:18-21; Mt 26:21-25). He then introduces rather abruptly (vv 24-26; cf. Mk 10:42-45; Mt 20:25-28) the disciples' dispute as to which of them was the greatest, with Jesus' rebuke, and adds a saying not found in the other Gospels: "For which is the greater, one who sits at table, or one who serves? Is it not the one who sits at table? But I am among you as one who serves" (v 27: cf. Jn 13:3-11).

After this Luke gives another saying, no part of which appears in Mark and only the last clause in Matthew (Lk 22:28-29; cf. Mt 19:28): "You are those who have continued with me in my trials; and I assign to you, as my Father assigned to me, a kingdom, that you may eat and drink at my table in my kingdom, and sit on thrones judging the twelve tribes of Israel." The word here translated "assign" is related to the Greek word for covenant. The meaning of this saying becomes clearer when we remember that the word translated "kingdom" often means "kingship."

243

The NEB reads, "and now I vest in you the kingship which my Father vested in me"; the NAB reads, "I for my part assign to you the dominion my Father has assigned to me." These renderings may suggest that Jesus abdicates in favor of the disciples. The TEV avoids that misunderstanding by a rather free paraphrase: "and just as my Father has given me the right to rule, so will I make the same agreement with you." The essential meaning is that Jesus will share his royal authority and power with the twelve.

What is the relation of this promise to the idea of the blood of the covenant? The covenant sealed by Jesus' blood is for many, whereas here he speaks of a special covenant with the twelve. If this is an authentic utterance of Jesus, it was probably not spoken at the last supper but, as in Matthew, at some earlier time before Jesus knew that one of the twelve would betray him. The clause "that you may eat and drink at my table in my kingdom" is lacking in Matthew. It may have suggested Luke's putting the saying here. The idea of a covenant does not imply a formal transaction, as though Jesus said officially, "By virtue of the kingship vested in me, I hereby confer kingship upon you."

Another statement not reported by the other evangelists follows in Luke (22:31-34). Turning to Peter, Jesus says, "Simon, Simon, behold, Satan demanded to have you, that he might sift you like wheat, but I have prayed for you that your faith may not fail; and when you have turned again, strengthen your brethren." Peter replies, "Lord, I am ready to go with you to prison and to death." Jesus, however, predicts that before morning Peter will deny him. Mark and Matthew report this after Jesus and the disciples have gone back to the Mount of Olives.

Now Jesus asks the disciples (Lk 22:35-38) whether they lacked anything when he sent them without purse, bag, or sandals on their mission of preaching and healing (Mk 6:8-9; Mt 10:9-10; Lk 9:3; 10:4). They reply, "Nothing." Jesus says that if one of them has a purse or bag now he must take it; and anyone who has no sword must buy one, even if he has to sell his mantle to do it. "For I tell you," Jesus continues, "that this scripture must be fulfilled in me, 'And he was reckoned with transgressors'; for what is written about me has its fulfilment" (Is 53:12; cf. Mk

15:28). The disciples tell him that they have two swords, and he says, "It is enough." What bearing this has on Jesus' attitude to the use of force, if any, is uncertain. Apparently Jesus, discouraged at the disciples' failure to understand, said, "Never mind; let it go." For us too it is hard to see what he meant. The sequel shows that it was not a call to armed resistance.

The story of the last supper ends with the singing of a hymn, after which "they went out to the Mount of Olives" (Mk 14:26-27; Mt 26:30-31; Lk 22:39). On the way, or after they got there, Jesus declared that all the disciples would forsake him, and quoted Zechariah 13:7: "I will strike the shepherd, and the sheep will be scattered." The quotation was appropriate and might well occur to him under such circumstances.

With all reasonable caution against trying to imagine Jesus' thoughts and feelings, one is surely justified in pausing to consider how profoundly discouraging the situation must have been for him, and to be grateful that there are such clear reflections of his disappointment and disillusionment. Here is no Docetic Christ, moving undisturbed through the frustrations and sorrows of human existence. Here is a real man, subject to the hopes and disappointments of our common lot, "a man of sorrows, and acquainted with grief" (Is 53:3).

In Mark and Matthew the quotation of Zechariah is followed by a promise: "But after I am raised up, I will go before you to Galilee" (Mk 14:28; Mt 26:32, cf. Mk 16:7; Mt 28:7; Lk 24:6). This points forward to the Galilean appearance of the risen Christ narrated at the end of Matthew (28:16). It implies also that Jesus knew the defection of the disciples would not be permanent.

Peter was still unwilling to admit that they would all desert Jesus (Mk 14:29-30; Mt 26:33-34; cf. Lk 22:33-34). "Even though they all fall away, I will not," he declared; but Jesus said to him, "Truly, I say to you, this very night, before the cock crows twice, you will deny me three times." (Matthew, Luke, and some manuscripts of Mark omit "twice.") Still Peter protested, "If I must die with you, I will not deny you"; and the rest echoed his words. Were they trying to reassure themselves? Vehemence of assertion is often in direct proportion to lack of conviction.

CHAPTER XVI

GETHSEMANE:
ARREST, TRIAL, AND CONDEMNATION

"And they came to a place which was called Gethsemane" (Mk 14:32; Mt 26:36; cf. Lk 22:40). Just where Gethsemane was is unknown. It is called a garden in the Gospel of John (18:1), but the Synoptic Gospels call it only a place. The name, which appears nowhere else and is omitted by Luke even here, means "oil press," suggesting that when the name was given the oil from the olives grown on the hill was extracted here. An ancient tradition locates the place in the valley, just north of the foot of the Mount of Olives, where a church now marks the traditional site of Mary's tomb. Two locations on the western slope of the hill are revered by different groups as the sacred place. Each has a church on it. On the modern road to Jericho, which runs around the bottom of the Mount of Olives, is the Roman Catholic church, with a small, reverently tended garden beside it containing some old, gnarled olive trees. Above this, in another enclosure, is the Russian Greek Orthodox church, surrounded by a quiet grove. There is no way to determine the exact site, but it must have been somewhere in this vicinity, though possibly farther up or even on the eastern side nearer Bethany.

When they came to Gethsemane, Jesus left most of the disciples and went on, presumably deeper into the garden or orchard, taking with him only Peter, James, and John (Mk 14:32-42; Mt 26:36-46; Lk 22:40-46). Then, "greatly distressed and troubled," he told these three to wait and keep watch. "And going a little farther, he fell on the ground and prayed that, if it were possible, the hour might pass from him. And he said, 'Abba, Father, all things are possible to thee; remove this cup from me; yet not what I will, but what thou wilt'" (Mk 14:35-36; cf. Mt 26:39; Lk 22:41-42; and Mt 26:42).

Just what the cup was that Jesus begged to be spared we cannot say. He had spoken before of a cup that he must drink and had told the sons of Zebedee that they would have to drink it too (Mk 10:38-39; Mt 20:22-23). The immediate reference both there and here may be to martyrdom; yet it can hardly have been only his death that Jesus wished he might avoid. He had long been prepared for that. More probably, if such speculation is permissible, it was his rejection and the frustration of his hopes for his people that he still could not help wanting to have changed. In any case, this prayer is a sublime expression of the devotion to his Father's will that governed Jesus' whole life.

After quoting the prayer, in the traditional text, Luke reports two unique items (22:43-44)—the appearance of "an angel from heaven, strengthening him," and the sweat "like great drops of blood falling upon the ground." Like the descent of the Spirit at his baptism, this may have been an inner personal experience. The reference to blood is merely a simile expressing the intensity of Jesus' wrestling with God and with his own feelings. Neither of these items is accessible to historical research; in fact the best text does not have these two verses.

When Jesus came back to the three disciples, he found them asleep (Mk 14:37-38; Mt 26:40-41); Lk 22:45-46). "Simon," he said, "are you asleep? Could you not watch one hour? Watch and pray that you may not enter into temptation." This is ambiguous. Some interpreters understand it as telling what is to be prayed for. This is clearly the meaning where in Luke (22:40) Jesus says on first reaching the garden, literally, "Pray that you may not enter into temptation." Now, however, the Greek uses a conjunction that usually means "in order that." The Aramaic conjunction back of the Greek would be as ambiguous as our English "that," but the meaning intended is almost certainly "Pray, in order that you may not enter into temptation."

The expression "enter into temptation" recalls the petition in the Lord's Prayer (Mt 6:13; Lk 11:4), "lead us not into temptation." The noun translated "temptation" in both places means being tried, put to the test. Our English words "tempt" and "temptation," as a matter of fact, were used in that sense when the KJV was made, as in the repeated statement that the Israelites tempted God (*e.g.*, Ex 17:7), or the story of the lawyer (Lk 10:25) who tempted Jesus (RSV "put him to the test"). The disciples were told in Gethsemane to keep praying in order that they might not be tried beyond their strength (cf. 1 Cor 10:13).

247

To this exhortation, in Mark and Matthew, Jesus adds a gentle expression of sympathetic insight (Mk 14:38; Mt 26:41) that has become proverbial: "The spirit indeed is willing, but the flesh is weak." The disciples meant well; but disappointment, perplexity, confusion, and sheer physical exhaustion were too much for them; they could not keep their eyes open. Probably also they could not quite believe that the end was so near or that it would be so disastrous as Jesus anticipated. They did not have his conviction that God so willed it.

A second and a third time, according to Mark and Matthew, Jesus went off by himself and prayed, and again came back and found the three disciples asleep. When he returned the third time (Mk 14:41-42; Mt 26:45-46), he said: "Are you still sleeping and taking your rest? It is enough; the hour has come; the Son of man is betrayed into the hands of sinners. Rise, let us be going; see, my betrayer is at hand." And as he spoke, a crowd armed with swords and clubs came from the chief priest and scribes and elders, with Judas at their head. Every reader knows who Judas was; but the evangelists add to his name "one of the twelve," as though to stress the horror of such a betrayal by one of the privileged circle.

The evangelists differ somewhat in their accounts of the arrest of Jesus, the variations consisting mainly of insertions or omissions (Mk 14:43-52; Mt 26:47-56; Lk 22:47-53). This time Mark's narrative is the shortest and simplest of the three. Mark and Matthew relate that Judas had agreed beforehand to identify Jesus by kissing him, and that he did so, at the same time greeting Jesus as Master (literally, Rabbi). Luke, however, suggests that Judas was not allowed to carry out his hideous intention: "He drew near to Jesus to kiss him; but Jesus said to him, 'Judas, would you betray the Son of man with a kiss?'"

One of the disciples, all the Gospels agree, drew his sword and cut off the ear of a slave of the high priest. The Fourth Gospel says that the disciple was Peter, and even gives the name of the slave, Malchus (Jn 18:10). Matthew reports (26:52-53) that Jesus said: "Put your sword back into its place; for all who take the sword will perish by the sword. Do you think that I cannot appeal to my Father, and he will at once send me more than twelve legions of

248

angels? But how then should the scriptures be fulfilled, that it must be so?'' According to Luke Jesus said only, ''No more of this!'' Luke adds, however, that Jesus touched the slave's ear and healed him. This is the last miracle related in the Synoptic Gospels, and the only healing miracle performed during the last days at Jerusalem. It is obviously a legendary embellishment of the straightforward tradition of Mark and Matthew.

Jesus then (Mk 14:48-49; Mt 26:55-56; Lk 22:52-53) spoke to ''the crowds,'' according to Matthew; Mark says only ''to them.'' Luke says, ''to the chief priests and officers of the temple and elders, who had come out against him,'' though according to Mark and Matthew the crowds came from the chief priests and elders. ''Have you come out as against a robber, with swords and clubs to capture me?'' Jesus asked scornfully, and reminded them that they had made no attempt to take him while he was teaching publicly in the temple. ''But let the scriptures be fulfilled,'' he concluded as reported by Mark. Matthew reads, ''but all this has taken place, that the scriptures of the prophets might be fulfilled.'' In Luke, Jesus says, ''But this is your hour, and the power of darkness.'' There is no way to tell which, if any of these, is correct.

''And they all forsook him, and fled,'' as Jesus had said they would (Mk 14:50; Mt 26:56; cf. Mk 14:27; Mt 26:31). The shepherd had been taken, and the sheep scattered. Mark alone adds the curious incident of the young man clad only in a linen cloth who tried to follow, and, when he was seized, slipped out of the cloth and fled naked (Mk 14:51-52). The conjecture that this was Mark himself is unfounded, but it is hard to see how the story arose unless it was a personal memory of someone.

In spite of the hour, Jesus was brought before the high priest and the chief priests, elders, and scribes, who were already assembled (Mk 14:53-54; Mt 26:57-58; Lk 22:54-55). Luke says that Jesus was taken to the high priest's house, and all three Gospels in the next sentence mention the courtyard of the high priest. Only Matthew among the Synoptic evangelists gives the high priest's name, Caiaphas.

There is much uncertainty concerning what ensued. Mark and Matthew agree closely, but what they report as occurring at a single appearance before the high priest is divided by Luke into two episodes, with a different order of events (Lk 22:56-62). Luke tells of Peter's denial of Jesus and the soldiers' mockery as taking place at the high priest's house, with no suggestion that the high priest or the other dignitaries put in an appearance until morning, when "the elders of the people . . . , both chief priests and scribes," assembled and "led him away to their council" (v 66). Luke in fact, does not mention the high priest at all; it is "they" who do everything. The Gospel of John also seems to have two arraignments (18:13-27), but they are not the same as those in Luke.

Contrary to the statement in John 18:16 that Peter stood outside at the door until he was brought in to the fire, the Synoptic Gospels agree that he followed Jesus and his captors at a distance, went directly into the courtyard, and sat with the guards by the fire (Mk 14:53-54; Mt 26:57-58; Lk 22:54-55). If he had fled with the other disciples when they forsook Jesus, he must have turned back immediately.

Mark and Matthew report that the council tried to get testimony against Jesus that would justify a sentence of death, but though many false witnesses were found, they did not agree in their testimony (Mk 14:55-59; Mt 26:59-61). Finally the high priest challenged Jesus directly to answer the accusations. Receiving no reply, he asked specifically, "Are you the Christ, the Son of the Blessed?" Matthew reads, "the Son of God," which of course is what Mark's expression means.

What Jesus said in reply is reported in different ways, and it is very difficult to interpret. We too should like to know whether he considered himself the Messiah. The evangelists never doubt it (cf. Mt 16:17, 20; Mk 8:30; Lk 9:21), but that fact makes it all the more remarkable that their records disclose so many reasons to question it—reasons that lead many New Testament historians to the definite conclusion that Jesus did not believe himself to be the Lord's Anointed. It is perhaps the greatest irony of Christian history that the affirmation that alone distinguished the first Christians from other Jews may have been after all contrary to Jesus' own intention and belief.

What may seem to be the strongest evidence that he did believe he was the Messiah is his reply to the high priest. In all three Gospels this consists of two distinct parts, but each part is reported in three different forms. According to Luke (22:67-68), when "they" said, "If you are the Christ, tell us," Jesus answered evasively, "If I tell you, you will not believe; and if I ask you, you will not answer." According to Matthew (26:64), Jesus said "You have said so," which in Aramaic would be understood as affirmative (cf. v 25).

There are seven places in the Synoptic Gospels where Jesus himself is reported to have used the term "Christ." Only in four places does he clearly use the term of himself; and two of these, being post-resurrection sayings, cannot be used as sayings of the historical Jesus. One of the remaining two speaks of being given a cup of water "because you bear the name of Christ," where the parallel in Matthew reads, "because he is a disciple." In the other, "you have one master, the Christ," the title seems obviously an explanation inserted by an editor, scribe, or later reader. The evidence that Jesus ever spoke of himself as the Messiah is thus decidedly weak. That he even approved or accepted the title when others used it is equally doubtful, as we have noted in relevant passages (*e.g.,* Mk 8:29 and parallels; Mt 11:2; Lk 4:41).

Many have held that Jesus believed he was the Messiah but rejected a type of Messianic hope that expected the Messiah to "restore the kingdom to Israel" (Acts 1:6). This is quite possible. Christians tend to overemphasize the military aspect of the Jewish Messianic hope. There were other kinds of expectation, more peaceful and more spiritual, and the term "Messiah" was used with them also. Warfare is not the only function of a king. From very ancient times a major responsibility of the ruler was to establish and maintain justice, to prevent the exploitation of the poor and weak by the rich and powerful, and in particular to maintain the rights of orphans and widows.

Under foreign oppression it was natural to feel, as the Zealots did, that only by rebellion could the Roman yoke be cast off; but many of the Jews must have agreed with the Pharisee that an attempt to take matters into their own hands would be both impious and futile. That this was Jesus' position is therefore no

251

evidence that he rejected entirely the idea of himself as Messiah. Quite possibly he only discouraged the public use of the term because of the danger of fomenting revolutionary acts and provoking punitive action by the Romans.

The second part of his reply to the high priest, as given by Mark (14:62), reads, "and you will see the Son of man seated at the right hand of Power, and coming with the clouds of heaven." (The use of "Power" here reflects the Jewish practice of avoiding a direct mention of God where it might seem anthropomorphic.) Instead of Mark's "and you will see," Matthew has (26:64). "But I tell you, hereafter you will see," as though Jesus said, in answer to the question whether he was the Messiah, "As you say, but never mind about me! From now on you are going to see the Son of man," and so on. There was the same quick shift from Messiah to Son of man in Jesus' response to Peter's confession at Caesarea Philippi. Luke (22:69) reads only, "But from now on the Son of man shall be seated at the right hand of the power of God." Both Matthew's "hereafter" and Luke's "from now on" suggest an extended process now about to begin rather than an instantaneous event. Neither Greek expression refers to an indefinite future time, such as the English "hereafter" suggests.

The image of sitting at God's right hand comes from the same verse (Ps 110:1) quoted earlier by Jesus in the temple (Mk 12:36 and parallels): "The Lord says to my Lord, 'Sit at my right hand, till I make your enemies your footstool.'" This was evidently understood as addressed to the Messiah. Jesus, however, is speaking here of the Son of man. This implies that for him they were the same.

The stress on the coming of the Son of man, here and throughout the New Testament, raises a difficult question: what is the relation of the coming of the Son of man to the coming of the kingdom of God? They are almost never mentioned together. Sometimes the problem is further complicated by references to the kingdom of the Son of man in connection with his coming. These may not be authentic, but it is quite probable that Jesus connected the idea of kingship with the coming of the Son of man. In some way, moreover, which is never made clear and may now be impossible to determine, the coming and kingdom of the Son of man and the coming of the kingdom of God are bound up together.

The whole question of Jesus' use of the term Son of man is an unresolved problem. Some scholars hold that Jesus did not use it at all, others that he used in one way but not in another. To me it still seems not at all improbable that the whole complex of ideas associated with the expression in the Gospels originated with Jesus himself. Its common idiomatic use by him, as by other Aramaic speaking people, may be taken for granted. Perhaps when he faced rejection and death he found an answer to the question "What then?" in Daniel's vision of the one like a son of man, to whom dominion and glory would be given. He might then think of himself as already the Son of man during his ministry. By the time he applied the term "Son of man" to the suffering servant prophecy, "the Son of man" must have meant to him practically "I." Obviously all this cannot be proved; other possibilities must be recognized. It is no more speculative, however, than current theories of the origin of the whole idea in the church.

In Luke's account (22:70) of the hearing before the elders, chief priests, and scribes, when Jesus was asked whether he was the Messiah and replied with the statement about the Son of man, they asked him, "Are you the Son of God, then?" (Mark and Matthew have combined this title with Messiah in the initial question.) He answered, "You say that I am." Like the high priest in Mark and Matthew, the council received this as a blasphemous affirmation that made further evidence unnecessary (Lk 22:71; cf. Mk 14:63-64; Mt 26:65-66). The high priest, say Mark and Matthew, tore his robe and called on the council to condemn the blasphemer, and "they all condemned him as deserving death." Here Mark and Matthew tell of the insults and abuse that Luke has already reported as inflicted at the high priest's house (Mk 14:65; Mt 26:67-68; cf. Lk 22:63-65).

The story of Peter's denial follows in the same two Gospels. Luke has reported it before the mockery and beating (Mk 14:66-72; Mt 26:69-75; cf. Lk 22:56-62). Otherwise the accounts are in substantial agreement. Only Luke has the poignant note, "And the Lord turned and looked at Peter." All three say that

Peter, hearing the cock crow, remembered what Jesus had told him and wept.

Regardless of discrepancies, this story surely bears the marks of historical truth. Not much later Peter became one of the foremost leaders in the church. Such a story about him would not have been invented or preserved without a solid historical basis, resting ultimately on his own acknowledgment. Perhaps when he said, "I do not know the man," he was not so much being a coward as expressing his confusion and despair. "I thought I knew him," he may have felt, "but I don't understand him at all. Why didn't he let me use my sword to defend him? Why didn't he call down the angels? Why does he let these men treat him like this without saying a word?"

Perhaps Peter and Judas shared something of the same disappointment; but the results were entirely different. According to Luke, Jesus had said to Peter after their final meal together (22:32), "I have prayed for you that your faith may not fail; and when you have turned again, strengthen your brethren." Peter did turn again and became a rock worthy of the name Jesus had given him, though, at least to Paul's way of thinking, he was still capable of hesitation and compromise (Gal 2:11-13).

Mark and Matthew now proceed with a statement that Luke made earlier in almost the same words (Mk 15:1; Mt 27:1-2; Lk 23:1; cf. Lk 22:66), to the effect that when day came the chief priests and the rest, after further consultation, bound Jesus and led him away. Luke says, however, "led him away to their council"; Mark and Matthew say, "led him away and delivered him to Pilate." Here Luke says simply "Then the whole company of them arose, and brought him before Pilate."

Matthew tells here (27:3-10) what happened to Judas after he betrayed Jesus. Luke gives another version of the story in the book of Acts (1:18-19). According to Matthew, Judas repented when it was too late, went back to the chief priests and elders, confessed that he had betrayed an innocent man, threw down in the temple the thirty pieces of silver they had paid him, and "went and hanged himself." The chief priests used the money to buy a field known as the potter's field, but the people of Jerusalem named it Akeldama, meaning in Aramaic "Field of Blood." In

Acts, Judas buys the field with his blood money, and it is called Akeldama because "falling headlong he burst open in the middle and all his bowels gushed out." Both stories may be legends.

Matthew adds that Judas' death fulfilled a prophecy of Jeremiah about buying the potter's field with thirty pieces of silver. As quoted by Matthew the prophecy combines bits from Jeremiah (18:2-3; 32:6-15) and Zechariah (11:12). Such combinations of verses from different books have been explained by the hypothesis that the evangelists quoted from collections of Messianic proof-texts. New support for this has been found in scraps of similar collections in the caves of Qumran.

Not much is known about Pontius Pilate, the Roman procurator before whom Jesus was now arraigned, but there is enough to show that he had little understanding and less concern for the sensitive pride of the Jewish people and their explosive mixture of religious devotion and nationalistic ardor. He allowed Roman soldiers to enter Jerusalem without removing the idolatrous images from their standards. Later he had golden shields bearing the emperor's name hung on the walls of the palace he occupied when in Jerusalem. In both instances he was compelled to rescind his orders. Luke mentions (13:1) some Galileans whose blood Pilate "mingled with their sacrifices."

Another act, which he doubtless considered beneficial, provoked rioting. To provide an adequate water supply for the crowds that filled Jerusalem during the festivals, Pilate had an aqueduct made to bring water from a place near Bethlehem. Unwisely he paid for it out of the temple treasury.

For ten years (A.D. 26–36) Pilate governed Judea until an oppressive act in Samaria brought his term of office to an end. When a crowd assembled on Mount Gerizim expecting to see the sacred vessels of the tabernacle excavated, Pilate's soldiers massacred them. In response to an appeal to the legate of Syria, Pilate was summoned to Rome. What effect the death of the emperor while Pilate was en route had on his reception at Rome is not clear, but he was not sent back to Palestine.

Such was the man before whom Jesus was now brought (Mk 15:2-5; Mt 27:11-14; Lk 23:2-5). The accounts of the appearance or appearances before Pilate involve as much uncertainty and confusion as those of his trial before the high priest. The quite different narrative in the Gospel of John only increases the complexity of the problem. Much intensive research has been done on this subject in recent years, without reaching clarity or certainty. Each item must be examined in the light of what is known about Jewish and Roman legal procedure, but we cannot assume that every recognized principle and precept was strictly observed. It seems clear, in fact, that there were some irregularities. For the present we can only follow the reports in the Gospels, noting what items are contributed or omitted by each evangelist.

Naturally Pilate would not have been interested in questions of Jewish theology or an individual's claim to be the person referred to by ancient prophecies. Jesus' accusers therefore alleged that he had been preaching sedition against the emperor. Luke says (23:2) that this accusation was lodged at the beginning of the hearing. Mark and Matthew imply that Pilate had heard of it, for they represent him as opening the proceedings with the question, "Are you the King of the Jews?" (Mk 15:2; Mt 27:11). But Jesus would say only, "You have said so," which Pilate took as a refusal to reply.

The persistent silence of Jesus in the face of the charges against him made Pilate wonder. He appears to have been reluctant to pronounce sentence against a man whom he regarded as at worst harmless. Only to appease the priests and elders and to avoid a charge that he himself was disloyal to the emperor (cf. Jn 19:12), and only after trying various expedients to evade responsibility for the decision, did he finally consent to have Jesus put to death.

One resort that seemed to offer a way out is related by Luke (23:6-12). When Pilate told "the chief priests and the multitudes" that he did not find the prisoner guilty of any crime, they insisted that Jesus had been stirring up the people from Galilee to Jerusalem. Learning that Jesus was from Galilee, the territory of Herod Antipas, Pilate recalled that Herod was in Jerusalem (no doubt for the Passover) and sent Jesus to him. Herod was curious to see Jesus perform a miracle but apparently no longer considered him dangerous. He therefore questioned him but could draw no response from him. At length, tiring of the effort, "Herod with his soldiers treated him with contempt and mocked him; then, arraying him in gorgeous apparel, he sent him back to Pilate."

By sending Jesus to Herod, Pilate achieved a more friendly relation with the puppet king; but he did not after all get rid of Jesus. He therefore summoned "the chief priests and the rulers and the people," announced that he had found Jesus innocent of any capital offense, and proposed therefore to chastise and release him.

All three evangelists tell of another expedient that may not have worked out as Pilate wished but did dispose of the annoying case (Mk 15:6-11; Mt 27:15-20; Lk 23:17-19). Pilate's proposal to let Jesus go, Luke says, was met by an outcry, "Away with this man, and release to us Barabbas!" Matthew calls Barabbas "a notorious prisoner"; Mark explains that he was one of "the rebels in prison, who had committed murder in the insurrection"; Luke says he had been imprisoned "for an insurrection started in the city, and for murder." Both Mark and Matthew say that it was Pilate's custom to release at the festival a prisoner chosen by the Jews. When the crowd asked that he do so at this time, he asked, as Mark has it, "Do you want me to release for you the King of the Jews?" That way of putting the question would of course ensure a refusal. According to Matthew, Pilate asked, "Whom do you want me to release for you, Barabbas or Jesus who is called Christ?" This slightly more diplomatic form of expression would still only harden the demand for Barabbas.

Matthew contributes a detail not reported elsewhere (27:19), a warning from Pilate's wife because of a dream in which she had "suffered much" because of "that righteous man." When the mob insisted on the release of Barabbas, Mark and Matthew report, Pilate asked what he should do with Jesus, and they replied "Crucify him!" (Mk 15:12-14; Mt 27:21-23; cf. Lk 23:20-23). Pilate asked, "Why, What evil has he done?" but they only demanded all the more loudly that he be crucified.

Again Matthew has a unique item. Seeing that the crowd was becoming disorderly, Pilate publicly washed his hands (Mt 27:24-25), declaring, "I am innocent of this man's blood; see to it yourselves"—as though letting an innocent man be crucified incurred no guilt! Matthew continues, "And all the people answered, 'His blood be on us and on our children.'"

All the evangelists went out of their way to relieve Pilate of the responsibility for Jesus' death and put it on the Jews. Current studies of Jesus' trial are much concerned with this fact, seeming sometimes as anxious to blame the Romans as the evangelists were to blame the Jews. Justified resentment on the part of Jews and shame on the part of Christians for the disgrace and horror of anti-Semitism make such a desire natural. A distortion of history in one direction, however, is not remedied by distorting it in the opposite direction. Only an earnest effort to find the truth can promote real understanding and mutual respect. No matter what was done or said by Jews or Romans nearly two thousand years ago, their descendants were not responsible. Even if the mob, or any of them, uttered the frightful curse ascribed by Matthew to "all the people," that would not make the Jewish people of that day guilty, to say nothing of later generations.

The reasons for the tendency of the evangelists to exculpate Pilate are fairly obvious. No doubt they felt genuine indignation at the injustice of Jesus' condemnation and death, but they were also anxious to counteract any impression that Christianity was a subversive movement and Jesus a political agitator against the Roman government. At the time when the Gospels were written, persecution was becoming a real danger for Christians. It was important to convince the rulers that the church was not a revolutionary organization.

As for the real responsibility of Pilate or the Jewish leaders for the crucifixion, perhaps the most we can say is that the Romans crucified Jesus, but the Jewish authorities probably desired his death and did what they could to bring it about. Both considered Jesus dangerous and had good reason to think so. Whether Jews or Romans were more responsible is a purely historical question, to be investigated without fear or favor.

To return to the narrative, Pilate released Barabbas, had Jesus flogged, and turned him over to the soldiers to be crucified (Mk 15:15-16; Mt 27:26-27; Lk 23:24-25). Matthew says that they "took Jesus into the praetorium"; Mark says, "led him away inside the palace (that is, the praetorium)." This is the only place

258

in the Synoptic Gospels where the word "praetorium" is used, but it appears in John and Acts, and Paul mentions "the whole praetorium" at Rome (Jn 18:28, 33: 19:9; Acts 23:35; Phil 1:13). Ordinarily the word designates the residence of the chief Roman official, where cases were often tried and judgment pronounced.

Not one of the places where these tragic events occurred can be identified with certainty. Some scholars believe that the praetorium was the fortified palace built by Herod the Great at the western edge of the city, where what is called the Citadel or Tower of David now stands. Herod's characteristic masonry can still be seen there in the foundations and the lower courses of the walls. This would be a natural place for Pilate to stay when he came up from Caesarea to Jerusalem.

There is another place, however, where he may have stayed, especially at times when it was important to keep an eye on the temple area. Herod had built a strong fortress, which he called Antonia, at the northwestern corner of the sacred enclosure. Some of the masonry of one of its towers is now visible, incorporated in a modern building. Here tradition puts the praetorium. In the courtyard of a Muslim school, on the rock where another tower stood, is the first of the fourteen traditional stations of the cross. Here Pilate is thought to have showed Jesus to the crowd, saying, "Behold the man!" (Jn 19:5).

According to the Gospel of John (19:13), when Pilate finally decided to have Jesus crucified, "he brought Jesus out and sat down on the judgment seat at a place called The Pavement, and in Hebrew, Gabbatha." There is a well-preserved and extensive stone pavement in what must have been the courtyard of the Fortress Antonia. It is clearly as old as the first century, for an early second-century Roman arch rests on it. On some of the huge paving stones are scratched diagrams of curious games, probably used by the Roman garrison. It is thoroughly probable that the Fortress Antonia was the praetorium, and that the pavement under the convent of Notre Dame de Sion is the very one on which Pilate placed his judgment seat when he condemned Jesus to death. If so, it was here too that the Roman soldiers mocked Jesus (Mk 15:17-19; Mt 27:28-30). There is no need to review the painful and familiar details.

259

CHAPTER XVII

JESUS' DEATH AND BURIAL

Having had their cruel fun with Jesus, Pilate's soldiers "led him out to crucify him" (Mk 15:20-21; Mt 27:31-32; Lk 23:26). For some reason not stated Jesus was not compelled to carry the heavy crossbar to which his hands were to be nailed. There is a tradition that he tried but was unable to carry it. The second station on the *Via Dolorosa,* the traditional route from the praetorium to Calvary, is the place where the cross is thought to have been laid upon him. The third station, a little way down the street to the west, marks the place where, according to the legend, he fell under the burden.

The Gospel of John (19:17) implies that Jesus carried the cross all the way himself. The Synoptic Gospels, however, say that a man from Cyrene named Simon was compelled to carry it for him. Mark calls Simon a passerby; Matthew says that the soldiers came upon him as they were starting out. Both Mark and Luke say that he "was coming in from the country." Mark further identifies him as "the father of Alexander and Rufus." Alexander is not mentioned elsewhere, but Paul sends greetings (Rom 16:13) to a man named Rufus, "eminent in the Lord," and his mother. Cyrene was in North Africa. Simon may have come to Jerusalem as a pilgrim for the Passover (cf. Acts 2.10), or perhaps he had come to Palestine previously and was living in one of the villages near Jerusalem.

Luke mentions (23:27) "a great multitude of the people" who followed, "and of women who bewailed and lamented him." Jesus turned to the women and told them to weep not for him but for themselves and their children, because a time was coming when to be childless would be considered a blessing (Lk 23:28-31; cf. Mk 13:17 and parallels). Quoting Hosea (10:8), Jesus added, "For if they do this when the wood is green, what will happen when it is dry?" Luke notes also that two criminals were led away at the same time to be crucified (23:32).

Like the site of the praetorium, the location of Calvary is at best uncertain. None of the stations of the cross between them, therefore, has any claim to historical validity. Only about half of the incidents thus commemorated are recorded in the Gospels. In fact, the records of early pilgrims show that the stations have not always been placed where they are now. Furthermore, the level of the ground in the central valley that is crossed by the *Via Dolorosa* is much higher now than it was in New Testament times. The whole series of events, however, so far as it is historical, took place not far from here, especially if the traditional sites of the praetorium and Calvary are authentic.

The place to which Jesus was taken was called Golgotha (Mk 15:22; Mt 27:33; Lk 23:33), which is a Greek transcription of the Aramaic word for "skull." The familiar name Calvary is from the Latin *Calvariae,* which is used in the Vulgate. The traditional site of Golgotha is just inside the door of the Church of the Holy Sepulchre, to the right as one enters. It is a portion of the native rock, left standing in approximately the form of a cube by cutting down the sides to the level of the floor of the church.

That this is indeed the place where Jesus was crucified can probably never be proved or disproved. There is much in its favor, as well as some reason for doubt. Unfortunately there was a radical break in the history of Jerusalem in the second century, which to some degree interrupted the local tradition of the sacred sites. When the emperor Hadrian, after putting down the Jewish revolt of A.D. 135, undertook to eradicate Palestinian Judaism and Jewish Christianity, he destroyed Jerusalem and built in its place a Roman city, which he named Aelia Capitolina. Where Jesus was believed to have been crucified and buried, Hadrian had the ground filled in and a temple to Venus built over Jesus' tomb. Not until the time of Constantine, two hundred years later, was this destroyed.

It may be, however, that the temple of Venus, intended to blot out the memory of what had happened there, served instead to preserve that memory. When the Jewish Christians were expelled from the city with the Jews, Gentile Christians were not banished. Among these there must have been many who had known the place before it was altered and desecrated. They could tell their children and grandchildren that the temple covered the place where Jesus was buried. When Bishop Macarius got permission from Constantine to excavate the area, he apparently knew where to dig.

The discovery of Calvary by Constantine's mother, the empress Helena, is another matter. She went to Jerusalem while Macarius was preparing to build the Church of the Holy Sepulchre. The story of her dream, leading to the finding of the cross, is not mentioned by Eusebius, who was bishop of Caesarea at the time and left the chief contemporary account of the discovery of the tomb. Perhaps Macarius had no such definite tradition concerning Calvary as he had for the tomb.

The main objection to the traditional site lies in the fact that it is now inside the city walls, whereas the crucifixion took place outside the city (Jn 19:20; Heb 13:12; Lev 16:27). Just where the northern wall was in the first century is not yet conclusively established, but it is difficult to find a convincing course for it that would leave the traditional Calvary and tomb outside. The persistence of the tradition in spite of this fact is a point in its favor. Some remains of what may have been a city wall have been found, but the area cannot be thoroughly excavated because it is covered with buildings. No other site, however, has any evidence at all to support it.

Some difficult questions are raised by the accounts of Jesus' death. Our brief review of the facts will have to give more attention to the data in the Gospel of John than was necessary or feasible in the earlier parts of the story.

The amount of variation among the Gospels is obscured by the traditional practice of "harmonizing." This is conspicuously evident in the "Seven Words" of Jesus from the cross, commonly used in Good Friday services. Only one of these appears in more than one Gospel, and it is the only one recorded by Mark or Matthew: "My God, my God, why hast thou forsaken me?" (Mk 15:34; Mt 27:46). Luke alone has three of the Words: "Father, forgive them; for they know not what they do" (23:34); "Truly, I say to you, today you will be with me in Paradise" (v 43); and "Father, into thy hands I commit my spirit" (v 46). The rest are in John: "Woman, behold your son!" and "Behold, your mother!" (19:26-27); "I thirst" (v 28); "It is finished!" (v 30).

Some of the Words are quotations from the Psalms. The cry of despair in Mark and Matthew is the first verse of Psalm 22. The statement, "I thirst," is said to have been made to fulfill scripture (Jn 19:28-29), in this case Psalm 69:21. The final expression of commitment (Lk 23:46) is a quotation of Psalm 31:5. Is it credible that in such moments Jesus would quote scripture? What might seem likely once becomes less so with three instances; yet it is not inconceivable. In any case, the variations among the Gospels show that we cannot know what Jesus said, if anything, as he hung on the cross.

Unlike the Seven Words, most of the sixteen incidents in the accounts of the crucifixion are found in at least three Gospels, though not always in the same order: six are in all four Gospels, five in all the Synoptic Gospels, and one in Mark and Matthew only.

According to Mark and Matthew, before Jesus was crucified he was offered wine mixed with myrrh or gall, but refused to drink it (Mk 15:23; Mt 27:34). Psalm 69:21 says in the Hebrew, "They gave me poison for food, and for my thirst they gave me vinegar to drink." Instead of "poison" the Greek version reads "gall," as Matthew does. Mark has no such scriptural reference; "myrrhed wine" was given as a humane measure to dull the pain of one crucified.

The crucifixion itself is mentioned almost incidentally in the Gospels (Mk 15:24; Mt 27:35; Lk 23:33; Jn 19:18). Matthew even puts it in a subordinate construction, making the division of the garments the main part of the sentence. The story of the soldiers dividing Jesus' garments by lot (Mk 15:24; Mt 27:35; Lk 23:34; Jn 19:23) is a reflection of Psalm 22:18. There is nothing intrinsically improbable in it; possibly, however, after Psalm 22 came to be regarded as referring prophetically to Jesus, the inference was drawn that his clothes had been so divided.

Mark and Matthew record next (Mk 15:26; Mt 27:37) "the inscription of the charge against him" (Mk): "The King of the Jews." Luke puts this a little later (23:38). Mark and Matthew note here also the crucifixion of the two robbers or bandits, which

Luke has already mentioned. The Romans used crucifixion for executing common criminals, especially slaves. It was considered unsuitable for a Roman citizen. Subjecting Jesus to this indignity was an expression of contempt.

As if the mockery he had already endured was not enough, Jesus had to endure the jeers of passersby, who "derided him, wagging their heads, and saying, 'Aha! You who would destroy the temple and build it in three days, save yourself, and come down from the cross'' (Mk 15:29-30; Mt 27:39-40). The words "wagging their heads" echo Psalm 22:7. The chief priests and scribes said: "He saved others; he cannot save himself. Let the Christ, the King of Israel, come down now from the cross, that we may see and believe'' (Mk 15:31-32; Mt 27:41-42; cf. Lk 23:35). Matthew adds (v 43) an almost exact quotation of Psalm 22:8.

Luke now says (23:36-37), "The soldiers also mocked him, coming up and offering him vinegar," which recalls Psalm 69:21, as Matthew did with the offer of mixed wine. Here the act is one of mockery. Mark and Matthew have later another drink of vinegar, apparently given in a different spirit. Here they report that the robbers crucified with Jesus joined in reviling him (Mk 15:32; Mt 27:44). According to Luke (23:40-42) only one of them railed at Jesus, and he was rebuked by the other, who then said to Jesus, "Jesus, remember me when you come into your kingdom." Jesus' response to this plea is the second of the Seven Words (Lk 23:43): "Truly, I say to you, today you will be with me in Paradise." Both the term Paradise and the idea of entering Paradise immediately at death are unique in the Synoptic Gospels and almost without parallel in the whole New Testament. Lacking any corroborative evidence, it is at best uncertain that the promise to the penitent robber represents Jesus' conception of the future life.

The crucifixion had taken place at about nine o'clock. From the sixth hour to the ninth (that is, from about noon until three o'clock in the afternoon) "there was darkness over the whole land" (Mk 15:33; Mt 27:45; Lk 23:44-45). The Greek noun may mean "earth," as the KJV reads in Luke but not in Mark or Matthew. Whether the darkness was a physical phenomenon or a poetic expression of horror at the death of Jesus is uncertain. Luke adds,

"While the sun's light failed." A solar eclipse, which could be exactly dated, would be a welcome help to the historian, fixing the year when Jesus was crucified. No such eclipse occurred, however, during Pilate's term of office. Many manuscripts and versions, in fact, have the reading followed by the KJV, "the sun was darkened," which might refer to a heavy cloud. Luke notes here also the rending of the curtain in the temple, which comes a little later in Mark and Matthew.

After Jesus' despairing cry and the misunderstanding of some who thought he was calling upon Elijah, Mark and Matthew relate the offer of a sponge soaked with vinegar (Mk 15:36; Mt 27:48-49), recalling again Psalm 69:21. This was an act of compassion, as also apparently in John (19:29). The variant versions of the story, however, make it appear likely that the verse in the Psalm suggested that Jesus had been offered vinegar.

The reserve with which the evangelists record the moment of Jesus' death is notable (Mk 15:37; Mt 27:50; Lk 23:46; Jn 19:30). Their simple statements of the fact are more moving than any emotional comment or any attempt to bring out the significance of the event. Here Mark and Matthew appropriately tell of the rending of the curtain in the temple (Mk 15:38; Mt 27:51; cf. Lk 23:45). Though recorded in all three Synoptic Gospels, this item is undoubtedly legendary, perhaps originally intended as symbolic, signifying the coming destruction of the temple and the end of the old dispensation.

Matthew alone adds (27:51-53) that there was an earthquake, which split the rocks; "and many bodies of the saints who had fallen asleep were raised, and coming out of the tombs after his resurrection they went into the holy city and appeared to many." Like the preceding phenomena, all this points up the cosmic significance of Jesus' death. For the prescientific mind it was easy (and still is) to assume that signs and wonders must have occurred at such a time.

The idea of a resurrection of "many" of the righteous who were "asleep" goes back to Daniel 12:2, where it is associated with the end of the age. These verses in Matthew stand alone in regarding such a resurrection as connected with the death and resurrection of Jesus and therefore already past. The phrase "after

265

his resurrection'' is confusing at this point, because the opening of the tombs is associated with the earthquake when Jesus died.

All three Synoptic Gospels tell of the Roman centurion's testimony (Mk 15:39; Mt 27:54; Lk 23:47), though differing somewhat as to what he saw and what he said. According to Mark and Matthew he said, ''Truly this man was the Son of God,'' or ''a Son of God'' (the Greek text omits the definite article). Being presumably a pagan, the centurion could have used the expression ''a son of God'' or ''a son of a god,'' meaning simply ''a god.'' In Luke, however, he says, ''Certainly this man was innocent!'' Possibly this is a paraphrase of what Matthew and Mark quote literally. By ''son of God'' the centurion might have meant a righteous man. In the Wisdom of Solomon the unbelieving enemies of a righteous man complain (2:13, 16-18) that he ''calls himself a child of the Lord'' and ''boasts that God is his father.'' Scornfully they say, ''Let us see if his words are true, . . . for if the righteous man is God's son, he will help him.''

The three evangelists go on to say that a group of women, who had ministered to Jesus in Galilee and followed him to Jerusalem, stood at a distance looking on while these things took place (Mk 15:40-41; Mt 27:55-56; Lk 23:55). Mark and Matthew mention Mary Magdalene and Mary the mother of James the younger and Joses (or Joseph). These two appear again later in connection with Jesus' burial and resurrection. A third woman also is named, Mark calls her Salome; Matthew, presumably referring to the same woman, calls her the mother of the sons of Zebedee (cf. Mt 20:20-21). Mark names Salome with the two Marys again in the next verse (16:1). She does not appear anywhere else in the New Testament.

The Fourth Gospel relates (Jn 19:31-37) that the Jews asked Pilate to have the legs of the crucified men broken and to have the bodies taken away, but the soliders found Jesus already dead and did not break his legs, ''that the scripture might be fulfilled, 'Not a bone of him shall be broken.' '' This refers to a law concerning the Passover lamb (Ex 12:46; Num 9:12); thus the idea that Jesus was the true Passover lamb finds expression again. One of the soldiers, John continues, pierced Jesus' side with his spear, ''and at once there came out blood and water.'' Thus another scripture

266

(Zech 12:10) was fulfilled: "They shall look on him whom they have pierced."

All four Gospels tell of Joseph of Arimathea, who asked Pilate for Jesus' body and gave it a proper burial (Mk 15:42-47; Mt 27:57-61; Lk 23:50-56; Jn 19:38-42). Joseph, we are told, was "a rich man" (Matthew), a "member of the council" (Mark, Luke), "respected" (Mark) and "righteous" (Luke), "who had not consented to their purpose and deed" (Luke). Matthew and John say that he was a disciple of Jesus; Mark and Luke say that he was "looking for the kingdom of God."

Mark adds that Pilate was surprised at Joseph's request and granted it only after learning from the centurion that Jesus was already dead. Joseph then took the body down from the cross, wrapped it in a linen shroud, and laid it in a tomb hewn out of the rock. Matthew says it was Joseph's tomb. Luke and John say that it had not been used before, and John says that it was in a garden in the place where Jesus was crucified. Perhaps the newness of the tomb is explained by Joseph's having moved to Jerusalem from Arimathea, where his family tomb would have been.

The tomb under the dome of the Church of the Holy Sepulchre is about 125 feet west-northwest of the traditional Calvary. The case for its authenticity is if anything somewhat stronger than the case for the traditional Calvary. No other place that has been suggested has as much in its favor as this site. That there was an ancient tomb here can hardly be doubted. What remains of it in the tiny chapel erected over it is so encased in marble that a visitor can see nothing of it. At the western edge of the rotunda, however, some ancient rock-hewn tombs are still to be seen, showing conclusively that the area was used as a burial ground before it was enclosed within the city wall.

In the fourth century, as at the nearby traditional site of Calvary, the rocky slope around the tomb was cut away, so that the floor within the rotunda was made level, and only a small mass of rock immediately around the tomb was left standing. In the eleventh century a fanatical Muslim ruler tried to demolish not only the chapel but the tomb itself, going so far as to have part of the rock in which it was cut removed. There is therefore no room for hope that the authenticity of the tomb can ever be proved or disproved by archaeological research. The evidence is cumulative and at best can establish only a relative probability.

Mark, telling of the burial of Jesus by Joseph of Arimathea, says "and he rolled a stone against the door of the tomb" (15:46). Matthew also mentions this (27:60), calling the stone "a great stone." There are still to be seen at Jerusalem several rock-hewn Jewish tombs of the Roman period with round stones like large millstones set on edge in grooves so that they can be rolled across the entrances. Mark concludes (15:47; cf. v 40), "Mary Magdalene and Mary the mother of Joses saw where he was laid." Matthew says (27:61) that they "were there, sitting opposite the sepulchre." Luke says in a more general way (23:55-56), "The women who had come with him from Galilee followed, and saw the tomb, and how his body was laid; then they returned, and prepared spices and ointments."

Matthew has a paragraph here (27:62-66) which begins, "Next day, that is, after the day of Preparation," which amounts to saying "the day after the day before the Sabbath." The chief priest and Pharisees, it seems, did not allow the observance of the Sabbath to interfere with taking precautions against a possible fraud by Jesus' disciples. They told Pilate that "that impostor" had said he would rise again after three days, and asked him to have the tomb made so secure that the disciples would not be able to steal the body of Jesus and claim that he had risen from the dead. Pilate assigned soldiers to go with them and told them to make the tomb as secure as they could. They went to the tomb, sealed the stone, and left the soldiers on guard.

No other incident in the Gospels seems quite so patently a bit of counter-propaganda. If the disciples had not proclaimed the resurrection, and the tomb had not been declared empty, no one would have thought of accusing them of stealing the body. The whole story of the guard and the sealing of the tomb was probably devised to refute that charge after it had been made (cf. Mt 28:11-15).

Since the eighteenth-century "Enlightenment" it has been suggested now and then that Jesus was not dead when he was taken down from the cross. A recent revival of this notion postulates that to fulfill prophecy, Jesus simulated death with the aid of a drug, and the disciples kept him hidden until he recovered. There is no sound basis for this fantastic theory. It is arrived at by inventing far-fetched rationalistic explanations of the most obviously legendary details in the biblical narratives. No fact in the whole Gospel story is more certain than that Jesus was crucified, dead, and buried under Pontius Pilate.

In all that the Gospels tell us about the crucifixion there is a notable lack of anything about the divine purpose of Jesus' death and what it accomplished. There have been scattered allusions to Isaiah 53 in the narratives; but when the evangelists come to the event itself, they are content to tell their story and let us deduce what they believe about it from the way they tell it. For doctrinal interpretations of the cross we have to read on into the rest of the New Testament.

CHAPTER XVIII

THE RESURRECTION

According to all the Synoptic Gospels, Jesus had repeatedly foretold not only his rejection and death but also his resurrection from the dead (Mk 8:31; 9:31; 10:34 and parallels; cf. 14:28; 16:7). Did he indeed expect to be raised from the dead? The evangelists had no doubt that he did. He was the risen Lord, now seated at the right hand of God in heaven and eagerly expected to return at any time. It would not have occurred to them to question his ability during his earthly ministry to foresee what had happened since then. A modern student of the Gospels, however, must consider the development of the tradition and the presuppositions and procedures of the evangelists themselves. We cannot enter into the mind of Jesus. We can and must examine the records.

The idea of resurrection was more familiar to Jesus' contemporaries than it is to us—not only the general resurrection for judgment at the end of the age, but separate individual resurrections, which we might call reincarnations. Herod Antipas had thought that Jesus was John the Baptist raised from the dead, while others thought that he was Elijah or some other prophet (Mk 6:14-16; 8:28 and parallels). Matthew's story of the saints who left their tombs and entered the city after Jesus' resurrection (27:52-53) is another case in point. Against this background it is quite possible that Jesus would tell the disciples that after his death he would rise again.

Is it likely, however, that he went to his death with such an expectation? Why should Peter so violently reject Jesus' warning of suffering to come if it ended with a promise of joyful victory? The words "and after three days rise again" or the like, which Luke omits in one instance (9:44), seem almost casual and out of keeping with the emotional tone of the predictions of rejection and death.

Within a very few years at most the resurrection had become so prominent and so firmly joined with the crucifixion in Christian faith that Paul would speak of "Christ Jesus, who died, yes, who was raised from the dead" (Rom 8:34), and would give as the substance of the gospel he had received and passed on "that Christ died for our sins in accordance with the scriptures, . . . and that he appeared to Cephas, then to the twelve," and to others (1 Cor 15:3-5). It would then be entirely natural for a preacher or teacher or writer, reporting Jesus' predictions of his death, to add almost as a matter of course, "and after three days rise again."

However that may be, the evangelists agree on the fact of the resurrection. All tell of the finding of the empty tomb (Mk 16;1-8; Mt 28:1-10; Lk 24:1-12; cf. Jn 20:1-18), with just enough differences among them to prevent an assured reconstruction of exactly what happened, while at the same time demonstrating the existence of independent traditions. All agree in naming Mary Magdalene as a witness. Mark names with her Mary the mother of James; Matthew says "Mary Magdalene and the other Mary." Luke, having said that the women from Galilee saw Jesus buried and went home to prepare spices and ointments, continues: "On the sabbath day they rested according to the commandment. But on the first day of the week, at early dawn, they went to the tomb." Later he names "Mary Magdalene and Joanna and Mary the mother of James and the other women with them" as those who told the disciples of their experience at the tomb.

According to Mark, the women were wondering as they went to the tomb who would roll the stone back for them. Finding the tomb open, they entered and "saw a young man sitting on the right side, dressed in a white robe; and they were amazed" (Mk 16:5). The "young man" then told them that Jesus had risen, and instructed them, "But go, tell his disciples and Peter that he is going before you to Galilee; there you will see him, as he told you" (cf. 14:28).

Matthew's account is more full. There was another earthquake, he says, and an angel of the Lord came down, rolled back the stone, and sat on it. In the customary language of angelic or divine apparitions (cf. Dan 7:9; 10:6), Matthew describes the angel as "like lightning, and his raiment white as snow." The guards, Matthew continues, "trembled and became like dead men"; but the angel reassured the women in practically the same words as given in Mark. According to Mark, the women fled from the tomb and "said nothing to any one, for they were afraid." Matthew, however, says, "So they departed quickly from the tomb with fear and great joy, and ran to tell his disciples."

Luke's account is quite different. The women entered the tomb, he says, but did not find the body. "While they were perplexed about this, behold, two men stood by them in dazzling apparel." They said to the women, "Why do you seek the living among the dead?" Most manuscripts add, "He is not here but has risen," as in Matthew and Mark. They did not say, however, that Jesus was going to Galilee, but, "Remember how he told you, while he was still in Galilee, that the Son of man must be delivered into the hands of sinful men, and be crucified, and on the third day rise." The women, Luke says, "remembered his words, and returning from the tomb they told all this to the eleven and to all the rest." After naming the women, Luke continues, "but these words seemed to them an idle tale, and they did not believe them."

Most of the manuscripts and versions have here a verse (Lk 24:12) not found in the "Western" text and therefore omitted by the RSV and the NEB. It reads, "But Peter rose and ran to the tomb; stooping and looking in, he saw the linen cloths by themselves; and he went home wondering at what had happened." Apparently this is a condensed account of an incident reported at greater length in the Gospel of John (20:1-10), where "the other disciple, the one whom Jesus loved," goes to the tomb with Peter.

As the women were running to tell the disciples about the resurrection, Matthew says, Jesus "met them and said 'Hail!' And they came up and took hold of his feet and worshiped him." Jesus then repeated what the angel had said: "Do not be afraid; go and tell my brethren to go to Galilee, and there they will see me" (Mt 28:9-10). The Fourth Gospel relates an appearance of the risen Jesus to Mary Magdalene, who did not recognize him but supposed he was the gardener (Jn 20:11-18).

The guard at the tomb, Matthew reports, went to the chief priests and told them what had happened (Mt 28:11-15; cf. 27:62-66). After taking counsel with the elders, the priests gave the soldiers money and instructed them to say that while they were asleep the disciples had come and stolen the body from the tomb. This, Matthew explains, was the origin of the story still current in his time among the Jews.

Matthew's final paragraph (28:16-20) records the reunion of Jesus and the eleven disciples in Galilee, according to his promise. When the disciples saw their risen Lord, Matthew says, "they worshiped him; but some doubted." Jesus then delivered to them what is often called "the Great Commission" (cf. Mk 16:15-20): "All authority in heaven and on earth has been given to me. Go therefore and make disciples of all nations, baptizing them in the name of the Father and of the Son and of the Holy Spirit, teaching them to observe all that I have commanded you; and lo, I am with you always, to the close of the age." This promise recalls an earlier saying (Mt 18:20): "For where two or three are gathered in my name, there am I in the midst of them."

Luke (24:13-35) reports an entirely different series of appearances of Jesus after the resurrection. After mentioning the incredulity of the disciples on receiving the news brought by the women, Luke continues, "That very day two of them were going to a village named Emmaus, about seven miles from Jerusalem, and talking with each other about all these things that had happened."

Assuming that there is some historical basis for this incident, we face a difficult question when we try to determine the location of Emmaus. The indicated distance of about seven miles (literally sixty stadia) from Jerusalem would narrowly limit the possibilities if its accuracy were not made doubtful by a different reading in a few important manuscripts, which read a hundred and sixty stadia, i.e., about eighteen miles. Corresponding to these two readings, traditions have attached themselves to two different places. One, about seven miles northwest of Jerusalem, was venerated at least as far back as the time of the Crusades. About eighteen miles from Jerusalem, however, in the plain near the mouth of a valley, there was a town named Emmaus in the time of the Maccabees (1 Macc 3:40, 57; 4:3-25; 9:50); and it still bore the Arabic name Amwas until it was destroyed a few years ago. In spite of the greater weight of textual evidence, it seems to me practically certain that the latter place was the one referred to by

Luke. Eighteen or twenty miles is not too much for a day's walk. All this applies to the geographical background of the story even if the incident is not historical.

As the two walked along, Luke tells us, Jesus joined them but was not recognized. When he asked what they were discussing, one of them expressed surprise that even a stranger in Jerusalem would not have heard of the events of the past few days. When Jesus asked what had happened, he was told about the prophet, Jesus of Nazareth, and his crucifixion. The disciples had hoped, they said, that he was the Messiah. They told also of the news brought by the women, and said that some of their companions had confirmed the fact that the tomb was empty but had not seen Jesus. Jesus reproved them for not believing what the prophets had foretold. The Messiah, he said, had to suffer these things; and he "interpreted to them in all the scriptures the things concerning himself."

On reaching Emmaus the two disciples urged the unknown traveler to lodge with them, and he went in and joined them at the table. Only when he "took the bread, and blessed, and broke it, and gave it to them," did they recognize him, whereupon he vanished. Returning at once to Jerusalem, they reported their experience and were told that the Lord had appeared also to Simon. Only here and in 1 Corinthians 15:5 is there any mention of an apperaance to Simon (Paul calls him Cephas).

An appearance to the group assembled in Jerusalem now follows in Luke (24:36-43). This too is mentioned elsewhere only in 1 Corinthians 15:5, unless Paul refers there to the appearance in Galilee related by Matthew (28:16-20). While the men who had been to Emmaus were telling their story, Luke says, "Jesus himself stood among them." He told the frightened disciples to look at his wounded hands and feet and touch him, and ate a piece of broiled fish.

In the Fourth Gospel there is a similar account (Jn 20:19-29), according to which Jesus showed the disciples his hands and side, and they were convinced. Thomas was not present on that occasion and declared that he would not believe unless he could see and feel Jesus' wounds for himself. Eight days later Jesus

274

appeared again to the disciples, and Thomas was convinced by the evidence of his own senses.

Luke's account of the appearance to the disciples at Jerusalem ends with what may be called his equivalent of Matthew's Great Commission (Lk 24:44-49; cf. Acts 1:1-5; Mt 28:18-20). Jesus reminds the disciples that what was written about him must be fulfilled, and continues: "Thus it is written, that the Christ should suffer and on the third day rise from the dead, and that repentance and forgiveness of sins should be preached in his name to all nations, beginning at Jerusalem. You are witnesses of these things. And behold, I send the promise of my Father upon you; but stay in the city, until you are clothed with power from on high." This looks like a deliberate correction of the immediate return to Galilee stressed in Mark and Matthew. Luke's final paragraph (24:50-53) says that Jesus led the disciples "as far as Bethany," where he blessed them and "parted from them, and was carried up into heaven." This is more fully related in the book of Acts (1:6-11).

We do not know how the Gospel of Mark originally ended. If verse 8 of chapter 16, ending with the clause, "for they were afraid," was not Mark's concluding sentence, what followed it was lost very early. The oldest manuscripts have different endings. What is commonly called the longer ending (16:9-20) appears in most but not all of the oldest and most important manuscripts and versions and became the standard text of later centuries. Instead of it, however, or combined with it, a few important manuscripts have a shorter ending, which reads: "But they reported briefly to Peter and those with him all that they had been told. And after this, Jesus himself sent out by means of them, from east to west, the sacred and imperishable proclamation of eternal salvation." Both endings differ notably in style from the rest of the Gospel of Mark and can only be considered attempts to supply a suitable conclusion to what seemed incomplete.

The longer ending includes a unique promise that those who believe will cast out demons, be immune to the venom of serpents and to poisons, and heal the sick by laying their hands on them (Mk 16:17-18). A brief statement of the ascension (v 19) ends with the assertion that Jesus "sat down at the right hand of God" (cf. Ps 110:1; Mk 12:36; Acts 2:33-35; 7:56; Rom 8:34). The last verse (v 20) says that the disciples "went forth and preached everywhere, while the Lord worked with them and confirmed the message by the signs that attended it. Amen."

The Fourth Gospel has another appearance of the risen Jesus in Galilee (Jn 21:1-23), not on the mountain mentioned in Matthew but by the Sea of Tiberias (that is, the Sea of Galilee). It is told in the appendix (chapter 21). Seven disciples, including Nathanael, who was not one of the twelve, and two others, whose names are not given, participated in a miraculous catch of fish with the help of the risen Christ, whom they did not recognize until "that disciple whom Jesus loved" said, "It is the Lord!" Reaching the shore, the disciples found a charcoal fire burning, and Jesus bade them bring some of the fish and have breakfast. He then gave them bread and fish, but it is not said that he ate with them.

With these varied accounts we must compare Paul's survey of the tradition that he had received (1 Cor 15:5-8). After recording that Jesus "appeared to Cephas, then to the twelve," Paul continues: "Then he appeared to more than five hundred brethren at one time, most of whom are still alive, though some have fallen asleep. Then he appeared to James, then to all the apostles. Last of all, as to one untimely born, he appeared also to me." The appearances to James and to more than five hundred people are not referred to anywhere else in the New Testament. Paul's account was written only about twenty years after the death of Jesus, and is thus probably earlier than the earliest of the Gospels by ten years or more. This makes it all the more noteworthy that Paul includes his own vision on the road to Damascus among the resurrection appearances, with no suggestion that it differed in kind from the others (1 Cor 9:1; Gal 1:15-17; cf. Acts 9:3-9; 22:6-11; 26:12-18).

Through all this confusing conglomeration of traditions three emphases stand out distinctly. The first is the stress on the incredulity of the disciples when confronted with the manifestations of the risen Christ. Such surprise may seem strange if Jesus had told them that he would rise again, but perhaps it was only natural.

276

Another emphasis in several of the stories is the reality and identity of Jesus' body. To convince the disciples that he was not a ghost, he showed them his hands and feet, or his side, and told them to touch him and satisfy themselves that he had flesh and bones. He is even said once to have eaten in their presence (Lk 24:43; cf. Acts 10:41).

At the same time, equal stress is laid on the difference between the risen Christ and the Master the disciples had known. Repeatedly they failed to recognize him. In Luke (24:18) the disciples on the road to Emmaus think the traveler who has joined them is a visitor to Jerusalem.

The Synoptic Gospels do not say, as the Fourth Gospel does twice (Jn 20:19, 26), that the doors of the room where the disciples assembled were shut when Jesus "came and stood among them." Luke does say that as soon as the two at Emmaus recognized him "he vanished out of their sight" (24:31); and while they were relating their experience to the others at Jerusalem (vv 36-37) he "stood among them" so suddenly and silently that "they were startled and frightened, and supposed that they saw a spirit." In short, the body in which Jesus appeared was the one that had been laid in the tomb, but altered.

What may be called the standard view of Jesus' resurrection (Acts 1:3, 9; 2:24, 32-33) involves three stages: the empty tomb, the forty days of intermittent association with the disciples, and the ascension to the right hand of God. Paul, our earliest witness, mentions none of these. He tells of appearances to many but speaks of "Christ Jesus, who died, yes, who was raised from the dead, who is at the right hand of God," as though the resurrection and the exaltation to heaven were immediately connected (Rom 8:34). In fact, apart from the circumstantial account in Acts, the ascension is mentioned only at the end of Luke's Gospel (where the text is doubtful) and in the longer ending of Mark (Lk 24:51; Mk 16:19).

Such are the records. What really happened? It has been fashionable lately to shrug that question off with platitudes about the inevitable subjectivity of historical judgments. As a preventive of dogmatism such considerations have their value, but they should not be used to evade responsibility for defining the limits of our knowledge and determining as far as we can the possibilities of the matter.

When we try to clarify our ideas on this subject, there are several important points to be kept in mind. One is that if we wish to come as close as possible to historical fact, we shall not do it by supposing that the faith of the first Christians was based on imposture and fraud. Of all conceivable explanations, that is the least plausible. In the history of religions there are demonstrable instances of oracles and miracles fabricated by professional religious promoters and officials. Far more often, however, legends and superstitions have been and are caused by wishful thinking and self-deception.

If we approach the narratives in the spirit of serious research, recognizing that they are at least in part legendary, but rejecting the assumption of deliberate imposture, we can hardly avoid the impression that something extraordinary must have happened to convince the disciples that Jesus had been dead but was alive again. That they did believe this, few if any competent historians would deny.

The question whether Jesus really came back to life cannot be answered by historical evidence. It is outside the area accessible to historical research. In all probability the Christian church would never have existed or survived without the conviction that Jesus had risen from the dead. It is hard to believe that the whole history of Christianity is grounded in a delusion, but we cannot prove that this was not so. Each person's position on that question necessarily depends on his presuppositions, his understanding of the kind of universe we live in and God's relation to it.

On that basis, speaking only for myself, I cannot believe that Jesus came back to life with the body that had been crucified and buried. What matters, after all, is that he is not dead but alive now. If he belonged to a different order of being from mankind, what is incredible and impossible for us might be possible for him; but then what bearing would his resurrection have on what is in store for humanity? How could it have such significance as Paul (1 Cor 15:12-15) insists it has? In explaining the resurrection of believers, Paul emphasizes the distinction between the physical body, which is buried, and the spiritual body, which will be raised (vv 35-50); and he says that Jesus has risen as "the first fruits of those who have fallen asleep" (v 20).

Assurance that Jesus was alive again was found by the disciples in experiences which they took to be personal encounters with him. What were these experiences? What was Paul's experience? Were they merely hallucinations brought about by mental and emotional stress? We do not have sufficient data for a psychological or physiological analysis. Even if we did, such an analysis would not necessarily be a full explanation.

The more the disciples endeavored to convince others of the reality of their experience, the more they would stress the identity of the risen Lord and the crucified Jesus. This might easily lead to emphasis on the physical reality of his body. The idea of his bodily presence might then suggest a bodily translation to heaven and a physical, bodily return (Acts 1:11).

Perhaps the tradition of the empty tomb grew out of this chain of ideas. That the tomb was actually entered and found empty is of course not impossible. The use of a new tomb near the place of execution might have been only a temporary measure taken in view of the approaching Sabbath. Guesses of this sort, however, are unnecessary. If it was believed that Jesus had appeared bodily to the disciples and had been taken up bodily to heaven, this would imply that he had left the tomb, and that inference would be read back into the accounts of what had happened when the women went to the tomb. At some time, somehow, the realization of what the angel is reported to have said to the women was borne in upon some of the mourners: "He is not here; he is alive."

To the disciples the resurrection meant that all was not lost; Jesus was not dead but living, not defeated but triumphant; he was Messiah after all. They were not forsaken and alone; he was with them (Mt 28:20). He was also reigning with the Father in heaven (Acts 2:33; 7:55-56); and at the end of this age he would return to judge the world (10:42; 17:31) and inaugurate the eternal kingdom of God on earth. Paul and later writers found also in the resurrection of Jesus assurance of resurrection for believers (1 Cor 15:12-23).

CHAPTER XIX

THE MAN JESUS

Our review of the Gospels has shown why competent New Testament scholars have given up hope of writing a biography of Jesus. The nature of the Gospels themselves and the relations between them make any serious attempt to reconstruct the history behind them tend to resolve itself into a discussion of a series of problems, largely insoluble. A biography, moreover, involves an interpretation of personality and character. Many scholars are even more skeptical about this than they are about Jesus' life and teaching.

From some points of view all this is not important. When stress is laid primarily on redemption by Jesus' death and resurrection, his life becomes merely an interim between birth and death; and what kind of man he was is comparatively irrelevant. If the essence of his mission on earth is found in his teaching, what he taught is true or false regardless of his conduct or character.

The Christian church has never been willing to go that far. From the beginning the example of Jesus has been held up for imitation, although with the exception of patient suffering and love for others, it has proved difficult to apply this principle to specific situations.

Certainly any attempt to recover from the Gospels even a dim picture of Jesus should be undertaken with a sense not only of facing a difficult problem but of treading on holy ground. Much of what will be said in this chapter may be condemned as unwarranted "psychologizing"; but when a meticulous academic procedure has taken us as far as it can go, there is still a legitimate place for imagination, properly guarded. Everything that is said in the Gospels about the character of Jesus must be subjected to the same tests of historical accuracy used in dealing with the events of his life and with his teaching. After all is said and done, however, it will be the total picture, visible through the screen of particular incidents and utterances, that must be our final evidence.

There is such a picture. Through all the variations and

280

uncertainties, the Gospels give us vivid glimpses of a definite, real, and extraordinary personality. After all, there was no sharp break between the ministry of Jesus and the experience of the church. The Lord of the church in the first generation was still the same Jesus who had lived among them and was still remembered. Colored by pious imagination, and perhaps also—God forbid that we should deny it!—by genuine spiritual communion, the memory was still there, and it is enshrined in the Gospels.

In the character of Jesus as it is reflected in the Synoptic Gospels, nothing is more certain or more typical than his devotion to the will of God. To fulfill the Father's purpose he was willing to make any sacrifice, and he demanded the same willingness in his followers. The disciple's eye must be single; having put his hand to the plow he must not look back; if an eye, hand, or foot should cause him to do wrong, he must get rid of it; he must even be prepared to hate those dearest to him.

Related to this utter devotion was the transparent sincerity and scorn of pretense or compromise shown by Jesus' attitude toward the hypocrisy of the scribes and Pharisees and the complacency and lack of compassion of the rich. His complete commitment was also the root of the courage that enabled him to set his face steadfastly to go up to Jerusalem and to stand with quiet dignity before the high priest and Pilate. The conviction that he must do what had been written of him by the prophets was of a piece with his consecration to the Father's wiill.

Throughout the tragic last events of Jesus' life, except perhaps in the anguish of Gethsemane and the desperate cry from the cross (if it is authentic), "Why hast thou forsaken me?" the Gospels picture Jesus as accepting everything with patient endurance. When the writers of the New Testament hold up this aspect of his life for imitation, they make clear allusions to Isaiah 53. Possibly in applying this prophecy to him they unconsciously drew from it some of the colors for their portrait; but if Jesus himself did not see in it the divine plan for his own mission, it must have been the fact that he so notably exemplified these qualities that reminded his followers of the prophecy, or that reminded them of him when they read it. If later they went on to assume that he must have

281

fulfilled everything in the prophecy, this could not have happened unless they remembered him as that kind of person.

The ultimate source of his devotion to God's will was his love for his heavenly Father, with his consciousness of being God's son. Not only did he say, as other Jews did, that the first of all the commandments was to love God with all one's heart and soul and strength. In his life "the law appears Drawn out in living characters" (Isaac Watts).

The second quality of Jesus' personality stressed by the evangelists is the impression of authority that he made on people. He spoke with a firm confidence that amazed those who heard him. The temptation story may dimly reflect a time or many times of doubt and earnest searching, but for the evangelists it was a demonstration of Jesus' Messianic authority.

In Mark and Luke the first explicit reference to Jesus' authority has to do with his teaching in the synagogue at Capernaum at the beginning of his ministry; Matthew makes the same statement at the end of the Sermon on the Mount. Jesus spoke with the conviction of immediate personal experience and knowledge. This must have seemed to his hearers either presumptuous or refreshingly new. The same sense of authority is heard in the characteristic and unique expression, "Amen I say to you" (usually, for lack of a better rendering, translated "Verily"—or "Truly"—"I say to you").

There is no suggestion of omniscience in such language. Jesus could be surprised. He marveled at the extraordinary faith of the Roman centurion, and at the lack of faith of the people of Nazareth. Several times he is said to have asked for information. "What is your name?" "Who touched my garments?" "How many loaves have you?" "Who do men say that I am? . . . But who do you say that I am?" "How long has he had this?" (referring to a boy's epilepsy) "What are you discussing with them?" "What were you discussing on the way?" "say to the householder, 'The Teacher says, Where is my guest room, where I am to eat the Passover with my disciples?'" When he said, "Heaven and earth will pass away, but my words will not pass away," he added, "But of that day or that hour no one knows, not even the angels in heaven, nor the Son, but only the Father."

He did not even claim to be good. To the rich man who addressed him as "Good Teacher" Jesus replied, "Why do you call me good? No one is good but God alone." Charged with exorcising demons by the power of Beelzebub, he said, "And whoever says a word against the Son of man will be forgiven; but whoever speaks against the Holy Spirit will not be forgiven, either in this age or in the age to come."

This is a very different picture from the one presented by the Gospel of John. In addition to such examples of apparently supernatural knowledge as Jesus' saying to Nathanael, "Before Philip called you, when you were under the fig tree, I saw you" (Jn 1:48), or telling the Samaritan woman that she had had five husbands and was then living with a man who was not her husband (4:18), the Fourth Gospel also stresses the "autonomy" of Jesus. Though he still says, "The Son can do nothing of his own accord" (5:19) and "I can do nothing on my own authority" (v 30), he will not do anything at the bidding of others but only on his own initiative and in his own way, as in turning the water to wine (2:3-4) or going up to Jerusalem for a festival (7:2-10). Equally characteristic of the Johannine Jesus and even more conspicuous is the series of "I am" discourses.

The Synoptic Gospels have two sayings that to some degree resemble these declarations. One is the "Johannine saying"; "All things have been delivered to me by my Father, and no one knows who the Son is except the Father, or who the Father is except the Son and any one to whom the Son chooses to reveal him." Following this in Matthew is the saying, "Come to me, all who labor and are heavy laden," with the promise of rest, an easy yoke, and a light burden. In neither case is the probability that the saying is authentic sufficient to outweigh the evidence that he considered his own knowledge limited.

The authority of Jesus in the Gospels is not only a matter of his teaching; it applies also to his acts. In the synagogue at Capernaum, when the people exclaimed, "A new teaching!" they continued, "With authority he commands even the unclean spirits, and they obey him." When the chief priests, scribes, and elders in the temple demanded that he tell them where he got his authority, what they questioned was his right to "do these things."

The Roman centurion takes it for granted that because he himself is "under authority" and obeys his superiors, and his soldiers obey him, Jesus can order a sick person to get well and he will. Jesus did not keep this authority to himself. When he sent the twelve out through the country, he "gave them authority over the unclean spirits"; and they exercised it.

Still another form of authority is attributed to Jesus. The healing of the paralytic is said to show "that the Son of Man has authority on earth to forgive sins." This authority, however, is not committed to the disciples, unless it is what is meant by the power of binding and loosing.

Jesus' authority is most prominent in Mark. The question has been raised, and it is a fair one, whether this emphasis, rather than being an authentic tradition, is an article of Mark's theology. It may be both. The fact that it is important for Mark does not prove that he invented it. He may have underlined, so to speak, what was already an important feature of the tradition. And that tradition probably had a solid basis in historical fact.

The same emphasis is found also in Luke, including his unique material. In the temptation story as he tells it, Satan, showing Jesus the kingdoms of the world, says, "To you I will give all this authority and their glory." When the seventy disciples return from their mission and report that the demons are subject to them, Jesus says, "Behold, I have given you authority to tread upon serpents and scorpions, and over all the power of the enemy."

One root of Jesus' sureness in word and act was his insight into human nature. His parables reveal a close and sympathetic observation of everyday life: the farmer's sowing and reaping, the shepherd and his flock, the house built on the rock, the leaven in the dough, the lost coin and the lost sheep, the father's joy in the return of a wayward son and the elder brother's peevish jealousy, the mother forgetting her agony for joy that a man has been born into the world, the workers standing idle in the marketplace because no one has hired them, and many other instances.

When the disciples argued about which one of them was the greatest, Jesus "perceived the thought of their hearts," as Luke says. There are many instances of his sharp insight into human nature. When he met a man who was sincere and dissatisfied with

284

himself, "Jesus looking upon him loved him." Yet he saw right through pretense and sham. People who encountered him found in him a disconcerting clearness and directness of perception. When his adversaries tried to trap him with the question about paying taxes to Caesar, he at once recognized their insincerity. This incident and the other conflict stories manifest a skill in debate partly explained by the same quick insight into motives and thoughts, and partly also by a notable keenness of intellect.

His own thinking, so far as we can judge, was characterized by directness and clarity rather than analytical subtlety. He went straight to the heart of an issue, brushing aside the incidental details and insisting on essentials. This is evident in his interpretation of Scripture and his attitude toward traditional interpretations. His independent use of Scripture was a part of the contrast between his teaching and that of the scribes. He could cite proof texts on occasion in debate with Sadducees or Pharisees, and it is entirely probable that from his youth he had read and deeply pondered the Scriptures for himself; but his ideas were not arrived at by deductive analysis of texts or compilation of pronouncements by recognized "authorities." Without the prestige of official position, without the sanction of precedents or the support of respected names, he declared with the confidence of immediate perception what God would do and what man must do. No less dedicated than the most earnest of the scribes to God's will, and to the Scriptures as the revelation of God's will, he was indifferent or opposed to the traditional definitions of what the law required.

His perception of real issues and his sense of proportion are exemplified by his rejection of asceticism. This is vividly expressed in his comparison of John the Baptist and himself. The people who have rejected both him and John, Jesus says, are hard to please. They ascribe John's austere way of life to demonic influence, but denounce Jesus because he enjoys eating with all sorts and conditions of men. They are like petulant children who will not join their playmates in playing either wedding or funeral. (Taken strictly, those who accept neither John nor Jesus are compared, not to the children who would neither dance nor mourn, but to those who complained of their attitude. The exact words, however, cannot be pressed. The piping and wailing clearly represent Jesus' and John's preaching, and the refusal to dance to the one or weep with the other corresponds to the rejection of both by the nation.)

The situation indicated fits perfectly the circumstances of Jesus' ministry, and devout tradition would never have invented the criticism of Jesus as a glutton and a drunkard. It is unnecessary, of course, to suppose that these terms correctly described Jesus' conduct. The fact that he did not conform to conventional ideas of what a religious teacher should do or should not do would be enough to evoke such opprobrious epithets.

The second part of the charge against Jesus was true enough: he was indeed a friend of tax collectors and sinners. The exclamation, "This man receives sinners and eats with them!" was no doubt a frequent expression of shocked surprise at the disreputable company he kept. His own answer to those who asked why he did so was that not those who are well but those who are sick need a physician. His conclusion to the stories of the lost coin and the lost sheep was, "Just so, I tell you, there will be more joy in heaven over one sinner who repents than over ninety-nine righteous persons who need no repentance" The parable of the prodigal son rebukes the self-righteous, uncharitable attitude of those who like the elder son, do not rejoice when a lost brother is found.

Jesus could also associate easily and naturally with the rich and prominent. When invited, he dined at their homes. These indications, it is true, are found in the editorial and traditional framework of the narratives, but the picture of Jesus as one who "came eating and drinking," quite willing to join high or low, rich or poor, at the table, seems to be a fixed feature of the tradition.

He evidently had no fear of contamination from associating with those called sinners. This is not a fact to be documented by specific texts; it is an implication of the whole story. He was not afraid that his purity would be soiled if he came into contact with tax collectors and harlots, or that their impurity would rub off on him. He was not concerned that people might think this had happened.

So far as we can tell, with the exception of the charge of gluttony and drunkenness, no one ever said of him, "He is just one of them, and no better than the company he keeps." Instead, observers expressed surprise that he would associate with people so obviously unlike him. When he spoke kindly to a notorious woman, the Pharisee in whose house he was dining did not think, "So *that* is the kind of man he is!" but "If this man were a prophet, he would have known who and what sort of woman this is who is touching him." Jesus' attitude is notably evident in his relations with women. There is never any indication of self-consciousness or condescension when women, good and bad, poor and rich, approached him. He was not a crusader for women's rights; he simply regarded them and treated them as people. How high his moral standard was could not be better demonstrated than by his declaration that to look at a woman with lust is to commit adultery in one's heart.

We have seen indications of strain between Jesus and his own family, but also reason to believe that the division was not permanent. Whether he ever married we do not know. Some argue that as a normal Jewish young man he would almost certainly marry, but there were Jews who did not—witness the Essenes. If he did, it is futile to speculate about what happened to the marriage. If he did not, it was not because he condemend marriage as a concession to the flesh, or regarded it as a lower, less holy state than celibacy. He considered it sacred and permanent, and based his conviction on the purpose of God in creating man and woman. If a statement reported by Matthew is authentic, he said there were some who made themselves eunuchs for the kingdom of heaven; but this did not mean abjuring all associations with women. His friendship with Martha and Mary, his many recorded conversations with women, and the accounts of the women who accompanied him and his disciples and served them are sufficient to prevent such a misunderstanding.

A very likable trait, the love of children and the ability to gain their confidence, is shown by two incidents. The first is Jesus' answer to the disciples' question about greatness in the kingdom of God, when he put a child in their midst. It is interesting that there was a child there within Jesus' reach or near enough to respond to his call, and that the child allowed Jesus to hold him while talking to the disciples. The other incident is the blessing of the children whose parents brought them to Jesus, with his indignant rebuke of the overzealous disciples who presumed to protect him from being bothered for such a purpose. He had younger brothers and sisters, and during their childhood he may have had to take the place of a father for them after Joseph died.

Another amiable and admirable quality, perceptible not in acts but in his sayings and parables, is Jesus' love of nature. It was not a mystical, Wordsworthian communion with nature as a personified abstraction, but a more common, everyday appreciation of natural beauty and awareness of the life about him. Its most notable expression is the passage in the Sermon on the Mount about God's loving care for his creatures. One can easily imagine that such thoughts had often occupied Jesus' mind in his boyhood and adolescence. But the reverent pondering of his earlier years was carried over into his mature manhood as a firm assurance that, despite all appearances to the contrary, the Lord is mindful of his own.

In keeping with his love of children and nature was his concern for animals. There is not much in the Gospels about this, but he assumed that the owner of an animal would lead it to water on the Sabbath as on every other day; and if an animal should fall into a pit on the Sabbath, the owner would pull it out without regard to any rule of Sabbath observance. Perhaps he was better acquainted with practical farmers than with theoretical expounders of the law, though on this point the Pharisees undoubtedly agreed with him. The Essenes had a regulation that he would certainly condemn: "Let not a man help an animal to give birth on the Sabbath day; and if she lets her young fall into a cistern or ditch, let him not raise it on the Sabbath" (CD xiii.14).

Attention has been drawn in several connections to another distinctive trait of Jesus, his keen sense of humor, manifested especially in grotesque hyperbole. In the light of such expressions it may be suspected that even the sternest demands for renunciation were spoken with a gentleness that took much of the sting out of them. This does not mean at all that he took lightly the sorrow and suffering and sin of mankind. Far from it. Even Mark never says that Jesus laughed or smiled. Jesus' humor was of the kind that springs from a sense of proportion, a clear perception of what is important and what is not. In spite of the lack of explicit statements, the very nature of his sayings and acts themselves makes it incredible that he did not sometimes smile and on occasion laugh freely.

With all his utter sincerity and scorn of compromise, a rather surprising spirit of tolerance is shown by his disapproval when John the son of Zebedee reported that they had forbidden a man to cast out demons in Jesus' name. A person who performed a "mighty work" in his name, he said, would not then speak evil of him. "For he that is not against us," he added, "is for us." He is reported also to have said, in a different connection, "He who is not with me is against me, and he who does not gather with me scatters." The two sayings are not contradictory if they mean that every person is either for Jesus or against him, there is no middle ground. In the same context with the second statement Jesus asks the Pharisees, "And if I cast out demons by Beelzebul, by whom do your sons cast them out?" He who said this might well say of a stranger who used his name to exorcise demons, "Do not forbid him."

Jesus did not react to all situations with humor or tolerance. One of the human traits that Mark mentions but Matthew and Luke pass over in silence is capacity for anger. In his account of the healing of a man with a withered hand Mark says that Jesus "looked around at them with anger, grieved at their hardness of heart." This is the only place in the Gospels where the Greek noun meaning "anger" is used of Jesus. Apart from such direct statements, however, his words and conduct are sufficient to show that he was capable of blazing anger, which found expression in vivid, scorching language and at least once in direct action. It is true that he pronounced one who is angry with his brother liable to judgment. (In adding "without cause" the KJV is supported by many manuscripts and versions, but not the best ones.) The statement does not imply, however, that anger is never justified. If it did, Jesus would stand condemned by his own words.

The angry language he is said to have used appears especially in two groups of sayings, the condemnation of the Galilean cities that failed to repent and the denunciation of the Pharisees and scribes. If Jesus said even a fraction of the things attributed to him in these passages, he was a master of eloquent invective. In the first group he may have been expressing grief and disappointment rather than anger. This can hardly be said, however, of his denunciation of the scribes and Pharisees. Here, especially in Matthew, he voices a flaming wrath and withering scorn undiluted by sorrow or pity except for the victims of Pharisaic hypocrisy.

One act of Jesus, the cleansing of the temple, can best be explained, I believe, as an unpremeditated explosion of righteous indignation like that of an Old Testament prophet. We have noted other, more widely held views of it. In defense of my interpretation I will point out only that when Jesus the next day indirectly suggested that his authority was from the same source and of the same kind as John's, he implied that he claimed and needed no other authority than that of a prophet, who spoke and acted on a divine impulse, reacting spontaneously to an immediate situation.

Sometimes it is not such fierce wrath but rather annoyance or disappointment that is manifest, as in some of the questions Jesus asked: "Have you no faith?" "Why did you doubt?" "How long must I bear with you?" When the disciples tried to prevent parents from bringing their children to Jesus to be blessed, Mark says, "he was indignant." Matthew and Luke, as usual, omit this reference to a common human emotion. The Greek verb used here by Mark expresses disapproval and displeasure rather than anger. When the Pharisees demanded a sign from heaven, Jesus "sighed deeply in his spirit," says Mark; and again Matthew and Luke omit the statement. We have observed that Jesus' denunciation of the Galilean cities was evoked by grief as much as anger, as in his expression of grief over Jerusalem. So too when he looked around at the bystanders with anger before healing the man with a withered hand, Mark says it was because he was "grieved at their hardness of heart."

Far different was the grief Jesus felt in Gethsemane, when, according to Mark and Matthew, he said to the three disciples, "My soul is very sorrowful." Luke omits this, but a few verses later he tells of Jesus' agony as he poured out the prayer that is the

290

supreme expression of his dedication to his Father's will. The evangelists stress this spiritual struggle in the garden much more than the physical pain he endured on the cross. What most of all caused his bitter anguish we can only dimly imagine. He had long faced the fear of death, and had set his face to go up to Jerusalem, telling his disciples that it awaited him there. Perhaps some hope that it might not be so never quite left him until that night in the garden. The desertion of those closest to him, and the treachery of one of those whom he had hoped to see judging the tribes of Israel, must have bulked large in his thoughts. Perhaps what was hardest to bear, however, was the fact that the whole consummation of his hopes, as he had contemplated it, seemed to be in doubt. He could accept the Father's will; but he had thought he knew what God intended, and now he must trust without knowing. In the end, the Son, who knew the Father as no one else knew him, had to take his Father's hand and step out into the dark.

Next to his dedication and the authority which it brought him, the quality of Jesus' character that stands out most sharply in the Synoptic Gospels is his ready and sympathetic responsiveness to the needs of others. If on the Godward side, so to speak, the motive power of his life was devotion to God's will, on the manward side "he was moved with compassion." It can be argued that the references to Jesus' compassion, like those to his authority, must be ascribed to the evangelists rather than the earliest tradition. Of the six places in which at least one Gospel speaks of Jesus' compassion, not one reference appears in all the Synoptic Gospels. The fact that the evangelists all refer to his compassion, though in different places, may indeed be attributed to editorial procedure; but it also attests a unanimous tradition that this was a distinctive trait of his character.

There is some suggestion of tension between Jesus' devotion to God and his compassion for men early in the story, when he goes out before dawn to a lonely place to pray, and says to the disciples, who tell him that every one is looking for him, that he must go on to other cities. The real tension, however, was between two aspects of the service of man to which God had called him. The physical needs of the people about him pulled one way; the inner compulsion to carry his good news to as wide an audience as possible pulled the other way. Moved as he was by the sight of distress, he steeled himself to sacrifice the immediate need to his wider mission.

Compassion was blended with insight in his readiness to forgive and to declare that God had forgiven. "My son," he said to the paralytic, "your sins are forgiven." When a woman anointed his feet while he was dining at a Pharisee's house, he said to host, "Her sins, which are many, are forgiven, for she loved much." And at the end there is the prayer on the cross, "Father, forgive them; for they know not what they do."

Whether Jesus' spiritual experience included ecstatic visions or auditions, such as prophets often have, is a very difficult question to answer with any assurance. The descent of the Spirit at his baptism can be so understood; but, as we have noted, the accounts differ in such ways that it is impossible to tell whether the Spirit was seen and the voice heard by Jesus alone or by the bystanders also. For him the experience may have been profound and decisive without being ecstatic; yet it may have been that too. Even the struggle with Satan in the wilderness can be interpreted as an experience involving hallucination. Fasting is a common part of the technique for inducing a trance. Altogether more likely, however, is a symbolic description of a completely conscious and rational inner conflict. The transfiguration bears a striking similarity to the experience at his baptism, but here the narratives indicate a vision seen and a voice heard by the three disciples rather than an experience of Jesus himself. The significance of the event is in any case much too uncertain to throw light on the nature of Jesus' spiritual life. Another possible but uncertain instance of ecstatic experience may be mentioned. When the seventy disciples reported to Jesus that the demons had submitted to them, he said, Luke reports, "I saw Satan fall like lightning from heaven." In spite of the shaky historical basis of this mission, the saying may be authentic.

Jesus was a Jew, not a Hindu. He was not a mystic in the sense of one who enjoys that "beatific vision" in which individual personality is absorbed in the undifferentiated unity of the All. There was mysticism in ancient Judaism: the tradition back of the Kabbala is its most notable manifestation. The characteristic form of Jewish mysticism, however, is the "I and Thou" type, in which the consciousness of distinct identity is maintained, if not heightened, and along with the feeling of communion there is also a keen sense of the distance between God and man.

If mysticism means "practicing the presence of God," then Jesus was a mystic. His praying is mentioned often by the evangelists. The children brought to him, Matthew says, were brought "that he might lay his hands on them and pray." Mark says twice and Matthew once that Jesus went out to a lonely place or up into the hills to pray alone. Twice Luke speaks of his withdrawing to the wilderness or the hills to pray, saying once, "and all night he continued in prayer to God." There are also five other places where Luke mentions Jesus' praying. If some or all of these references express a special interest of Luke or of the circle he represents, they also reflect something that must have been characteristic of Jesus.

Such general statements do not indicate the content of Jesus' prayers. Just before the prediction of Peter's denial of his Master, Jesus tells him, according to Luke, that Satan has desired to win the disciples (the "you" here is plural), and adds, "But I have prayed for you" (here it is singular) "that your faith may not fail." Such intercessory prayer may well have been a frequent theme in Jesus' devotional life.

How much use Jesus made of regular prescribed prayers is unknown, but he evidently followed the Jewish practice of giving thanks at meals. We have also one report of a special, spontaneous thanksgiving: "I thank thee, Father, Lord of heaven and earth, that thou hast hidden these things from the wise and understanding and revealed them to babes; yea, Father, for such was thy gracious will." Matthew and Luke report this in quite different connections but in exactly the same words. It is entirely probable and in keeping with all we know about him that Jesus thanked God, perhaps often, for revealing to simple folk what the learned scribes could not perceive.

The climax of what is recorded about Jesus' prayers is the story of his agony in Gethsemane. Here is a soul wrestling in bitter torment and perplexity, yet with unshaken commitment to the Father's will. One word is preserved by Mark in the language that

Jesus spoke, the Aramaic word *abba*. As he does elsewhere, Mark gives with the original word its Greek equivalent. Matthew and Luke give only the Greek translation. If nothing else in his recorded sayings could be accepted with confidence as the very word Jesus used, we could be quite sure that he used this word constantly in addressing God and in speaking of God. So great was the impression made by the way he used it that even the Greek-speaking church evidently continued to use it in worship, for Paul quotes it twice (Rom 8:15; Gal 4:6). Like Mark, Paul adds the Greek translation. Perhaps Greek-speaking Christians commonly did so in prayer.

According to Matthew, when the mob came with Judas to take Jesus, and one of the bystanders cut off an ear of the high priest's slave, Jesus condemned the act and spoke of a prayer he might have made but did not: "Do you think that I cannot appeal to my Father, and he will at once send me more than twelve legions of angels? But how then should the scriptures be fulfilled, that it must be so?"

The last prayers of Jesus reported in the Gospels are some of the words from the cross, which we have discussed in connection with the crucifixion. Of these the first and the last seem most in keeping with the other prayers that we have been considering. Both are reported by Luke: "Father, forgive them; for they know not what they do"; and "Father, into thy hands I commit my spirit!"

In the picture of Jesus as we encounter him in the Synoptic Gospels, how much is tradition? How much is editing or interpretation? Each may claim many details, but in the aggregate the records reveal a real personality. Not only the lack of evidence, or the kind of evidence available, prevents giving a satisfying description of him. A sense of his incomparable greatness strikes us dumb.

After all, listing and documenting characteristics can no more convey a vital perception of a person than a face can be visualized through describing its features one by one. To get a clear and vivid impression of the man Jesus we have to live with the Gospels and let the whole picture take possession of us. When we do that, we sometimes receive an overwhelming impression of a

294

person who almost frightens us. To me this has come in a few widely separated experiences. Such an experience, like the disciples' vision on the Mount of Transfiguration, cannot last. The splendor fades, because human nature is not capable of retaining it. Yet something is left that can never be lost, unless one becomes utterly unfaithful and estranged, and perhaps not wholly even then. Some day perhaps we shall really see Jesus, not as reflected in the dim mirror of our knowledge but face to face, know him as we are known, and see him as he is (1 Cor 13:12; 1 Jn 3:2). Meanwhile we can at least try to see him as he was. That is all the more important if he is indeed (Heb 13:8) "the same yesterday and today and for ever."

SUGGESTIONS
FOR FURTHER STUDY

Inclusion of a book in the following list does not necessarily indicate that I agree with the writer's views. The works named, all fairly recent and all available in English, have been chosen primarily for information on important matters dealt with lightly if at all in the present volume, particularly bibliography, background, methods, and theological implications. Abundant references to the literature for more intensive study will be found in these books. *Jesus in the Church's Gospels,* by John Reumann (Fortress Press, 1968) is a remarkably complete critical review of research to the time of its publication. Later works are noted in *Jesus: The Man, the Mission, and the Message,* by C. Milo Connick (Prentice-Hall, 2nd edition, 1974), a comprehensive textbook.

For the background of Jesus' ministry an outstanding work is *Jerusalem in the Time of Jesus: An Investigation into Economic and Social Conditions during the New Testament Period,* by Joachim Jeremias (translated by F. H. Cave and C. H. Cave, Fortress Press, 1969; paperback, 1975;. The political and religious background is thoroughly presented in *The New Testament Environment,* by Edouard Lohse (translated by John E. Steely, Abingdon, 1976). The vicissitudes and developments of Judaism in Jesus' day are portrayed in *First Century Judaism in Crisis: Yohanan ben Zakkai and the Renaissance of Torah,* by Jacob Neusner (Abingdon paperback, 1975), a popular abridgement and condensation of the author's biography of Yohanan ben Zakkai. Excerpts from primary sources in translation are assembled in *The Origins of Christianity: Sources and Documents,* by Howard Clark Kee (Prentice-Hall, 1973).

Interpreting the New Testament Today by R. C. Briggs (Abingdon, 1973), an expanded revision of the author's *Interpreting the Gospels,* presents well the procedures, results, and limitations of textual criticism, source analysis, form criticism, reaction criticism, and literary criticism. (Structuralism

296

came a little too late to be included; the word "structure" is much used but not in the sense in which the structuralists use it.) Helpful introductions to the newer methods are provided by the *New Testament Guides*, edited by Dan O. Via, Jr., and published by the Fortress Press: *What Is Form Criticism?* by Edgar V. McKnight (1965); *What Is Redaction Criticism?* by Norman Perrin (1969); *Literary Criticism of the New Testament*, by William A. Beardslee (1970); and *What Is Structural Exegesis?* by Daniel Patte (1976). Special numbers devoted to Structuralism have appeared in *Interpretation* (April, 1974), *Semeia* (No. 1, 1976), and *Soundings* (summer, 1975), the last named being reissued as *Structuralism: An Interdisciplinary Study* (Pickwick Press, 1975).

The "new quest" is propounded in *A New Quest of the Historical Jesus*, by James W. Robinson *(Studies in Biblical Theology 25, Alec R. Allenson, 1959)*. A pioneer statement of results is *Jesus of Nazareth*, by Gunther Bornkam (translated by Irene and Fraser McLuskey with James M. Robinson; Harper, 1959; paperback, 1975). British scholarship is represented by another compact summary of conclusions from a different point of view, *The Founder of Christianity*, by C. H. Dodd (Macmillan, 1970).

A trailblazer in hermeneutics is *Early Christian Rhetoric: The Language of the Gospel*, by Amos N. Wilder (SCM Harper, 1964; Harvard University Press, 1971). *The New Hermeneutic*, edited by James W. Robinson and John B. Cobb, Jr. *(New Frontiers in Theology*, vol. II, Harper, 1964), is a manifesto of the movement so designated. An illuminating review of ongoing research and discussion in literary criticism and hermeneutics is *Jesus and the Language of the Kingdom: Symbol and Metaphor in the New Testament*, by Norman Perrin (Fortress Press, 1976).

A Future for the Historical Jesus, by Leander E. Keck (Abingdon, 1971), is a very thoughtful examination of the theological aspect of contemporary research in the Gospels. *Jesus: Inspiring and Disturbing Presence*, by M. de Jonge (translated by John E. Steely; Abingdon, 1974), being a collection of essays and lectures, lacks clear unity and movement but is full of excellent observations on this subject.

INDEX OF REFERENCES
TO THE GOSPELS AND ACTS